From
ICE FLOES
To
BATTLEFIELDS

Scott's 'Antarctics'
in the First World War

ANNE STRATHIE

The
History
Press

*In memory of my late parents, Jack and Marion Strathie,
and all those who have died in or suffered due to wars or in
exploring the wonderful world which we all share.*

First published 2015

The History Press
The Mill, Brimscombe Port
Stroud, Gloucestershire, GL5 2QG
www.thehistorypress.co.uk

British Library Cataloguing in Publication Data.
A catalogue record for this book is available from the British Library.

ISBN 978 0 7509 6178 3

Typesetting and origination by The History Press
Printed in Great Britain

Contents

Acknowledgements

———

I owe a considerable debt of gratitude to numerous organisations and individuals who have contributed in a wide range of ways to this book and have made researching and writing it both enlightening and enjoyable.

I thank the museums, archives, libraries and galleries that conserve and interpret the documents, artefacts and images which lie at the heart of biographical and non-fiction writing. I particularly thank the following, including for permission to quote from documents in their custody or use images from their collections.

In Britain: Scott Polar Research Institute, University of Cambridge (Naomi Boneham, Lucy Martin); Blandford Museum (Bridget Spiers and fellow volunteers); The Wilson, Cheltenham (Ann-Rachael Harwood); Cheltenham Library; Haslar Heritage Group (Eric C. Birbeck MVO); King's College, Cambridge (Rupert Brooke Archives); Imperial War Museum; National Archives, Kew; National Portrait Gallery; Natural History Museum; Plymouth City Museum and Art Gallery; Royal Geographical Society (Eugene Rae, Sarah Evans and colleagues); Royal Signals Museum (Adam Forty); The Alliance Boots Archive and Museum Collection; University of St Andrews Library (Group 22–2, Rachel Hart and colleagues).

Outside Britain: Canterbury Museum, Christchurch, New Zealand (Sarah Murray, Nicolas Boigelot); Akaroa Museum; Archives New Zealand; In Flanders Field Museum, Ypres, Belgium (Dominiek Dendooven, Annick Vandenbilke); Queen Elizabeth II Library, Memorial University, St John's, Newfoundland, Canada (Bert Riggs); Royal British Columbia Museum, Canada (Marion Tustanoff, Kelly-Ann Turkington); University of Melbourne Archives, Australia (Georgina Ward); Waitaki District Libraries and Archive, Oamaru, New Zealand.

I also thank the descendants and family members of Harry Pennell and others who served on the *Terra Nova* expedition, and writers, historians, explorers and others who have provided guidance, information, encouragement and, in several cases, permission to use written material or photographs. They include:

David and Virginia Pennell; June Back and family; Christopher Bayne and other relatives of Edward Atkinson; Dr Paul Baker; John Barfoot; Sarah Baxter (Society of Authors); Christopher Bilham; Dr Steven Blake, David Elder and other members of the Cheltenham Wilson centenary committee; Sheena Boese; Julian Broke-Evans; Robin Burton; Stephen Chambers (Gallipoli Association); Jeff Cooper (Friends of Dymock Poets); Peter Cooper (SEA. Ltd); David Craig; Wendy Driver; Angela Egerton; Tony Fleming; Mike Goodearl; Luci Gosling (Mary Evans Picture Library); Hermann Gran; Signora Francesca Guarnieri; Dr Henry Guly; Andrew Hay and family; Trevor Henshaw; Steven Heyde; Dr Max Jones; Heather Lane; Jo and Ian Laurie; Neela Mann; Karen May; Katherine Moody (Christchurch Public Libraries); Sir Andrew Motion (Trustee, Rupert Brooke Estate); David Newman; David Parsons; Graeme Pearson; Thérèse Radic (University of Melbourne); Adrian Raeside; Dr Stephen Ross and Dr Pearl Jacks; Leonard Sellers; Caroline Strange (Australian National University, Canberra); George and Valerie Skinner; Roy Swales; Michael Tarver, Joan Whiting-Moon, and (alphabetically last, but certainly not least) Dr David Wilson.

I am also grateful to the authors whose books have provided invaluable information on and background to events covered in this book. I also thank those involved in the BBC's First World War programmes and those working at the BBC and elsewhere on websites and blogs covering different aspects of the First World War and polar exploration.

My thanks go also to family members and friends who have supported me on my Antarctic and First World War voyages of discovery. They include (but are not limited to): Jean Strathie; Roberta Deighton, Fiona Eyre, Jill Burrowes and families; Michael Bourne, Ali Rieple, the Nuttalls, Isaacs, Nops and other Cranfield friends; Helen Brown; the Cairncrosses; Lin and Robert Coleman; the Fortes family and Margaret Douglas; Tracey Jaggers, Pauline Lyons, Moira and Martin Wood, Penie Coles, Jackie Chelin, Simon Day and other Cheltenham friends; Charlotte Mackintosh and her fellow godchildren; Jan Oldfield; the late Clive Saunders and Eva Borgo Saunders; Joanna Scott; Ann Watkin, the Leggs and other St Andrews University friends; Roz and John Wilkinson; Sophie Wilson.

Thanks also to Mark Beynon, Naomi Reynolds and their colleagues at The History Press for commissioning this book and helping bring it to fruition. I also thank them, other publishers, bookshops and libraries who continue to make books widely available.

As the above acknowledgements show, this book is the sum of many parts; any errors within it are of my own making.

Introduction

—◦◦◦◦—

About five years ago, during my research for *Birdie Bowers: Captain Scott's Marvel*, I noticed that the name of Harry Pennell appeared regularly in Bowers' letters and journals from the early part of the *Terra Nova* expedition. Bowers always wrote warmly of Pennell, as did Scott, Edward Wilson and other members of the expedition. Pennell, who had joined the expedition as navigator on the *Terra Nova*, was clearly a much respected, admired and liked member of the team.

In February 2013 I visited Oamaru, New Zealand, where events were being held to commemorate the centenary of the clandestine landing by Pennell and his friend Edward Atkinson with the news that Scott, Bowers, Wilson, Lawrence Oates and Edgar Evans had died on their way back from the South Pole. A conversation with members of Harry Pennell's family, the discovery that Pennell had several connections with Gloucestershire (where I live) and the availability of previously unpublished letters and journals combined to inspire this book. When I realised the extent to which Pennell kept in regular contact, often from a great distance, with his *Terra Nova* expedition companions (the 'Antarctics' of the title) and others, including Bowers' mother and that he had died in one of the major engagements of the First World War, I decided that the book should take the form of a group portrait rather than a simple biography. I have a feeling that Pennell, a modest man who valued his friends and colleagues, would not have objected.

In outward appearances Pennell and Bowers were very different – Pennell was tall and lean, Bowers short and stocky – but they shared a love of and capacity for sustained hard work, a profound Christian faith and a deep sense of devotion and duty to family, friends and colleagues. They were both highly intelligent and fascinated by the world they lived in; both saw ships and the sea as their element and calling.

Bowers and Pennell met in London in June 1910 and took their leave of each other in early January 1911, with Bowers heading south from Cape Evans to lay food depots along the Ross Sea ice shelf and Pennell sailing north to New Zealand. Both hoped that Scott would allow Pennell to join the landing party the following year but events conspired against Pennell and Bowers meeting again.

The first part of *From Ice Floes to Battlefields* tells the story of the *Terra Nova* expedition (largely from Pennell's standpoint) and its bitter-sweet aftermath, which is interrupted when 'trouble in the Balkans' leads into the First World War. The following section consists of a series of interconnected (though largely self-contained) chapters which follow Pennell and his friends as they once again expand their horizons, push themselves to their limit and deal with death.

No man, even the apparently ubiquitous Winston Churchill, saw and understood every aspect of the war. Pennell and his friends kept in touch with each other but when on active duty sometimes did not know what was happening on a nearby ship, in a trench a few miles away or to their families. In writing of Scott's 'Antarctics' and their experiences I have largely done so from their viewpoints, which combine to produce a series of 'in the moment' snapshots rather than a comprehensive panorama or in-depth analysis of a globe-encompassing war.

During the *Terra Nova* expedition Pennell and many of his companions kept journals and wrote long letters, many of which are held by the Scott Polar Research Institute, Cambridge, or other archives in Britain and elsewhere. The wartime writings of Scott's 'Antarctics' are less easily traced and, as a result, the source material for the second part of this book ranges from affectionate family letters to brusque regimental diaries and, where no primary material has been identified, from detailed analyses of a single engagement to century-spanning regimental histories.

In the First World War, as in Antarctica and on the Southern Ocean, some of Scott's men thrived, others struggled and a few died. The five men who died on their return journey from the South Pole are, perhaps inevitably, the most famous members of the expedition. When I embarked on writing this book, I viewed Pennell and other 'Antarctics' largely through the prism of the *Terra Nova* expedition; now, as I finish it, I am full of admiration for what they achieved both in Antarctica and during the war and touched by the efforts they made to keep in touch with and support their fellow 'Antarctics'.

I hope that readers will also share my sense of discovery – and, on many occasions, enjoyment – as they follow Harry Pennell and his companions from the ice floes of Antarctica, by way of London's theatres and restaurants and the British countryside, to the battlegrounds of Europe and the Seven Seas and into the hard-won peace which followed.

Anne Strathie, Cheltenham

Antarctica, showing surrounding countries. Map © and courtesy of Michael Tarver, Mike Goodearl.

Prologue

—⟨∾⟩—

In February 1911, on the Ross Sea ice shelf in Antarctica, Norwegian mariner and ski expert Lieutenant Tryggve Gran found himself sharing a tent with Captain Lawrence Oates of the Inniskilling Dragoons and Lieutenant Henry Bowers of the Royal Indian Marine.[1]

The three men, who had met in London in June 1910, were all members of the shore-based party of Captain Robert Scott's second Antarctic expedition. They were on their way back to the expedition's headquarters at Cape Evans after several weeks of laying food depots to be used during the following season's attempt to reach the South Pole.

As the Antarctic winter approached, days shortened and temperatures dropped. Day by day, they plodded onwards, following in their snow-filled outward tracks, peering into the misty gloom for route markers they had planted on their way south. At the end of each day's march, after building walls of snow to shelter their weary ponies, the three men pitched their tent and crawled into their cramped quarters. They would then light their portable stove, wait patiently while ice and snow melted into their first drink since their midday break and prepare some simple hot food. They would then climb into their sleeping bags for some well-earned rest.

During the long journey from Britain 'Birdie' Bowers and 'Soldier' Oates had become good friends. Bowers owed his nickname to his large, beak-like nose; Oates was the expedition's only military man. Tryggve Gran, whose first name most of his fellow explorers found hard to pronounce, was known as 'Trigger'. Gran, one of the youngest men on the expedition, had been recruited by Scott as a ski expert; his ability to move quickly and fluently across the snow was much admired, but he had gained a reputation (including with Scott) for a tendency to conserve his energy between journeys. Bowers and Oates were, by contrast, recognised as two of the hardest-working and most robust members of the expedition.

Gran hoped that the current period of enforced proximity would enable him to develop more of a bond with his two British companions. As all three men had travelled widely, he decided to initiate a discussion on international relations, including those between Britain and Germany. Gran recalled an occasion when, as a young midshipman, he had arrived in Hamburg to find German dockers standing on the quayside shouting 'Down with England and the damned Englishmen!' When he had tried to find out what had given rise to the demonstration he learned that the owners of Germany's main transatlantic shipping line had tried to break a local strike by bringing in British dockers.

Oates said he would not be surprised if Gran, like most other 'foreigners', was also anti-British. Bowers, in an effort to keep the peace, suggested that if Britain ever found herself at war with Germany, Gran could join him in taking a commission with Oates' regiment. Bowers was so sure that Gran would agree to the prospect of the three men fighting together against the Germans that he wagered Oates some of his soup that evening if Gran proved him wrong.

After Gran confirmed that Bowers was correct, Oates and Gran shook hands to seal their bargain – and Bowers began looking forward to his soup.

* * *

On 29 October 1912, after the long, dark Antarctic winter was over, Gran and other members of the expedition's landing party set out from Cape Evans to try to establish what had happened to Scott and the other members of the South Pole party, which had, they knew, included Bowers and Oates.

On 12 November Gran and his companions spied the tip of a tent above the snow. Inside they found the bodies of Scott, Bowers and Edward Wilson, Scott's Chief of Scientific Staff. There was no sign of the bodies of Oates or Petty Officer Edgar 'Taff' Evans.

Scott's journal entries showed that Evans had died in mid-February and that Oates, whose feet had become so badly frostbitten that he could hardly walk, had limped out of their shared tent a month later. Oates had hoped that by sacrificing his life he would give Scott, Wilson and Bowers a better chance of survival. But they had died in their blizzard-bound tent towards the end of March 1912.

On the way back to Cape Evans Gran wore Scott's skis, so that they at least would have completed the return journey to the South Pole.

* * *

On Thursday, 30 July 1914, on a beach at Cruden Bay, near Aberdeen, Gran waited for the weather to clear so he could embark on his potentially record-breaking flight over the North Sea. He knew this was his last chance as British aviation authorities had announced that all commercial flights from Britain would be banned from that evening due to the tense international situation.

Just over a month previously Archduke Franz Ferdinand of Austria had been assassinated in Sarajevo, the capital of Bosnia. Since then, the situation had escalated and it now seemed possible (at least according to the newspapers) that major powers, including Germany and Britain, might become involved in what had initially seemed to be an isolated incident in a troubled but distant region.

As Tryggve Gran waited for the North Sea mist to lift he remembered his conversation with Bowers and Oates in a tent at the other end of the world – and the promise he had made to them.

New Zealand, showing places associated with the *Terra Nova* expedition. Map © and courtesy of Michael Tarver, Mike Goodearl.

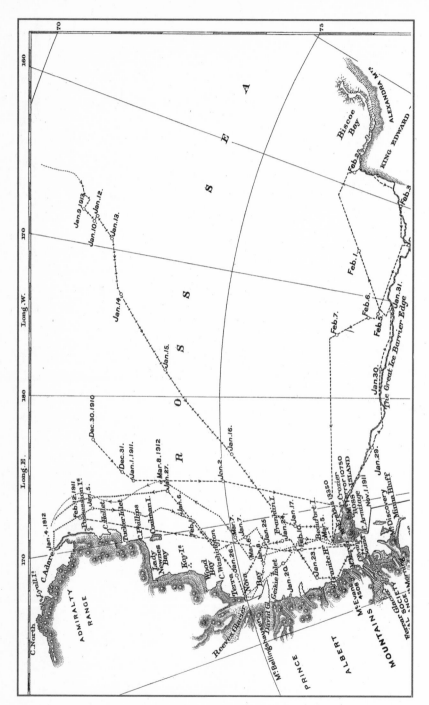

Voyages of the *Terra Nova* during the expedition: the years appear at the northerly end of each voyage; the voyage towards King Edward VII Land took place in early 1911. Map by Stanfords, image © private.

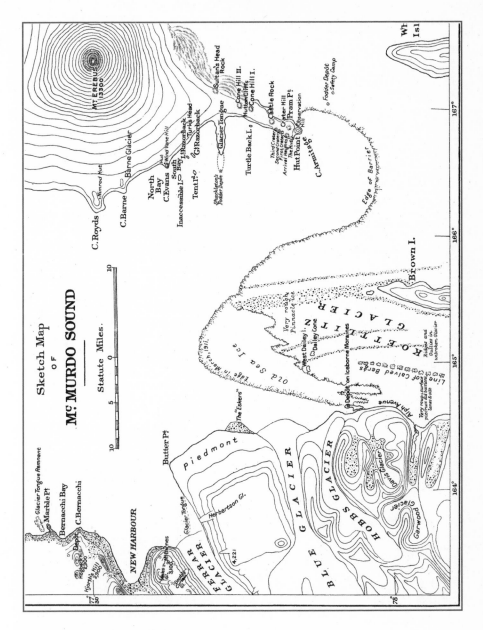

McMurdo Sound, showing (on right) Ross Island, with Cape Evans and Hut Point. Map by Stanfords, image © private.

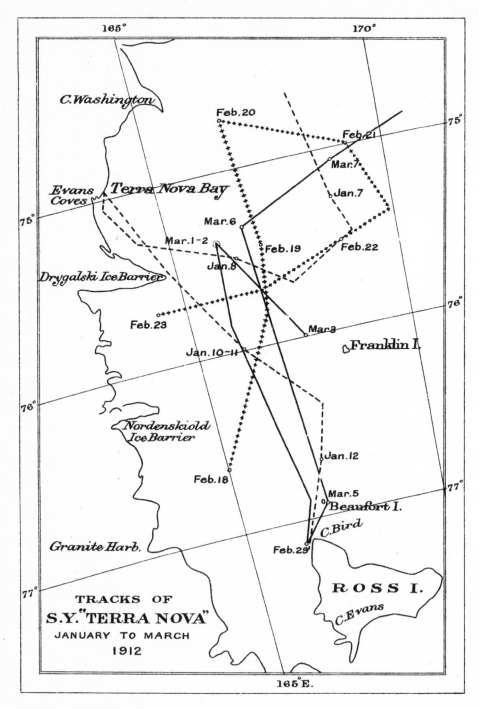

Voyages of the *Terra Nova*, January–March 1912, showing the journeys made when depositing Campbell and his Northern Party at Evans Cove and attempting to relieve them; where lines stop short of the coast, this indicates that pack ice was blocking the route. Map by Stanfords, image © private.

1

Southward Ho!

In London, on Friday, 20 May 1910, Captain Robert Scott, Lieutenant Edward Evans, Lieutenant Henry Bowers and other naval officers who would soon be travelling to Antarctica on SY *Terra Nova* took part in the funeral parade of King Edward VII.

The late monarch's son, now King George V, was joined in his mourning by members of his extended family, including the rulers of Germany, Norway, Denmark, Belgium, Spain, Portugal, Greece and Bulgaria and members of the ruling families of Austria-Hungary, the Ottoman Empire, Russia, Yugoslavia, Montenegro, Romania, Italy, the Netherlands, Japan and Egypt.

Their duty done, Scott and his men returned to West India Docks or the expedition's office in Victoria Street. Men had travelled from all over the world to join the expedition and were still arriving. Bowers had been released from his duties with the Royal Indian Marine in Bombay and the ship's navigator, Lieutenant Harry Pennell, was still on his way back from Australia.

When Pennell had applied to join what had initially been known as the 'Scott–Evans Antarctic expedition' in summer 1909 he had been serving with the navy's Mediterranean Fleet.[1] Now 27, Pennell had gone to sea at the age of 16 and won a medal for his services on Britain's China Station during the Boxer Rebellion. He had then passed out from HMS *Britannia* (where Scott and the new monarch had also trained) with five first-class certificates, full marks in piloting and navigation, and a £10 prize. When Pennell learned that his application to join what was now officially called 'The British Antarctic Expedition' had been successful, he had been completing a round of duty with the Australasian station.[2]

Edward 'Teddy' Evans, Scott's naval second in command, was two years older than Pennell. He had, following a somewhat eventful school career, failed to secure a *Britannia* cadetship, but, after training on HMS *Worcester* (where Bowers had also trained), had won a scholarship to Greenwich Naval College. Evans and Scott had first met on HMS *Majestic*; in 1902 and 1903 Evans had served on the *Morning*, the relief ship which had helped release Scott's main expedition ship from the grip of the pack ice during his *Discovery* expedition. Whilst in New Zealand between voyages, Evans had met and married Hilda Russell, the beautiful daughter of a prominent Christchurch lawyer. On his return to Britain he had initially concentrated on his naval career; he resisted the temptation to join Ernest Shackleton's *Nimrod* expedition, but soon started organising an Antarctic expedition of his own.

When Scott learned that Shackleton had established a new 'Furthest South' record but failed to reach the Pole, he began planning a second expedition. Sir Clements Markham, past president of the Royal Geographical Society and staunch supporter of Scott, persuaded Evans to combine forces and resources with Scott for another attempt on the Pole and a major scientific programme. Although Evans was less well-known than Scott he brought to the expedition feast substantial support from members of the Cardiff business community, who were keen to support an expedition involving a naval officer of Welsh extraction.

Evans agreed to Markham's proposal, in return for which he was appointed captain of the *Terra Nova* and Scott's naval deputy. When Evans and First Mate Lieutenant Victor Campbell joined the expedition's landing party, it would fall to Harry Pennell to captain the *Terra Nova* back through the pack ice and Southern Ocean to New Zealand. Pennell would then return to Antarctica in early 1912 and again in early 1913, on which last voyage he would pick up any members of the South Pole or scientific parties still on the ice. Although fuel costs would be heavy, this would be a small price to pay to reduce the risk of the *Terra Nova* becoming frozen in, as this time there was no permanent relief ship.

* * *

On 15 June 1910 the *Terra Nova* was cheered away from Cardiff, her final British port of call. Scott, who was not on board, was staying on in London to complete final financial arrangements for the expedition, before travelling by steamer to Cape Town and trying to raise further funds before the *Terra Nova* arrived. Scott's wife, sculptress Kathleen Scott, Hilda Evans and Oriana Wilson, wife of Chief of Scientific Staff Edward Wilson, would travel with him.

As the ship headed south, Teddy Evans proved to be a convivial captain who joined in and often instigated officers' wardroom 'entertainments'. Pennell spent most of the time on the bridge or in the crow's nest, but found time to work on the zoological log and perform the occasional hornpipe.[3] At Cape Town, Scott, who had barely met some of the men who might accompany him to the South Pole, decided to join the ship for the next leg of the voyage. Edward

Wilson, much to the disappointment of Pennell, Bowers and others, left the ship to accompany 'the wives' (as they were sometimes referred to outside their hearing) on the steamer to Melbourne.

The voyage south had given Pennell (now known as 'Penelope') the chance to get to know his fellow travellers, particularly the scientists (mainly Cambridge graduates) he now regularly encountered in the wardroom.[4]

Edward Wilson was, Pennell felt, 'a real expert' in seabirds and marine wildlife and an 'extraordinarily well read and pleasant man'. Of the expedition's two marine biologists, Edward Nelson (who had worked on a North Sea 'Fishery Investigation') would land on Antarctica, while Dennis Lillie (a specialist in whales) would remain on the ship and trawl the Southern Ocean and waters round Antarctica for samples.

George Simpson (known as 'Sunny Jim'), who had been seconded from the India Meteorological Department, appeared to be 'a really clever man, well up in the job' of recording Antarctic weather conditions. The other scientists had their own specialisms: Murray Levick and Edward Atkinson were both naval doctors (although Atkinson was also a parasitologist); Griffith Taylor, Frank Debenham and Raymond Priestley were geologists; Charles Wright was a physicist and Apsley Cherry-Garrard a zoologist.

Although Pennell sometimes felt 'rather a worm and appallingly ignorant' in comparison to the scientists he soon gained the impression that every man aboard seemed keen to do 'his best for his messmates & for the expedition'.

* * *

On 28 October the *Terra Nova* sailed into Lyttelton, the port for Christchurch, New Zealand. She would remain there for a month while cargo was reloaded, repairs were carried out and more expedition members, and sledge-dogs and ponies (from Manchuria and Siberia) joined the ship.

Scott and his men were well looked after by Joseph Kinsey, the English-born shipping agent who had handled local arrangements for Scott's *Discovery* and Shackleton's *Nimrod* expeditions. Scott, like Teddy Evans, had family connections in New Zealand and Edward and Oriana Wilson had forged firm friendships there during their belated honeymoon which followed the *Discovery* expedition. One of Pennell's fellow lieutenants, Henry Rennick, also had friends from his time serving in New Zealand waters with HMS *Penguin* of Britain's Australasia station. Lyttelton was also an established recruiting ground for crew with previous Southern Ocean experience.

Pennell was pleased to see Edward Wilson again, but was less sure about how he felt about 'the wives', in particular Kathleen Scott. In Cape Town Pennell had found Scott and Evans to be rather susceptible to the 'petticoat influence' and he suspected that Kathleen Scott ('an ambitious lady') was trying to persuade Scott to appoint her brother, Lieutenant Wilfred Bruce (whose experience was on large passenger ships), as captain of the *Terra Nova* in place of Pennell on the return voyage to New Zealand.[5] Kathleen Scott and Hilda Evans also took sides whenever Scott and Evans disagreed about expedition matters (a not infrequent occurrence). At one point matters reached such a pitch that it looked as if Teddy Evans might resign before the ship left New Zealand but Wilson and Campbell had, thankfully, managed to smooth things over.[6]

Although Wilson was a clear favourite amongst expedition members he was closely followed, in Pennell's opinion, by Edward Atkinson.[7] Pennell considered Atkinson (known as 'Atch' or, for less obvious reasons, 'Jane') to be 'an out and out gentleman with the quiet self-assurance that makes a man without making him offensive'. Although Atkinson, like Wilson, 'lent a sympathetic ear to everyone's trouble', he could, Pennell noticed, also take a dislike to someone 'on very short acquaintance' or (in Pennell's view) on 'very insufficient grounds'. But Pennell respected Atkinson's judgement and views, particularly in relation to 'the mess-deck feeling' on specific issues. And, Pennell felt, he could be trusted to honour confidences.[8]

While the ship was docked, Pennell dined regularly with Atkinson, Bowers and Oates at their boarding house in Sumner, across the hills from Lyttelton. Pennell enjoyed himself on these occasions but noticed that Atkinson, if he over-indulged, had the tendency to become obstinate or, as he had done at a farewell dinner for London expedition agent George Wyatt and his attractive wife, somewhat comically over-amorous.[9]

On 29 November 1910, with everyone and everything aboard, the *Terra Nova* embarked on her 2,500-mile voyage across the Southern Ocean. While Kathleen Scott, Oriana Wilson and Hilda Evans waved their husbands away from a tug, a spray-soaked young lady in the bow of their vessel waved and called out her farewells to Henry Rennick.[10]

When the *Terra Nova* entered the 'Roaring Forties' and 'Furious Fifties' Pennell and his fellow mariners were in their element.[11] The ship, weighed down with coal and the wherewithal to support men and animals in Antarctica for up to three years, sat low in the water. As she ploughed through the Southern Ocean, waves crashed over her gunwales, washed across her decks and found the slightest gaps between her groaning deck-planks.

Pennell now had the opportunity see how the men he would soon be commanding performed in such conditions. In the bowels of the ship, Chief Artificer William Williams ('a really good man') and his stokers and firemen managed to keep fires alight and engines turning.[12] On deck and aloft, boatswain

Alfred Cheetham and his men wrestled valiantly with winches, rigging and sails, using favourable winds to help conserve precious coal stocks. 'Alf', a wiry, cheery merchant seaman from Hull who was of an age with Scott, had served on the *Morning* under Evans and *Nimrod* under Shackleton. Cheetham, who had been spotted helping himself to a length of Nelson's brand-new trawling rope and splicing it into the rigging, seemed to be 'an absolute magpie', albeit for the general good.[13]

As the *Terra Nova* rocked, rolled and yawled through the Southern Ocean Pennell tried to hold a steady course while Rennick and Bruce organised 'bucket crews' of scientists and other non-mariners who were not confined to their bunks by sea-sickness.[14] Below decks, Bowers and Teddy Evans were trying to help Williams and his men clear the soot-clogged pumps. On deck, Cecil Meares, the expedition's much-travelled dog expert, cavalry officer Lawrence Oates (in charge of ponies) and their Russian assistants tried to ensure the expedition's land-based animal transport reached their destination in fit states. Bowers and Bernard Day (in charge of motor-sledges) lashed additional ropes round items of heavy equipment that seemed at risk of being washed overboard.

In early December, just outside the Antarctic Circle, the ship entered the pack ice. For almost three weeks Evans, Pennell, Bowers and others coaxed their ship through the tightly packed ice floes, weaving through leads of open water, punching their way through intransigent pancake ice. Pennell and his shipmates celebrated Christmas Day 1910 in some style on a motionless ship, but by New Year's Day 1911 they had made it through to the open waters of McMurdo Sound.

Scott had hoped to establish his base around his *Discovery* expedition quarters at Hut Point but they were inaccessible due to the ice. He gave orders to return north to a sheltered, sloping shelf which he immediately named 'Cape Evans' in honour of his naval second in command. Pennell's job now was to hold the *Terra Nova* steady adjacent to the sometimes unstable sea-ice so that animals, provisions, building materials, sledges and other equipment could be unloaded and, with the assistance of dogs and ponies, moved quickly to solid ground.

On the higher ground, ship's carpenter Francis Davies and a team of helpers had begun building the main expedition hut, stables and outbuildings. Scott had thoughtfully arranged for a library of books, a gramophone and a Broadwood pianola (donated by the makers) to be installed in the hut to help while away the long, dark Antarctic winter evenings. Rennick, who had regularly played the pianola on the voyage south, now disassembled and reconstructed it, a job he did cheerfully, despite having no prospect of playing it again in the foreseeable future.[15]

During the voyage south Scott had approached Rennick and asked him to step down from the landing party (for which he had been recruited) so that Bowers could be transferred from the ship's party to the landing party (within which Bowers would now serve as quartermaster). Rennick was unable to hide his disappointment, but showed no resentment towards Bowers and completed his task on the pianola with a lively rendition of *Home, Sweet Home*.[16] Pennell had initially been disappointed about the change of plans. He had looked forward to working with Bowers, a natural seaman and shipboard favourite, but decided that Rennick was 'an A1 chap' whose surveying expertise would also be of great value.

On 17 January 1911 the Cape Evans hut was declared ready for occupation – a landmark event which meant that the ship (on which most of the men were still living) could be made ready for departure and the expedition proper could begin.

On 24 January Scott set out south with Wilson, Teddy Evans, Atkinson, Bowers, Oates, Meares, Demitri Gerof (Meares' assistant), Gran, Apsley Cherry-Garrard (a young scientist recruited by Wilson, nicknamed 'Cherry') and three petty officers, Tom Crean (a *Discovery* veteran), Pat Keohane and Robert Forde. Over the next few weeks they would deposit caches of provisions and animal fodder on the ice shelf (to around 80°S), which would be used during the following season's attempt to reach the Pole.

Scott knew he was not the only one with Antarctic aspirations over this and the coming season. Lieutenant Wilhelm Filchner of Germany and Lieutenant Nobu Shirase of Japan had both announced their intentions to claim the Pole for their nations. Australian scientist Douglas Mawson, a member of Shackleton's *Nimrod* expedition, had discussed joining forces with Scott but decided to mount his own expedition to Cape Adare, some 400 miles north of Cape Evans. Scott, who felt he had the advantage over all three in terms of both reaching the South Pole and his scientific programme, had been surprised to receive a cable in Melbourne, announcing that Norwegian explorer Roald Amundsen was now also heading to Antarctica.

Amundsen had been a member of the 1897–99 Belgian Antarctic expedition, but owed his fame to having discovered the elusive North-West Passage. He had announced his intention of flying his country's flag on the North Pole but, possibly due to recent claims by Americans Frederick Cook and Robert Peary to have reached the earth's northernmost point, had decided to race Scott to the South Pole instead.

Scott, who saw reaching the Pole as a means of publicising his expedition's scientific work as well as a goal in itself, decided not to change his plans in response to Amundsen's implied challenge. He would, as intended, return from the South Pole not just with proof that he had been there, but with a full set of navigational and other observations and geological specimens collected on the way there and back.

Once the depot-laying party had departed, the *Terra Nova* (now under First Mate Victor Campbell) deposited a 'Western Party' at Butter Point, where they would explore glaciers in the area. This international group consisted of two Australian scientists, Griffith ('Griff') Taylor and Frank ('Deb') Debenham, a Canadian geologist, Charles ('Silas') Wright and a Welsh petty officer, Edgar Evans (a *Discovery* veteran). Wright and Taylor knew each other from Cambridge, where Wright had heard Douglas Mawson's tales of the *Nimrod* expedition and been persuaded to walk to London to apply for Scott's expedition.

The *Terra Nova*'s next port of call was to be King Edward VII Land, where Campbell and his 'Eastern Party' would disembark and explore land discovered and named by Scott during the *Discovery* expedition. Campbell's party consisted of Raymond Priestley (a *Nimrod* expedition scientist), George Levick, Petty Officers George Abbot and Frank Browning and Able Seaman Harry Dickason.

As the *Terra Nova* sailed along the immense Ross Sea ice-barrier Pennell saw something which was new to him:[17]

a large mass of ice calving from the Barrier not a mile from us. The noise was … rather like a heavy gun firing & then near the Barrier appeared a huge mass of spray & snow that took fully a minute to subside, when 3 fairly large bergs could be seen & a vast accumulation of débris of ice. Our photographers got the cameras to work though the light was very bad.

As they approached King Edward VII Land, Campbell and Pennell climbed to the crow's nest to spy out a suitable landing place. The 700ft cliffs of ice looked impenetrable, so Campbell gave orders to go about and return to the Bay of Whales, where they could moor while he considered his options.[18]

Just after midnight on 3 February, Bruce, who was on watch with Dennis Lillie, spotted what initially looked like an ice-bound shipwreck but soon revealed itself as the *Fram*, the ship which veteran Norwegian Arctic explorer Fridtjof Nansen had loaned to Amundsen, originally for his attempt on the North Pole. Campbell, who spoke Norwegian fluently, went over to the ship and returned with the news that Amundsen was at the expedition's hut on the ice shelf but would be back in the morning.

The following morning, Campbell, Pennell and Levick joined Amundsen and his companions for breakfast:[19]

The shore party consisted of 9 including Amundsen and Johannsen & were a fine looking body of men both in physique & appearance … Their sole idea is the Pole, for which they have 100 dogs, from Greenland … The dogs are to be fed on fish. The men will follow on ski and say that they can even then hardly keep pace.

Apparently no depots will be laid out this year ... Amundsen returned the visit ... & we also had a look at the *Fram*. Her oil fuel has not been replenished since Europe & her little motor gives her 5 to 6 knots in a flat calm; they also say that she has proved herself a better sea boat then they had reasonably expected.

The encounter with the Norwegians had been cordial enough, but Campbell decided to abandon his plans for exploring King Edward VII Land and return to Cape Evans with a message for Scott about the unexpected encounter. He would then make a decision as to where his party would land.

Pennell, meanwhile, was considering the allocation of duties amongst his *Terra Nova* 'afterguard'.[20] Williams and Cheetham would now be short of several hands each, so Rennick would take every third watch in addition to carrying out his regular soundings. Expedition secretary Francis Drake would deal with his customary paperwork, serve as meteorologist, keep ice logs, tally provisions, act as postmaster and take photographs as and when required. On the scientific front, Lillie would take and analyse specimen dredgings, keep a tally of whale species and 'lend a hand' as required. Bruce would, in addition to sailing duties, maintain the overall zoological log and keep the fair copy of the survey book. Pennell knew from his experience of working on the zoological log with Wilson on the southern voyage, that this record was somewhat a collegiate effort, with final entries only agreed following heated debates as to whether, for example, 'a whale was *Sibbaldii* or *Australis*, etc., when one & all have learned the little knowledge they possess from Lillie'.

Campbell returned from Cape Evans, where he had left his note about Amundsen to be given to their leader when he returned from the ice shelf. Campbell and his party would now sail north with Pennell until a suitable location for investigation and over-wintering could be identified.

On 9 February 1911 the *Terra Nova* headed out of McMurdo Sound in thick snow. Gale-force winds and newly formed ice floes hampered their progress but eventually they made it through to Cape Adare, which Campbell regarded as a possible suitable site. Priestley and others were aware that Mawson had already declared his intention of exploring the area but, with coal stocks shrinking and the sea showing signs of freezing over, Campbell knew that, if he did not land immediately, he and his party might have to return to New Zealand with the ship.

As Campbell and his men prepared to land, Pennell caught up with his journal.[21] He had found it hard to say farewell to Atkinson and others who had become friends on the voyage south. Pennell had, he felt, taken longer than he should have to realise that Levick's somewhat slow demeanour concealed an excellent mind. Pennell's main concern regarding the Cape Evans' party was that Teddy Evans was still getting 'ruffled at small things' with Scott, which suggested that tensions might arise during long sledge journeys 'when everyone's temper gets up a bit!' Pennell was aware that Scott had never really forgiven Shackleton after a quarrel during the *Discovery* expedition's southern journey but that Wilson usually managed to keep the peace and Atkinson and others would try to keep out of any rows.

As to who would reach the South Pole first, Pennell considered Scott to be 'a certainty'. Amundsen he thought was a 'likely runner' who, if his skiers and dogs did not let him down, could reach the Pole a few weeks ahead of Scott. But Pennell felt that, even if Scott was second to the Pole, his expedition would still have considerably greater overall value, particularly given Amundsen's behaviour, which Pennell felt had not been 'entirely straightforward'.

On 20 February 1911, with Campbell and his party safely ashore, Pennell gave orders to set sail. He agreed with Campbell that he would, ice permitting, return in January 1912 and move what was now the Northern Party to another location which they could explore before returning to Cape Evans. Should Pennell return and find Cape Adare cut off by ice, Campbell and his party would make their way back to Cape Evans overland.

During the first day of Pennell's first command the *Terra Nova* almost ran into an iceberg in thick fog, but swift thinking and hard work by Cheetham and his men brought the ship round in the nick of time.[22] The following day, as they headed west, Bruce called out from the bridge that he could see uncharted land. By nightfall 'Oates Land', 'Mount Bruce', 'Bowers Mountains', and glaciers named for Rennick, Lillie and Dennistoun had been marked on the ship's charts. As the ship entered 'the home or mortuary of icebergs', even Pennell's sharp eyes were fooled into believing that a collection of weathered icebergs was 'an archipelago of snow covered islands'.[23]

Whenever it appeared that the *Terra Nova* might become frozen in, Bruce would muster all spare hands on deck to 'rock ship', a process which involved men dashing in unison across the deck until the ship's hull swung like a pendulum. As longer nights and daytime blizzards limited their sailing hours, Lillie would pass the time by helping with coal trimming.[24] Pennell, who suspected that the sea might freeze over completely sooner rather than later, tried to ride a northerly swell out of the pack. His manoeuvre failed but he enjoyed watching whales at close quarters:[25]

rorquals close alongside the ship … have to thrust their noses up vertically & blow in a sort of standing-on-their-tails position. All day we have been watching them, photos taken & the men have amused themselves at times by pelting them with coal ashes or other little missiles. Several times one rested its head on a floe …

The grooves on their throats were plainly seen, & one sometimes even saw their 'moustaches' … we have passed an exceptional number of seals … it appears to be their courting season, for they go through the most extraordinary movements without any apparent reason except … showing off.

On 9 March, over seven weeks after leaving Cape Evans, the *Terra Nova* finally emerged from the pack. Pennell hoped for fair winds to New Zealand but found himself faced with a combination of inky-dark nights, ferocious gales, scattered icebergs and high seas. As the ship bobbed like a cork and water leaked in, everyone's skills and nerves were tested, but by 21 March the storm had abated and they had not seen an iceberg for a week.

Suddenly and unexpectedly, after the barometer had plummeted 'into its boots', they found themselves in a Force 9 squall. As massive waves pounded the ship and swamped the decks, the ageing pumps once again clogged up with a mixture of salt water and coal-dust:[26]

Mr Williams … had to lie flat on the boiler room plates & when the ship rolled to Starboard, stretch right down, with his head below the plates & clear as much coal away from the suction as possible; this often meant that the water surged back before he could get his head out, and there can be few nastier liquids to be ducked in than that very dirty bilge water.

* * *

On 28 March 1911, almost five weeks after leaving Campbell's party, the *Terra Nova* arrived at Stewart Island, 20 miles off the southern tip of New Zealand. Pennell and Drake went ashore and sent cables to Joseph Kinsey in Christchurch and to Central News Agency in London (who had purchased exclusive rights to Scott's expedition reports). When they returned Pennell and Drake reminded everyone aboard not to speak to anyone (particularly newspaper reporters) until reports on the expedition based on the cable to Central News Agency had appeared in New Zealand newspapers.

Pennell could now take time to consider his first voyage as captain and how his crew had performed:

our N.Z. men have proved themselves real seamen … The E.R. [Engine Room] department are not one jot behind the U.D. [Upper Deck] party. The afterguard have turned up on every occasion to lend a hand … Lillie has taken his [turn] on the pumps & on deck. Drake ha[s] taken over all the writing and meteorological observations … Bruce & Rennick have been perfect treasures … Mr Cheetham makes an ideal watchkeeper always alert & on the lookout & absolutely reliable & what is more loves the ship for her fine qualities & watches over her as boatswain with the greatest care … We all say that [steward] Archer ought to take on the motto … 'while she swims I'll cook' … he has never been defeated …[27]

By the time the *Terra Nova* docked at Lyttelton the Christchurch *Press* and other newspapers were running reports on the expedition based on Central News Agency's cables from London. Although the main focus of interest was on the progress of Scott and the landing party, Pennell's account of the return voyage and encounter with Amundsen's party also appeared to be newsworthy.

There was also news of other Antarctic expeditions.[28] Mawson, who was in London fundraising for his expedition, was reported to be unhappy that Campbell would be exploring Cape Adare before he could do so. Shirase had passed through Wellington in early February and was on his way to the Ross Sea. Filchner, who could only claim the Pole for Germany if both Scott and Amundsen failed this season, would be working around the Weddell Sea until he knew the position regarding the Pole. Kinsey and Pennell, when asked by reporters what effect Amundsen's presence would have on Scott's plans, responded that everything would proceed as previously announced.[29]

Pennell arranged for the *Terra Nova* to go into dry dock for repairs, gave everyone a period of shore leave and began finalising arrangements for the surveying and sounding work which Scott hoped might be commissioned by New Zealand's maritime authorities.[30] Pennell gratefully accepted the hospitality of the Kinseys (in Christchurch) and of the Dennistouns, friends of Kinsey, who invited him to spend weekends at their farm station at Peel Forest, near Timaru, south of Christchurch. He was pleased to be invited back since, on an earlier visit, his borrowed horse had kicked out and broken the leg of George Dennistoun, his hosts' elder son. Dr Hugh Acland, whom Pennell had recently met in Christchurch, also invited him to spend a weekend at his family's estate at Mount Peel, which was close (in farm station terms) to Peel Forest.[31]

By 9 July, after Pennell had agreed everything with the maritime authorities, a spick and span *Terra Nova* set sail for Three Kings Islands, off the tip of North Island.[32] The islands, a recognised shipping hazard which lacked a lighthouse or fog warning system, had never been fully surveyed and mariners claimed that (as confirmed by a recent preliminary survey) official charts were inaccurate.

Rennick knew Three Kings Islands well. Ten years previously, when serving on HMS *Penguin*, he had been near them and spotted a life-raft with eight thirsty, starving, sun-burned people aboard. Once rescued, they explained that they were survivors from the SS *Elingamite*. Their ship had run into fog-shrouded cliffs at

Three Kings Islands several days previously and sunk with the loss, they believed, of almost fifty crew and passengers.[33] At the subsequent enquiry Ernest Attwood, the *Elingamite*'s English-born captain, had been found guilty of 'reckless navigation' and stripped of his master's certificate, despite his protestations regarding the accuracy (or lack thereof) of the charts with which he had been issued.

For ten weeks Rennick, working with helpers, took hundreds of measurements on, around and between the Three Kings Islands. When the *Terra Nova* returned to Lyttelton he plotted his soundings and distances on a fresh chart showing the dimensions of the islands and their positions in relation to each other and the coast. After he had submitted his chart to the British and New Zealand maritime authorities it was used at a new hearing on the wrecking of the *Elingamite*. Ten years after his ship had gone down Captain Attwood's name was cleared and his captain's certificate was reissued to him.

As he prepared to leave Lyttelton, Pennell bought newspapers so that Scott and the others could read about the outside world and other expeditions. The *Fram* had already left her winter quarters in Buenos Aires, bound for the Ross Sea, from where, according to the newspapers, she would bring Amundsen back to either Stewart Island or Lyttelton. Filchner was in the Weddell Sea, carrying out scientific work. Shirase had left Sydney on 19 November, heading for King Edward VII Land; before leaving he had presented a samurai sword to Professor Edgeworth David (under whom Taylor, Debenham and Mawson had studied) as a sign of gratitude for his support for their endeavours. On 2 December Mawson left Hobart in the *Aurora*; he was now planning to chart and explore the coast between Kaiser Wilhelm II Land and Cape Adare.[34]

On 15 December 1911 Harry Pennell gave orders for the *Terra Nova* to cast off from Lyttelton harbour. All being well, and ice permitting, he and his shipmates would soon have news of their own expedition's progress.

2

Battling Through the Pack

As Harry Pennell embarked on his second voyage as captain of the *Terra Nova* he restarted his 'official' captain's journal.[1] George Wyatt, the expedition's London agent, had performed 'wonders' and, despite strikes in Britain and Australia, everything had arrived in Lyttelton in time. There had been several changes of local crew, something Pennell had expected to have to deal with; he had also managed to dissuade John Mather, a promising young RNVR seaman, from leaving to join Mawson's expedition.

There would also be a new addition to Pennell's afterguard. Jim Dennistoun, the younger son of Pennell's Peel Forest hosts, would act as 'general caretaker of the animals', looking after mules (to replace deceased ponies) and sledge-dogs, which Scott had requisitioned for the coming season's work.[2] Pennell had written to Dennistoun explaining that there would be no remuneration and that, although food, ski-boots and mittens would be provided, Jim would need to bring with him certain items of clothing:

> plenty of head gear ... merino drawers and flannel vests ... sweaters, etc., and a good supply of socks ... gumboots, oilskin and sou'wester ... boots and slippers, or whatever foot-gear you fancy ... a good supply of neckerchiefs ... [or] strips of flannel stuff ... a greatcoat of any age and shabbiness ...

Scott had given Pennell his orders for this voyage almost a year ago:[3]

1. Pick up Campbell and party about January 1 [1912] at Cape Adare.
2. Re-land them in the vicinity of Woods Bay.
3. Relieve the geological party [led by Taylor] at about 15 January at Granite Harbour.
4. Land mules, dogs, stores, &c., at Cape Evans.[4]
5. Lay out various depôts according to the orders to be received at the Hut, in readiness for the next season's work.

6.   Consistently with carrying out the above, make biological collections, sound, and carry out other scientific work to as large an extent as possible.

During the first leg of the voyage the weather was fine and calm, which allowed Dennistoun and Lillie to exercise the animals and Rennick to rescue the ship's cat, after it had jumped overboard during an altercation with a sledge-dog.[5] The animal had been sodden and shivering when brought back on board but a stiff dose of brandy and snooze in the warm engine room worked wonders.

On Christmas Day 1911, the first iceberg of the voyage drifted past the *Terra Nova*. Two days later, Pennell and his companions were just north of the Antarctic Circle and in the pack ice, but by New Year's Day 1912 they were back in clear water.[6] They encountered more ice floes on the approach to Cape Adare but Campbell, Priestley, Levick, Abbott, Browning and Dickason were soon aboard, 'safe & sound, all in perfect health & spirits'. Campbell and Pennell agreed that Evans Cove (named by Shackleton for his *Nimrod* captain) in Terra Nova Bay would be a good base for the Northern Party's second, shorter geological campaign.

On 8 January 1912, after landing Campbell, Priestley, Levick, Abbott, Browning and Dickason with their equipment and over a month's provisions, Pennell agreed that he would (ice permitting) return and take them back to Cape Evans before he set sail for New Zealand.[7]

As the *Terra Nova* continued south towards McMurdo Sound, fog descended and ice closed in, leaving Pennell in little doubt that his next three tasks might be more difficult to achieve than the first two.[8] Now, day after day, stuck fast in the ice, all he and his crew could do was trim coal and exercise the mules and dogs. To while away the time Rennick chased an emperor penguin around an ice floe, Pennell stared at the mock suns and several people joined in a lively discussion about the similarity between the calls of 'the inevitable skua' and the farmyard duck.

On 21 January, after Pennell had conducted on-board church service, they made 2 miles over six hours, which brought their progress over four days to 3 miles in total. As they languished in the pack, the wildlife offered welcome diversion:[9]

Yesterday a large school of Killers were round the ship … [a] question that the Killers raise is as to whether the Adélie is afraid of them. The Penguin is quite inconsistent in this as in other matters, occasionally a flock of the birds will be gambolling in the water quite close to the whales, while at others they will rush out on a floe apparently terrified when a Killer comes in sight.

By 30 January the ice had pushed them north to 76°S, which latitude they had passed three weeks previously. On 3 February Pennell managed to bring the ship sufficiently close to Cape Evans for Atkinson, Meares and Simpson to sledge over to meet them.[10] Atkinson, who had 'good news of everyone', was delighted to be able to pick the bundles of mail Pennell had brought south with him.

Pennell and his men were equally keen to learn what had happened since they set sail from Cape Evans twelve months previously.

* * *

On 1 November 1911, the last members of a long convoy of men, ponies, dogs and sledges had left Cape Evans, heading south. Scott had not given any indication as to who he might take to the South Pole with him but he had made it clear that anyone chosen risked not being back at Cape Evans until late March 1912. Unless the weather was unexpectedly warm, the *Terra Nova* would need to have left by then to avoid being frozen in – and Pennell would need to return again in early 1913.[11]

Teddy Evans, motor engineer Bernard Day, William Lashly and steward Hooper had left with the motor-sledges several days ahead of the main party. The main convoy had only been marching for a few days when they came across the remains of two broken-down machines and notes from Teddy Evans. He and his three companions were now faced with marching for hundreds of miles, pulling what provisions and equipment they could until they reached the agreed meeting point just south of 80°S.

On 24 November, after everyone was reunited, Day and Hooper turned back to Cape Evans, leaving a somewhat exhausted Teddy Evans and Lashly to continue south with the rest of the party. Due to the demise of the motor-sledges and several ponies, Scott asked Meares to continue south with the party for further than they had both originally planned.

Scott's original plan had been for Meares, on his return to Cape Evans, to take provisions for men and sledge-dogs to One Ton Depot. Now Scott wrote a note for Day to take back to Cape Evans explaining the situation and asking Simpson to arrange for a sledge-hauling party to take additional provisions from Cape Evans to One Ton Depot (a round trip of over 200 miles). This would leave Meares with a less onerous task to do on his return.

Day and Hooper arrived back at Cape Evans on 21 December which, if the original plans had been adhered to, was around the time Scott had expected Meares to be back. After a brief rest Day, Hooper and Cape Evans 'residents' Edward Nelson and cook Thomas Clissold piled a sledge with provisions and hauled it to One Ton Depot.[12]

On 5 January 1912 Meares, his assistant Demitri and the dogs finally returned to Cape Evans after a difficult return journey. Having travelled for a longer period and over a greater distance than originally planned, they all needed time to recover before setting out with another load of provisions to One Ton Depot.

Meares had already made it clear to Scott and other members of the expedition that he would not be staying for another season. He was a seasoned traveller and accomplished linguist but he had unhappy memories of waiting for relief ships in polar regions. He had been working on an isolated trading post on the remote Kamchatka Peninsula in 1904 when the Russo-Japanese war had broken out.[13] When the ship which was due to pick him up had failed to return, Meares and his companions avoided starvation and scurvy thanks only to a passing American ship which found them and took them to Nome, Alaska. After Meares had recovered, he went to do business in Mukden but found himself embroiled in a huge clash between Russian and Japanese forces. As he made his way to the relative safety of Shanghai he met photographer-cum-war-correspondent Herbert Ponting, who invited Meares to join him on a photographic expedition covering Burma, India and Ceylon. So, when Scott later hired Meares as expedition 'dog expert', Meares had suggested that his friend Ponting would make an excellent expedition photographer.[14]

On 17 January Ponting, during one of his daily walks, spotted the mirage of the *Terra Nova* through his 12x magnifier lens.[15] It became evident that she was stuck in the ice, leaving Meares reluctant to set out for One Ton Depot and risk missing her arrival.

On 26 January Atkinson, Cherry-Garrard, Wright and Keohane arrived back at Cape Evans. When Atkinson's party had turned north, Scott, Wilson, Oates and 'Taff' Evans (a foursome in place since the outset) had been pulling one sledge while the newly formed team of Bowers, Teddy Evans, Lashly and Crean pulled the second sledge. Scott had still not indicated who would accompany him to the Pole. Everyone at Cape Evans agreed that Scott's remaining seven companions all had good claims for inclusion.

Just over a week after Atkinson's party returned, the *Terra Nova* finally arrived. Now everyone at Cape Evans had their mail from home – but they would only know who would be going to the South Pole with Scott when the second returning sledge-party arrived off the ice-barrier.

* * *

By 6 February 1912 Pennell had managed to bring the *Terra Nova* sufficiently close to Cape Evans that dogs and mules could be landed and important items of cargo unloaded and taken by dog-sledge to the hut.[16] Pennell was handed a bundle of letters, which turned out to be from Scott, Atkinson, Bowers and Teddy Evans. All had been written in the expectation that the writer would not be at Cape Evans to greet Pennell when he arrived.

Atkinson's now somewhat redundant letter opened with a description of an incident which had occurred towards the end of the depot journey:[17]

> the sea-ice had gone out with Cherry, Birdie and Crean. They did a very plucky thing. They were trekking for the hut over sea-ice when they realised the ice was going out. Birdie sent Crean to tell the Owner and he and Cherry with all food and four ponies made for the Barrier. They were rescued, all fine, but lost 3 ponies unavoidably. I had better tell you now Birdie, Cherry and Uncle and Titus are quite the pick of the whole bunch.

By contrast, Atkinson continued, Teddy Evans did not seem well suited to on-shore expedition life. Atkinson had therefore taken the liberty of telling Scott about a matter the two friends had discussed before Pennell had left the previous year:

> About the 2nd year I have let the Owner know your wishes off my own bat and he told me that he had been considering it, would like it very much but that it was a very difficult question. You would like the life it is good and hard.

Bowers' letter opened with lists of goods in short supply or overstocked and requests for items Pennell might have to hand, including boot-leather, reindeer skins, china mugs and new gramophone records. Having dealt with his duties as quartermaster Bowers told Pennell who he thought might return to New Zealand with the ship and who might stay on for another season:[18]

> I don't think [Scott] is particularly keen on coming home this time … if you have brought the beasts [mules] down he will certainly stay … Bill [Wilson] I believe has decided to stay … provided he gets good news of Mrs Wilson's health, etc. Teddy [Evans] I think is keen on leaving once the polar show is over. I am staying anyhow, so is Sunny Jim [Simpson], Silas, Deb, Day, Nelson, Atkinson & probably Titus, Cherry & Trigger. Meares, Ponko [Ponting], & Griff [Taylor] are returning in the ship … I think Anton [the groom] will go home, he is a good little chap but gets depressed at times. Demitri is staying & is a great success with the dogs.

Bowers had warm words for many of his companions, including 'Taff' Evans ('perfect godsend'), Lashly ('equally good in his line'), Clissold ('a great success'), Hooper ('filled out & become quite a hefty chap'), Cherry-Garrard and Wright (now both 'great sledger[s]'), Ponting ('indefatigable with his photography') and Day ('a marvel at all mechanical jobs'). Wilson and Atkinson were, Bowers confirmed, 'just the good chaps' they had first appeared to be. Scott and Wilson made 'an ideal pair' and Simpson had made a 'sporting effort' in joining one of the shorter expeditions from Cape Evans.

Others had not, Bowers felt, taken so well to life on the ice:

Teddy has changed a good deal[;] he is just as enthusiastic & energetic as ever but inconceivably quiet for his mercurial nature. One hardly ever hears him & we have [not] had a single sing-song since you left us. Trigger [Gran] was a little flattened out by the cold in the autumn but has bucked up considerably since. Titus [Oates] is much more cheerful than he was at the start of the depôt journey … the great 'Griff' [Taylor] … is up & down like a barometer always … an enthusiast as well as an egoist & probably the cleverest fellow in the party by a long chalk.

Bowers, like Atkinson, hoped that 'wheels within wheels' would result in Pennell joining the landing party for what would certainly be the final season of the expedition.

Scott's letter was also encouraging in that and other respects:[19]

I guess that you yourself would like to have a turn at shore work and I have it in my mind to arrange it but it is a delicate matter and best left to one of my Southern notes or for my return. I needn't tell you I should be delighted to have you here. I have written to the Admiralty to commend your services … I know you will do your best and I want you to feel confident that I shall support your actions whatever they may be. Don't ever worry yourself by wondering whether I should approve this or that; if you think it is the right thing I shall be satisfied. Goodbye for the present. I shall be writing from the South I suspect.

Teddy Evans' letter made it clear he was not entirely happy and would not be averse to exchanging duties with Pennell:[20]

Dear old Penelope

I shall be awfully glad to see you again. I asked Capt. Scott to write & ask the Admiralty to promote you early[;] this he has done. Excuse a short note I am tired out. I have been away sledging for the past month, or I would have written more fully. Good bye, don't hurry out of [McMurdo Sound] too soon. If we stay a 2nd year I don't mind exchanging with you if you like, as I am rather afraid it is not quite fair to my dear little Hilda.

But Pennell knew that, regardless of what he or the others wanted, nothing could be counted on unless Scott sent a written instruction back, as he had suggested he might, with the second returning party sledge-party.

In the absence of Wilson and Bowers, Cherry-Garrard had a tale to tell. On 27 June 1911, in the depths of the Antarctic winter, Cherry, Bowers and Wilson had set out to trek to the emperor penguin colony at Cape Crozier. Wilson wanted to collect specimen eggs, which would, he hoped, show whether there was an evolutionary link between birds and reptiles.[21] During their five-week expedition howling gales had shattered their 'igloo' shelter, their tent had blown away, they had fallen down crevasses, and, in temperatures as low as 70°F below freezing point, their helmets had frozen into blocks of ice and they had suffered frostbitten extremities and cracked teeth. They had staggered back into Cape Evans on 1 August, starving and virtually unrecognisable, but bearing three specimen eggs. The expedition, during which Wilson and Bowers had 'celebrated' their 39th and 28th birthdays respectively, had tested Cherry's endurance to the limits but he would never forget the resilience and kindness of his two companions.

On 14 February 1912, with most of the unloading completed, Pennell decided to make another attempt to pick up Taylor's geological party (the still unfulfilled third task on his list). As he sailed, Atkinson and Demitri also left Cape Evans for Hut Point with a dog team. Given the uncertainty as to when the ship would leave, they would travel south to meet Scott and the South Pole party and rush back with their news in the hope the ship had not yet left McMurdo Sound for New Zealand.

On 16 February, Pennell welcomed Taylor, Debenham, Gran and Forde aboard the *Terra Nova*.[22] They had seen the ship in the distance during Pennell's first attempt to reach them and had since been making their way across the ice floes in anticipation of Pennell's return.

When a 'snow and blow' made an immediate return to Cape Evans impossible, Pennell decided to head for Terra Nova Bay in case he could retrieve Campbell's party. But the pack was still heavy and there was no sign of open water. He had no option but to retreat, but it took four hours to turn the ship and three hours of alternating reverse thrust and 'full steam ahead' to make a mile through the overlapping pancake ice. Pennell knew it was no help to Campbell or anyone else if the *Terra Nova* became frozen in, so he decided to return to Cape Evans.

When he arrived on 25 February, Pennell asked those on board who were planning to stay for a further season to gather their belongings and disembark and those who were planning on returning to New Zealand to disembark, pack quickly and tell anyone else who wanted to leave to prepare for departure.

If everyone did as asked, he might be able to make one more attempt to relieve Campbell.

Suddenly Simpson arrived on board with news of the second returning sledge party. They were off the Barrier but Teddy Evans was desperately ill with scurvy and needed to be brought onto the ship immediately. Atkinson and Evans were both at Hut Point, where Atkinson was treating him with scorbutics. But it was to Bill Lashly and Tom Crean that Evans owed his life.

* * *

On 4 January 1912 Teddy Evans, Lashly and Crean had waved Scott, Wilson, Bowers, Oates and Taff Evans away to the Pole and then turned north. As the days and weeks passed it became clear that Evans was gradually losing strength, but Lashly and Crean were still pulling strongly. On 13 February, about 100 miles from Hut Point, Evans collapsed completely.

Lashly and Crean decided what films, personal possessions and non-necessities they could safely take off the sledge and loaded the comatose Evans onto the sledge. For the next week they dragged Evans, their tent, vital equipment and a diminishing stock of rations at an average speed of 10 miles a day for ten hours' pulling. Eventually Lashly and Crean began to weaken. Evans roused himself sufficiently to order them to abandon him, but they decided to disobey him and instead to put themselves on half rations and continue marching towards Hut Point. With any luck, they thought, there might be someone waiting there to meet them or the South Pole party.

After four days on half-rations Lashly and Crean worked out that they would not, at their current rate of progress, reach Hut Point before their rations ran out completely. They agreed that Lashly would stay with Evans while Crean, armed with two sticks of chocolate and three biscuits, would set out to walk the remaining 30 or so miles to Hut Point.

On 19 February Tom Crean staggered into Hut Point to be greeted by an astonished Atkinson and Demitri. Crean had walked for eighteen hours with only a five-minute break to eat his chocolate and two biscuits.

Now Atkinson needed to reassess his priorities. Of his two fellow doctors, Wilson was on his way to or from the South Pole and Levick was marooned at Evans Cove. Only Atkinson was available to try to save Teddy Evans' life.

Atkinson and Demetri set out with a dog-sledge and brought Evans back to Hut Point. Knowing he also needed to think about who would travel south to meet the South Pole party he sent Crean to Cape Evans with a note asking Cherry-Garrard and Wright to come to Hut Point. With the ship due to leave,

Atkinson had little choice. Meares was packed and ready to go; Simpson had been prepared to stay (as Bowers suggested) but Pennell had brought him a letter from the India Meteorological Department summoning him back to work.[23] Simpson was keen for Wright (who was staying) to take over his meteorological work straight away. Atkinson knew he could not expect Lashly and Crean to return immediately to the barrier. He also knew that, as a doctor, he was duty bound to stay with Evans until he was out of danger. That left Cherry-Garrard and Demitri. The latter was an experienced dog-driver; the former could be trusted to do his utmost to meet up with the South Pole party, which included Wilson and Bowers, two of his best friends on the expedition.

On 23 February Atkinson gave his Cherry his orders. As the South Pole party was by now almost certain to have passed 83°S (the most southerly meeting point Scott had specified to Meares), Cherry and Demitri should travel as fast as possible to One Ton Depot, with supplies for themselves, their dogs and the South Pole party. If they met the South Pole party at or before reaching One Ton Depot they should dash straight back with Scott's news and reports in case the *Terra Nova* was still in the area.

On 26 February Atkinson saw Cherry-Garrard and Demitri off from Hut Point, then settled down to wait for Pennell to bring the *Terra Nova* round from Cape Evans to collect him and Teddy Evans. By now the ice between Hut Point and Cape Evans had floated out to sea, so the only way out was by ship.

* * *

On 27 February Harry Pennell was waiting for a gale to die down so he could get round to Hut Point and pick up Evans and Atkinson. To pass the time he had started a letter to Edward Wilson, which he would leave at Cape Evans for Wilson to find on his return. Having assured Wilson that his wife, Oriana, was in good health and would be well looked after by Joseph Kinsey and others in New Zealand he told Wilson about his current concerns:[24]

> Here we are in a gale, hove to and waiting to pick up Evans & Co. ... he has scurvy & Jane is with him and got back a note to C. Evans just in time as the ice is now out. All approach to Campbell has been cut off up to date ... I should be landing in place of Evans but if he is an invalid of course cannot do so. Naturally though desirous of landing I shall feel quite satisfied if the expedition has the best use of my services in whatever capacity. The non-relief of Campbell up to date is rather a worry ... either the pack has cleared & he can be reached or it is there & he cannot ...

Once he had brought Evans and Atkinson on board Pennell was able to consider making another attempt to relieve Campbell's party and try to bring them back to Cape Evans. But when Pennell encountered a 35-mile wide band of compacted ice floes and frozen slush between him and Campbell's location he was forced to admit defeat.

Scott had, it transpired, given Evans a written order confirming that the two lieutenants could exchange duties. As Pennell wrote in his journal:[25]

> The slip between cup & lip in this case has been a narrow one and however much one would like to have landed there can be no doubt as to my duty keeping me in the ship. A year with Jane & Bill etc. would indeed have been bliss.

* * *

On 4 March 1912 the *Terra Nova* left McMurdo Sound with Teddy Evans, Ponting, Meares, Taylor, Simpson, Day, Forde, Clissold and groom Anton all aboard. Pennell had safely stowed away home-bound mail from those still on the ice and a report Scott had left at Cape Evans for Pennell to pass on to Central News Agency.

Pennell, his crew and passengers had bade farewell to Debenham, Nelson, Wright, PO Thomas Williamson (replacing Forde) and steward William Archer (replacing Clissold) at Cape Evans. Atkinson and Keohane travelled with the ship to Hut Point, where they disembarked to await the return of Cherry-Garrard, Demetri and the South Pole party.

On 7 March, following a final, frustrating and failed attempt to reach Evans Cove and pick up Campbell's party, Pennell set course for New Zealand. Now all he could do was hope that when the *Terra Nova* returned to McMurdo Sound in early 1913 all those still on the ice would be safely gathered at Cape Evans.

3

Breaking News – and a Mysterious Death

——⟨⟨⟨⟩⟩⟩——

On 10 March 1912, as the *Terra Nova* headed north, Harry Pennell considered what had happened since the ship had arrived in McMurdo Sound.[1] The fact that Teddy Evans had fallen prey to scurvy obviously gave rise to concerns about the health of the South Pole party. The early onset of ice had forced an early departure from Cape Evans (without knowing whether Scott and his party had reached the Pole) and prevented Pennell from relieving Campbell's party and returning them to Cape Evans. On the positive side Pennell felt that Scott had chosen the best men to take to Pole and that Wilson, Bowers, Oates and 'Taff' Evans all merited their places. On the scientific side, Simpson's meteorological results had exceeded expectations, Lillie's marine biology work was going well and Taylor's party had brought back specimens of coal and fossil traces. With strong sledgers, mules and additional dogs available, the prospects for the 1912–13 season's scientific work also looked promising.

As for his own situation, Pennell looked forward to captaining the *Terra Nova* back to Cape Evans the following season and to working with Rennick on his dredging and surveying work. In terms of his personal disappointment about not landing, Pennell reminded himself that two years ago he considered 'the ship billet all that could be desired'. He was determined not to succumb to the 'promotion craze' which appeared to be infecting his fellow-officers:

> Teddy Evans thinks of it incessantly, even Scott seems to think one is down here to get promotion & Rennick is disappointed with his billet because it will not help him on his promotion. [Atkinson] originally thought it would help him but now has had a sickness of promotion-catching talk …

By 21 March the *Terra Nova* had crossed the Antarctic Circle and icebergs were increasingly few and far between.[2] The repeated attempts to relieve Campbell's party had taken their toll on coal stocks but they were making good progress and everyone, bar 'the few exceptions who are not so keen on civilisation', was looking forward to an early arrival in New Zealand.

The next day Pennell and his shipmates found themselves in the middle of the worst storm they had experienced since leaving Britain.[3] Force 11 gales sent them bobbing to the crest of 50ft waves, then crashing down into the trough between them. But as helmsman McCarthy wrestled with the wheel, all the sailors stuck to their task and everyone accepted 'a good dose of work and plenty of spray on them … as part of the day's joke'. Ponting even managed to capture some 'capital cinematograph films' and Lillie to stop his 'multitudinous bottles' from hitting the deck.

Pennell was rather enjoying himself:

> The sight of the ship in the sea particularly during the night, with the howl of the wind, formed a spectacle that few are now privileged to see and nearly all spent some time on the bridge … so this gale will probably not lose out in the telling in future. A curious feature of the squalls at their worst was that they come up absolutely black, as if there was heavy snow or rain in them, while as a matter of fact there was little precipitation & the blackness was that of the squall itself; so dark that one could see nothing more than a ship's length off.

The storm lasted for four days but by 29 March they were within 400 miles of New Zealand with just enough coal in hand to reach Akaroa, where Pennell would hand over his and Scott's reports to a representative of Central News Agency.[4] As the ship approached land Pennell wrote to relatives of the South Pole party, explaining that the latest news they would have was on letters dated 3 or 4 January 1912. This did not, he assured them, suggest anything amiss, other than that the early onset of ice had hastened the *Terra Nova*'s departure from Cape Evans. Pennell knew that newspapers would report the fact that Teddy Evans had scurvy, so he also assured them that this did not mean that members of the South Pole party would succumb to it.[5]

Pennell told Emily Bowers that her son was the 'heart and soul' of the expedition's work and that Wilson had sung his praises after they had returned from the Cape Crozier journey. He explained to her and others he was writing to that there would now be no further news until early 1913, after the *Terra Nova* had completed her final return voyage and brought all the remaining members of the landing party back to New Zealand.

In the early hours of Monday, 1 April 1912, under cover of darkness, the *Terra Nova* slipped into Akaroa's 'remarkably pretty' natural harbour.[6] Ponting was quite moved to see green foliage and pasture-covered hills after over a year photographing the barren ice and lava rocks of Antarctica.[7]

Pennell and Drake took the cutter ashore to meet Central News Agency's representative. Bertie John (byline 'B.J.') Hodson had served as a soldier in the 2nd Boer War before learning his craft on his local paper and moving to London, where he lived with his German-born wife and young son. Having travelled the world on behalf of Central News Agency, he hoped to be the one to secure what could be CNA's greatest 'scoop' since 1885, when they announced the fall of Khartoum and General Gordon's death twelve hours ahead of rival agencies.[8] Hodson had already been in Akaroa for several weeks and had, to avoid arousing the suspicions of local journalists, registered at his lodgings as 'Mr Newbury', an English tourist who played tennis and enjoyed mountain-climbing.

Pennell and Drake explained that Scott was not on the ship and that they did not know whether he had reached the Pole. Hodson told them that the *Fram* had arrived in Hobart on 7 March with Amundsen aboard. Amundsen and his team of skiers and dog-sledges had, it seemed, reached the South Pole on 14 December 1911.

By the time Pennell and Drake had finished discussing matters with Hodson the harbour foreshore was swarming with residents, some armed with cameras or binoculars. As only Pennell, Drake, Hodson and those on the *Terra Nova* knew whether or not Scott was aboard, Pennell agreed to remove the ship from prying eyes until Central News Agency's exclusivity period had passed.

Pennell and Drake returned to the *Terra Nova*, ready to break the news to their shipmates and show them the newspaper reports about Amundsen's triumph. But some locals had already rowed out to the ship and shouted, by way of greeting, 'Why didn't you get back sooner? Amundsen got to the Pole in a sardine tin on 14th December!'[9]

After Pennell dropped anchor outside the harbour, Teddy Evans emerged from his cabin for the first time. As he sat in a deck chair in the sunshine, Jim Dennistoun took some final photographs, Rennick gave Lillie a haircut and others discussed Amundsen's achievement or began sprucing up themselves and the ship, ready for their arrival in Lyttelton.

Ponting decided to take some final group photographs of the afterguard and crew. The afterguard squinted in the sunshine: Dennistoun (holding his own camera), Cheetham, Rennick, Drake, Williams (in his woollen hat), Pennell (in his favourite carpet slippers), Bruce and Lillie. After the shutter clicked, Ponting dismissed the afterguard and began corralling the seamen for their photograph.

On 3 April 1912 the *Terra Nova* steamed into Lyttelton harbour, where a tug, with Hilda Evans and Oriana Wilson on board, came out to meet them. Pennell transferred to the tug so he could explain the position regarding their husbands. After the *Terra Nova* came alongside the wharf, Teddy Evans was helped down to where Joseph Kinsey was waiting with his list of names and rail passes for those travelling to Christchurch.[10]

Pennell, his afterguard and Kinsey spent much of the following days responding to the demands of the press and photographers. Pennell freely acknowledged that Amundsen had achieved 'priority' at the Pole, but maintained that Scott's scientific programme would be of lasting value. There had been suggestions, largely in British newspapers, that Amundsen had unfairly encroached on Scott's 'sphere of influence'. Fridtjof Nansen had defended his fellow-countryman; Sir Clements Markham had denied the existence of a 'race' but suggested that Scott's scientific endeavours outweighed Amundsen's 'dash' to the Pole.[11] To try to put an end to all talk of a 'race to the Pole', Kinsey released a copy of Scott's letter of 28 October 1911 to the newspapers:[12]

> We shall leave with high hopes of accomplishing our object, despite the reverses of last season, but as there is a chance that we may not catch the ship, I have decided to arrange for her to return in 1913. I am fully alive to the complication of the situation by the presence of Captain Amundsen, but as an attempt at a race might be fatal to our chance of getting to the Pole at all, I decided, long ago, to do exactly what I should have been done had Amundsen not been here. If he gets to the Pole he is bound to do it rapidly with dogs, and one foresees that his success will justify him. Anyway he is taking a big risk and deserves his luck if he gets there.

Alongside the letter, *The Press* reported from Sydney that Edgeworth David, whilst presiding at a lecture by Amundsen, had stated that Amundsen's behaviour had been 'fair and square' and that he was sure Scott would, on his return, 'send hearty congratulations to the champion who had beaten him'. David also noted that Scott and Shackleton had both found coal traces, which suggested that Antarctica contained the largest unworked coal field in the world.

Pennell caught up on news of other expeditions. Mawson had arrived in Hobart on the *Aurora* on 12 March to find the *Fram* in harbour and everyone talking of Amundsen's triumph. Shirase had returned to Wellington on 23 March, happy to have explored King Edward VII Land and seen the *Fram* and met some of Amundsen's men in the Bay of Whales. There was no news of Filchner.

The *Fram* was now on her way to Buenos Aires, leaving Amundsen to meet the Australian prime minister and continue his series of illustrated lectures. Amundsen had originally stated that he would not give lectures in New

Zealand (which he described as 'Captain Scott's ground'), but shortly after it became known that Scott was not on the *Terra Nova* a cable arrived from Australia confirming that Amundsen would give some talks in New Zealand before rejoining the *Fram*.

Most of Scott's men would have left New Zealand before Amundsen arrived. Griff Taylor was heading for Australia to join the Bureau of Meteorology; Simpson was going to visit Australia on his way back to India.[13] Ponting was returning to London and, as arranged with Scott, would publicise the expedition through his photographs and films. Teddy Evans, after further recuperation at his wife's family home, was going to sail back with her and Francis Drake; the two men would then carry out some expedition work at the Victoria Street offices. Meares had accepted an invitation from Dennistoun to visit Peel Forest for some mountain climbing, following which he was going to sail back to Britain with Bernard Day.[14] Clissold would help tidy the ship then travel back to England with Cheetham who, with Pennell's permission, was making a short visit to his family following the death of Frederick, his tenth child, who had been born six months after Cheetham left on the *Terra Nova*. Anton the groom, who disliked long dark Antarctic and Russian winters, had decided to try to find work in New Zealand rather than return to Russia.[15] As others made their plans, Pennell discussed arrangements with the New Zealand marine authorities for the coming winter's surveying work, which would start in June near Marlborough Sound.

As soon as Amundsen arrived in Auckland he was asked for his views on the recent sinking of the luxury liner *Titanic* following a collision with an iceberg during her maiden voyage.[16] Since the accident, in which over 1,000 crew and passengers had died (about half of those aboard), enquiries had been convened and memorial services held in Britain, the United States and other countries; London's Lord Mayor had established a Mansion House Relief Fund to provide for needy dependents of crew and others who had died.

When Amundsen arrived in Christchurch on 26 April, Kinsey met him at the station. During the day Amundsen visited Kinsey's office (where he met Teddy Evans), the *Terra Nova* (where he was introduced to the crew) and Kinsey's house in Sumner (where he met Pennell and members of the afterguard).[17] Pennell found Amundsen to be 'a quiet, unassuming man'. Although he still felt the Norwegian's lack of openness regarding his plans had undermined Scott's expedition, he decided there was 'no use in belabouring the point'.[18] Following his short lecture tour, Amundsen returned to Auckland to join the *Remuera*, on which Cheetham and Clissold had also booked their passages.

As his duties in Lyttelton became less onerous, Pennell paid more attention to what was happening in Britain:

The great coal strike with its attendant miseries was over at home and the political world is in a ferment over Home Rule, Disestablishment, Insurance Bills, etc. There can be no question that Home Rule must come to the kingdoms of the United Kingdom to relieve the awful congestion of the Imperial Parliament; all I ask is that the schemes should be well thought out & not schemes to buy support.

Pennell awarded himself two weeks' leave with the Dennistouns at Peel Forest, where he played tennis, rode, climbed mountains with Jim and his sister and generally enjoyed 'a quiet life'.[19] In Christchurch he met up regularly with Hugh Acland of Mount Peel and expanded his knowledge of medical matters by joining Acland at a lecture on sleeping sickness.

Towards the end of May, Pennell reconvened his depleted afterguard. Drake and Cheetham were still in England, Dennistoun was back working at Peel Forest and Lillie was due to leave for five months' whaling on a Norwegian ship. But William Williams was ready for duty and Rennick was back from Dunedin, where he had visited Isobel Paterson, the young lady from the Port Chalmers tug. Over the past few weeks Bruce had stayed in Christchurch as several thespians he knew were taking part in a visiting production of *The Whip*. Bruce went to see the 'spectacular' (which featured live horses) several times and showed his friends round the *Terra Nova*.[20]

By early June Pennell had confirmed that the surveying team would be working around French Pass, a notoriously fast-flowing neck in the Cook Strait, between Wellington and Nelson. Since the late 1880s a dolphin known as Pelorus Jack had guided sailors through the pass; he had not been seen for months and there were fears that he might have died.

During the winter the *Terra Nova* would remain at Lyttelton undergoing repairs, while crew members Parsons, Balson and McKenzie guarded her and repaired storm-damaged sales. The marine authorities would provide two motor launches for Pennell and his team, which included Rennick, Bruce, Williams, Mather, carpenter Davies, engineer Brissenden, stoker Burton, Leese, Forde and three other seamen.

Pennell and the surveying party soon settled into Alexander Stuart's boarding house at Elmslie Bay, the remote, small settlement which served the French Pass area. Life there was generally quiet but on Saturdays French Pass fishermen and other locals gathered on the wharf to take delivery from Nelson of copious quantities of beer and rum, which they then shared out with friends. Pennell made it clear to everyone that alcohol was forbidden on the surveying launches or in their boarding house.[21]

While he was at Elmslie Bay, Pennell received a telegram from the expedition's honorary treasurer, Sir Edgar Speyer.[22] His message was brief: 'Evans promoted

Commander returning with Drake time to take ship South in December'. Pennell struggled to marshal his thoughts:

> [Evans] is singularly fortunate in getting his promotion[,] I never believed it possible. If he is really coming out it would seem that I am getting my congé.[23] To stop in the ship after being suspended [as captain] would make an awkward position as I shall have been in command for nearly two years; on the other hand to leave the ship before the relief is accomplished would be very disappointing. I still hope the telegram was a mistake & that Evans will stick to his original intention of leaving me alone.

Apart from the personal slight, Pennell felt that Evans did not regard scientific trawling (which used up coal) as being worthwhile; Pennell, on the other hand, was keen to do as much as possible on the *Terra Nova's* final return voyage to Antarctica, given that Lillie was there 'to make the most of whatever is got'. But he decided that there was 'no use creating trouble in the expedition' and that, although the telegram had depressed him, he should accept this development 'loyally & cheerfully'. Pennell's final lingering hopes that the telegram might be 'a mistake' were dashed by a second message from Speyer, but he decided that 'the pill must be swallowed with grace'.[24]

But in the middle of August something happened which put things into perspective – it was hard to know exactly what had happened, but Pennell tried to set it out clearly in his journal:[25]

> We have had the great misfortune to lose Brissenden by drowning.
>
> On Saturday [17 August 1912] we were out at work as usual till 5.0. After tea he was mending his jersey in the dining room & went to the store to get some wool to go on with his work. Here he met with the Kassebaums (local fishermen) who were all more or less (mostly more) drunk & lent one of them a friendly hand. That is as far as we can get.
>
> On Sunday morning his roommates saw that he had not slept in his bed and made a search themselves but thought it quite possible that he had been drinking & so were not really anxious.
>
> Rennick & I were in D'Urville Island [near French Pass] all day Sunday & on our return the fact of his being missing was reported, but as the *Nikau* [the local steamer] had been on Saturday night & it was always possible he might have taken an involuntary passage on her we were still not really anxious. Early on Monday morning, at daybreak & low water, the body was seen under the pier head.

The day after Brissenden's body was found Coroner Evans and Dr Johnston came from Nelson to conduct an autopsy and inquest. Pennell, Bruce, several members of the *Terra Nova* crew and local witnesses were summoned to give evidence in the Elmslie Bay schoolroom. William Williams and Bill Burton, who were close friends and long-time shipmates of Brissenden, had been excused due to their distress at their friend's death.

During his testimony Pennell described Brissenden as 'a most reliable and steady man'. He was 34 years old, a married man with two children, a temperance man who had never been brought before Pennell or reported as being drunk. He could swim, appeared 'perfectly healthy' and did not, to Pennell's knowledge, suffer from fits.

The Coroner, after listening to testimonies and reports for over nine hours, concluded that:

> The said Robert Brissenden was drowned at the French Pass, New Zealand, on Saturday the 17th August 1912 while in an unconscious condition either from a fall or a blow but there is no evidence to show how he was injured, or how he got into the water. He was himself sober.

Following the inquest Pennell arranged for a visiting Methodist minister to come to Elmslie Bay to take the funeral service. Locals placed fresh flowers over the coffin, which Williams, Burton and other shipmates of Brissenden carried to the Elmslie Bay burial ground, high on a hill above the sea.

Pennell remained perplexed as to what exactly had happened to Brissenden. Evidence given at the inquest had convinced him that 'Kassebaums & party were hilariously drunk'; on the other hand the very thorough post-mortem had shown no sign of Brissenden's having been hit with 'a bottle or other missile' and marks on his body could have occurred in the water or from falling down the pier steps. Pennell suspected, however, that George Kassebaum 'if less drunk – or possibly if he wanted to – could throw some more light on the matter'. Even if there had not been 'foul play', Pennell wondered if Brissenden might have been given 'a drunken shove when not expecting it'.

Pennell sent a copy of the coroner's report to the Admiralty and ordered a marble cross from a local monumental sculptor to place over Brissenden's grave. He tried to comfort Bill Burton as best he could and encourage the young man to 'step up' and accept the role of engineer previously occupied by his best friend. Pennell sent a message to Lyttelton, where another of Brissenden's close friends, Edward McKenzie, was on the *Terra Nova*; the ship's flag was lowered to half mast. When the news reached the expedition's London office, it was arranged that Kathleen Scott (who happened to be staying in Kent, where Brissenden lived) would break the news to Brissenden's wife.[26]

By the end of September, despite poor weather, the surveying work was complete; they had surveyed 24 square miles and taken over 10,000 soundings, which Rennick would plot on new charts of the French Pass area to be issued to ships as soon as possible.

In late October there was more good news for mariners who regularly negotiated French Pass – Pelorus Jack, the famous dolphin, had been seen guiding a ship in the area.[27]

4

Final Journeys

—⟡⟡⟡—

On 30 October 1912 Teddy and Hilda Evans and Francis Drake arrived back in Christchurch. Evans was, as far as Pennell could see 'practically well again' but his heart was still weak.

Pennell had recently returned from Peel Forest, where he enjoyed climbing local mountains with Jim Dennistoun, playing tennis, riding around the farm station and learning more about foresting techniques.[1] With Evans back, he was keen to find out how they were going to deal with the situation regarding command of the *Terra Nova*.[2] Pennell suggested that one solution would be for Evans to be 'Commander of the Expedition' for the duration of the voyage, leaving Pennell in his current role as ship's captain. The only alternative was, as far as Pennell could see, for Evan to take command of the ship and discharge Pennell completely. But Evans, whose new rank of commander had been conferred on him by the king, had the final word on the subject:[3]

> I am now in the position of Navigator. The position is of course a very awkward one, one might almost say humiliating, even, but will have to be made to work and as he is a man of considerable tact and we are good friends should not be hard.

Pennell concluded his *Terra Nova* captain's journal with a long entry summarising the winter's work and acknowledging the service, over two years, of his afterguard and crew.[4] He formally handed the ship over to Evans and returned to Peel Forest. Over the next few weeks Pennell went to see *Kismet* with Jim Dennistoun's father and visited Hugh Acland and his wife ('one of the sweetest women I have met'), who had rearranged one of their rooms so Pennell, Atkinson and Lillie could stay in Christchurch whenever they wanted. During one visit, Pennell and Atkinson 'had the great honour of being asked to be godfathers to the Aclands' expected baby', which, all being well, was due to be born in July.[5]

There was also happy news from Henry Rennick, who was now engaged to 'Miss Paterson' of Dunedin; although this was supposed to be a secret, Isobel

Paterson was now living in Christchurch – which made Pennell suspect that Rennick would be paying noticeably less attention to his plotting duties until the *Terra Nova* set sail. Meanwhile, Lillie had returned from his months of whale-watching and fossil-hunting and Alf Cheetham was back from visiting his family in Hull.

Amundsen, who had been on Cheetham's homebound ship until South America, was now in Britain, where he had been lecturing to members of the Royal Geographical Society and the Royal Scottish Geographical Society. The latter had welcomed him warmly, but RGS members had been more reserved, as many still felt that Amundsen's sudden switch from North to South Poles and his use of dogs had unfairly disadvantaged Scott. Amundsen went on to lecture elsewhere in Britain (including Cardiff and Cheltenham) and in France and Italy.[6] He then planned to travel to the United States where he would give more lectures before rejoining the *Fram* in San Francisco in mid-1914 and heading north into Arctic waters.

On 14 December 1912 the *Terra Nova* left Lyttelton wharf, waved away by Kinsey, Hilda Evans, Oriana Wilson, other friends and well-wishers and a crowd of onlookers.[7] Evans and Pennell had carefully stowed bundles of letters for those still on the ice, as well as champagne and a range of delicacies with which to celebrate the return of the South Pole and Northern parties.

On the first evening out of Lyttelton they found a stowaway aboard, a local 'rabbiter' who seemed uncertain as to why he wanted to sail south; they turned around, but the captain of a passing sailing barque kindly agreed to take the man aboard and land him. There were no mules or dogs aboard this time but Rennick had, in the hope of enjoying fresh eggs, brought with him three hens. Meanwhile Cheetham was laying 'a break-back trap and meat with a little aniseed on it' to deal with the few rats remaining on the ship.

On this voyage the *Terra Nova* was following the easterly route which James Ross had taken on his 1842 voyage to the sea which bore his name.[8] Pennell was glad to see that Evans now seemed keen to have a 'good scientific record' and was giving Rennick and Lillie the time they needed to take new soundings and trawl new waters respectively. Evans also seemed 'madly keen' to make sure that Pennell and Rennick were promoted after the expedition, but Pennell was happy to take his chance. During the voyage Pennell could spend as much time as he wanted in the crow's nest, as Teddy Evans' weak heart prevented him from clambering aloft. With only navigator's duties to keep him busy, Pennell was able to spent hours watching out for seabirds for the zoological log he was keeping. On 22 December, Pennell's 30th birthday, Evans produced 'a little parcel from home' containing neck-ties from his mother and handkerchiefs, which Pennell thought was 'a very pleasant surprise … on the high seas'.[9]

Christmas Day fell on a Wednesday and was, in Pennell's view, 'rather a failure'.[10] On recent voyages he and Rennick had organised a rest day, with minimal duties for everyone, which had allowed everyone to join in 'a little service & Xmas hymns'. Evans had decided instead to order 'Sunday routines' which had meant the day not feeling particularly special. But on Boxing Day they saw their first iceberg.

For a few days they managed to skirt the pack but by New Year's Eve they were at a complete standstill. They celebrated the coming of 1913 with 'a very jolly evening', during which they had a 'sing-song' and were able (due to being stationary) to play the new gramophone records they had bought in Christchurch.[11]

As they inched their way through the pack, the antics of two Adélie penguins provided some light relief:[12]

Two examining a tin, thrown overboard to the ice yesterday, were screamingly funny. Each was very jealous of the other & very anxious to see the tin & each one's antics in trying to drive away his companion … [were] ridiculous beyond words. Wonderfully peaceful it is here without the hubbub and disturbance of our over specialised civilisation.

By 18 January 1913 the *Terra Nova* was through the pack and anchored a short distance off Cape Evans. Much to Pennell's relief, Campbell was visible from a distance; he was, like Teddy Evans, armed with a megaphone. Evans asked, across the distance, whether everyone was well. Campbell shouted back that the South Pole party had reached the Pole in January 1912 but had died on the way back to Cape Evans.

In the hush which followed, the bunting in the *Terra Nova* wardroom was taken down and the champagne, cigars and chocolates which had been laid out for immediate consumption were stowed away again.

Everyone then set to loading the ship and by the following day the *Terra Nova* was ready to leave Cape Evans for Hut Point, where Atkinson and others who had wintered at Cape Evans had one last thing to do.[13] They dragged a heavy wooden cross up to the top of Observation Hill and drove it into the ground. Carpenter Frankie Davies had already carefully chipped out the names of the members of the South Pole party and a text from Tennyson's *Ulysses* chosen by Cherry-Garrard: 'To strive, to seek, to find, and not to yield'.[14] After Atkinson came down the hill, he checked the hut was secure and well-stocked for any future travellers.

The *Terra Nova* left Hut Point on 21 January and embarked on a circuit of McMurdo Sound, punctuated by stops for scientists to pick up heavy specimens they had deposited over the past two seasons. Pennell finally had time to commit to paper what he understood to have happened since early 1912:[15]

Seaman Evans died at the foot of the Beardmore and his illness was the real reason of their loss, though even this would not have had this effect if the weather had been normal, but the season was very early and very severe.[16]

Oates got badly frostbitten and one night left the others as being their only means of safety; the other three got to within 11 miles of 1 Ton Depot where there was a month's supply of food. Here a nine days blizzard raged and killed them.[17]

Cherry & Demitri, who had left with the dogs when we left Hut Point finally last year, were unable to get beyond 1 Ton Camp owing to the appalling weather and on their return to Hut Point Cherry's heart gave out from overstrain though now, thank God, he is alright again.

Jane [Atkinson] & Keohane went out man-hauling but could not get beyond Corner Camp and were fortunate in getting back ... there being now no hope at all of the Southern Party [Jane] tried to work up towards Campbell in case he was coming down the coast. They (J, Silas, Keohane & Williamson) had a very bad time but struggled to Butter Point, after which there was no clear ice and they had to return.

Jane has had a very bad winter, but has risen to the occasion and kept his party in spirits under the most trying circumstances ...

As soon as possible this season [Atkinson and a party] went out with the mules & found Scott, Wilson & Bowers.[18] The two latter were peacefully asleep and had died a quiet death, the Owner [Scott] had had more of a struggle.

Campbell's party expected the ship till the beginning of March last year & then on her non-arrival set to prepare for the winter. The sea did not freeze over and sledging south was impossible, so they dug out an igloo and started to kill seal and penguins ... Browning was the only one who became really ill ... at one time it seemed as if he must die. The party kept very cheerful and nothing in this expedition is finer than their story. Every Sunday they sang hymns ... and on birthdays etc. made much of a dozen raisins each. Scott's original description of Campbell as 'a refined & cultivated gentleman' has been borne out to the full under the greatest stress — when the man appears naked & unashamed in his real character.

Atkinson had told Pennell that, from what he had seen at One Ton Depot and read in Scott's journal, the evaporation of fuel (vital for melting snow and ice into water) and the early onset of winter had been the main contributory factors to the deaths of Scott, Wilson and Bowers.

By now, Atkinson and the other scientists, knowing how much store Scott and Wilson had set by their huge programme of scientific work, had resolved that the *Terra Nova* expedition should not be seen as a failure:

> if (as everyone is determined it shall be) it is properly cleaned up it will be a very great success in every way. The Southern party brought all records & their geological specimens with them, & so though the cost has been great – far greater than the most pessimistic has feared – yet the success is complete. The principal [scientific] work was done during the first season on the whole, this splendid achievement during the second.

The *Terra Nova* made a final stop at Evans Cove. Campbell picked up specimens and equipment and showed 'visitors' round the 'igloo' which the Northern Party had carved out of the ice as a shelter from the worst of the winter weather. Pennell was amazed and full of admiration:

> No written description can conjure up what the 5 minutes inspection fixed on one's mind. Size 9' x 13' & everything done that ingenuity with no material could devise, but in spite of their thought and care it was almost a shock to see this little dugout in the snow and realise that 6 men had lived there from March 1st to mid-September with a depot of 1 months sledging rations …
>
> The whole thing is splendid – their resourcefulness, unselfishness, humour & quiet heroism. Campbell has indeed proved himself in as dire straits as man could ever be in & win through, but every one of the party has come out with credit.

When he arrived at Cape Evans Pennell had immediately noticed that the past year's events had taken a physical as well as a mental toll on both Campbell and Atkinson. But, as the ship sailed north, Pennell noticed something strange happening:

> Campbell's wrinkles are coming out of his face fast and now he looks younger than when he first joined the ship in London. Jane is much more marked – lines all over his face, which now, in repose, has a thoughtful almost sad look. The expedition will I think affect him more (personally) than any other member.

Teddy Evans had by now set up an ad hoc committee which consisted of himself (as chair), Pennell, Campbell, Bruce, Atkinson and Drake. Their most immediate task was to pull together a dispatch to transmit to Central News Agency from New Zealand covering the period from 4 January 1912, when Teddy Evans had brought back Scott's journals covering the first part of the journey to the South

Pole. Since then, Scott had been sledging or trapped in blizzards and his journals had become increasingly difficult to read. He had also expended much of his energy in the days before he died writing personal letters to members of his family, to his companions' relatives and to close friends and former colleagues, including Kinsey, J.M. Barrie and Sir Edgar Speyer.

Scott had, however, written a 'Message to Public' which was clearly intended for publication. In this he suggested that his death and those of his companions had been the result of a combination of factors including the loss of several ponies during the depot journey, unexpectedly poor and cold weather conditions, and delays on the way to and from the South Pole.

Atkinson and those who had seen the leaking fuel containers at One Ton Depot felt that Scott had not perhaps taken everything into account. But Teddy Evans argued that Scott's message should be published as written. As chair of the committee, he had the casting vote, should one be required.

As they sailed north, the pack was less dense than on previous northbound voyages, but some large icebergs gave them some heart-stopping moments. On one occasion, as they tried to skirt an iceberg, they sailed for 21 miles alongside a 200ft high wall of ice before they reached the end of it; on another, they were forced into a narrow gap between two icebergs without having any idea whether they were entering an open-ended channel or a cul-de-sac.[19] But, all in all, everyone seemed in good heart and members of the landing party enjoyed watching the flocks of Southern Ocean birds which they had not seen for over two years. Pennell, who had helped Wilson keep the log of birds on the first southern voyage, was also pleased to have seen so many different species.

By early February 1913 the *Terra Nova* was clear of the pack and heading for Oamaru, a port 150 miles south of Christchurch, where Pennell and Atkinson would land with the news of Scott's South Pole party.

5

From Oamaru to Awliscombe

In the early hours of 10 February 1913 Tom Crean rowed Harry Pennell and Edward Atkinson from the *Terra Nova* into Oamaru harbour.[1] When Crean had returned, the *Terra Nova* weighed anchor and sailed north. She would dock in Lyttelton only after Evans was sure that the news carried by Pennell and Atkinson had been published in New Zealand newspapers. But the arrival of two strangers in Oamaru under cover of darkness did not escape attention:

> The night watchman … telephoned to Captain Ramsay the Harbour Master who … took us up to his house for the remainder of the night, where we had blankets & sofas in the dining room. The first express did not pass through till about 11.0 and so Jane [Atkinson] & I after sending a wire to Kinsey went & sat in a field. In the train going up we met Mr Dennistoun … quite half a dozen reporters were onboard but after asking us for information and being refused they left us alone.

In Christchurch, Pennell and Atkinson headed for Kinsey's office, from where they sent several more cables.[2] They tried to contact Oriana Wilson, who was staying with friends in Dunedin, but she had already left for Christchurch and would not arrive for some time. Pennell and Atkinson went to Kinsey's Christchurch home; after an early night and a good night's sleep they returned to Kinsey's office.

It fell to Atkinson, as leader of the search party which had discovered Scott's tent and the bodies of Scott, Wilson and Bowers, to explain to Oriana Wilson what had happened. Pennell could see how difficult this was for Atkinson but felt that Wilson's widow 'behaved splendidly throughout, proving herself a fit wife for Bill'.

That night Pennell and Atkinson went to Sumner and stayed at the Marine Hotel, the scene of happy evenings with Bowers, Oates and Wyatt and where Bowers and others had left surplus personal effects. The next morning, 12 February, they walked over the hills to Lyttelton wharf, from where a tug took them out to the *Terra Nova*. By now news of the expedition was in all the newspapers and it seemed that everyone wanted to meet, interview or photograph Scott's men. The atmosphere in Kinsey's office was initially rather chilly as Kinsey seemed to have taken against Evans and vice versa. There was also the issue of potential overlaps of duties and responsibilities (including between Kinsey and Drake), but gradually everyone settled down.[3] Pennell felt that 'no man or lady could have behaved better than Mr & Mrs Kinsey with Mrs Wilson', particularly as they had been 'very much upset' themselves. It was not easy for anyone, particularly during a memorial service at Christchurch cathedral – the sight of flags flying at half-mast was also a constant reminder of what had happened.

Pennell and his companions were now public figures, so it was a relief to get away at weekends. Pennell, Atkinson and Campbell spent their first weekend at Kinsey's house in Sumner and Pennell, Atkinson and Bruce spent the second at Peel Forrest. Pennell was busy during the week as he, rather than Teddy Evans, would be sailing the *Terra Nova* back to Britain. Rennick went to see his fiancée in Dunedin, but would return in time to make final preparations for the voyage.

Campbell, the scientists and Gran all decided to travel back to Britain by steamer rather than with the slower *Terra Nova*; before leaving Gran climbed Mount Cook in a record time of fourteen-and-a-half hours.[4] Atkinson travelled to Wellington with Wilfred Bruce, Teddy and Hilda Evans and Oriana Wilson to meet Kathleen Scott off her ship from San Francisco. She had learned of Scott's death whilst at sea and was, according to Atkinson, 'wonderful' about what had happened; she decided, however, not to go to Christchurch but to sail straight back from Wellington to Britain.

Teddy and Hilda Evans also left direct from Wellington, but Oriana Wilson and Atkinson returned to Christchurch. After a farewell weekend with the Kinseys, Pennell accompanied Atkinson and Oriana Wilson and her sister to Wellington, from where Atkinson was going to escort the two ladies on their voyage back to Britain.

Pennell returned to Christchurch to make final preparations for the long homeward voyage. After writing a number of letters of thanks, including one to the prime minister of New Zealand, he reflected that, 'In some ways this has been a very happy month: no one could have imagined how nice everyone could be until this sort of thing occurred, the thoughtfulness, the sympathy of all our neighbours, the press & the public has been wonderful.'

On 13 March the *Terra Nova* set sail from Lyttelton, heading east to join the old 'Great Circle' clipper route to Britain, by way of the Pacific Ocean, Cape Horn, South America and the Atlantic. Of Pennell's original afterguard, only Rennick, Cheetham, Williams and Lillie remained, so Pennell was glad that Edward Nelson had offered to serve as Second Mate and that stalwarts like Levick, Lashly, Crean and Keohane were back on board.[5] Levick, as well as acting as ship's doctor, was in charge of the meteorological log, while Nelson would write up the 'fair copy' ship's log. Pennell had put himself in charge of the zoological log and would, as he had done when previously in command, be taking Sunday morning services.

On Monday, 17 March, St Patrick's Day, Pennell gave the order to 'splice the main brace' so that Irishmen Crean and Keohane and others could enjoy an additional tot of rum.[6] As they were now exactly twelve hours behind Greenwich Mean Time the following day was also Monday, 17 March, but there was no second extra rum ration. Pennell was pleased to see a song thrush alighting on the ship. He added it to his sightings of wanderers, grey shearwaters and black-bellied petrels in the zoological log and, as the sun went down, remembered his Southern Ocean bird-watching partner, Edward Wilson: 'The sunset tonight was very beautiful … it was one of the subdued nights that he appreciated so much.'

By 19 March, 1,000 miles out from Lyttelton, they were ahead of schedule. But a few days later Pennell became aware of a problem on board:[7]

> Four days ago Abbott became obsessed with the delusions that the hands were talking about him; apparently he has been 'anxious' for over 3 weeks but the hands thought he would get alright and said nothing. He now varies from about normal with a slight unknown grievance in his mind … Tonight for the first time he is inclined to be violent.

Sometimes Abbott had to be pinned down or confined to the wardroom. At night (when he was at his most violent) Levick would sit by him; others took turns at sitting by him by day. Pennell could see that Abbott was passing through stages, including 'grievance, religious mania, imagining himself God', but by the beginning of April the patient was sleeping a lot and eating well.[8] Pennell noted that the seamen looking after their shipmate in pairs, were 'extraordinarily good … gentle and firm'.

Edward Nelson meanwhile had taken to his new post 'like a duck to water' and seemed 'keen as mustard'; he was, as far as Pennell was concerned, 'far and away the most brainy person on the ship'.[9] As for the original afterguard, Rennick seemed to be missing his fiancée, but boatswain Cheetham (who had acquired a pet canary in New Zealand) and engineer Williams were 'as happy as sand boys'; Lillie was also enjoying trawling new waters. Tom Crean was, as Pennell had expected, 'absolutely splendid'.

By mid-April they were round the Horn and on course for Rio de Janeiro, where they would make a coaling stop.[10] Pennell had recently spied some flying fish, but was disappointed in his tally of seabirds, because he had seen no mollymawks or 'sooties'.

In Rio, somewhat to Pennell's surprise, the *Terra Nova* was not quarantined.[11] He and Levick immediately went to the British Consulate to ask for help in booking a passage home for Abbott. The Consul General, Sir Roger Casement, was away investigating 'rubber atrocities' in Peru, but his deputy, Ernest Hamblock, was 'simply splendid and of enormous assistance'.[12] Pennell (who had not been to Rio before) was impressed by the fine harbour with its rugged surrounding hills and the city's wide 'show street'. Just as they were in the midst of loading coal, Britain's Minister to Brazil, Sir William Haggard, arrived on a surprise visit.[13] Pennell thought he seemed genuinely interested in the expedition and not to have minded scrambling over coaling barges to reach the ship.

As they sailed out of Rio in beautiful sunshine, Pennell pondered the paucity of birdlife compared with the Southern Ocean. This thought in turn reminded him of Edward Wilson and a poem he had written – which Pennell now copied into his journal:[14]

The silence was deep with a breath like sleep
As our sledge runners slid on the snow,
And the fate-full fall of our fur-clad feet
Struck mute like a silent blow,
On a questioning 'hush', as the settling crust
Shrank shivering over the floe;
And the sledge in its track sent a whisper back
Which was lost in a white fog-bow.

And this was the thought that the Silence wrought
As it scorched and froze us through,
Though secrets hidden are all forbidden
Till God means man to know,
We might be the men God meant should know
The heart of the Barrier snow,
In the heat of the sun and the glow
And the glare from the glistening floe
As it scorched and froze us through & through
With the bite of the drifting snow.

As the *Terra Nova* entered equatorial waters Pennell and the afterguard took watches in the engine room to allow stokers and firemen time away from the searing heat.[15] Pennell hoped that as temperatures dropped and days lengthened he would have more entries for his zoological log, but there was 'not a bird or a dolphin seen' until a little wheatear alighted on the ship.

Fayal, in the Azores, was their final stop before re-entering British waters. This time the *Terra Nova* did not escape being quarantined, but the doctor allowed Pennell, Levick and Archer ashore to send cables and purchase provisions.[16] Pennell thought the town seemed 'really quaint'; he was intrigued by the hooded outfits worn by local women and enjoyed a drive into the countryside to see the volcanic crater. Other aspects of the countryside seemed more familiar and the sight of stone boundary walls and the sound of robins and blackbirds singing in the bushes made him think of his home in Devon.

On 11 June, a week after leaving Fayal, the *Terra Nova* arrived at the Scilly Isles, where Teddy Evans and Francis Drake boarded the ship for the final leg of the journey to Cardiff.[17] Teddy Evans had sad news: his wife Hilda had died of peritonitis during their homeward voyage. Since returning from France (where his wife had been buried), Evans had kept himself busy at the expedition's Victoria Street offices, making arrangements for the return of the *Terra Nova* and finalising details of her resale to her previous owners, Bowring Brothers.

In a few days the expedition would be over and Pennell could go home.

* * *

On Saturday, 14 June 1913, a day short of a year since leaving Cardiff, the *Terra Nova* returned to her point of departure, where Pennell's sisters, Winifred, Dorothy and Neeta, were there to greet him. There was a sizeable crowd on the wharf, but the presence of Kathleen Scott, her young son Peter and Oriana Wilson seemed to discourage cheering. Atkinson and his aunt, Lady Nicholson, were also there, along with other friends and relations of those on board. Once the ship had docked, temporary railings and the presence of policemen kept those with no direct connection with the expedition or its members at bay.

Pennell and his sisters stayed with a Mr and Mrs Miles, who obligingly also provided accommodation for visitors. Edward Nelson came to stay, as did Harold Hodson, one of the six brothers of Gerry Hodson, Pennell's best friend from HMS *Britannia*. Mr and Mrs Miles took Pennell and his sisters to see Tintern Abbey, but gave Pennell the chance to 'slack it' after his long voyage. On 16 June Pennell attended two 'compulsory' formal events; he felt that both the official welcome and dinner at the Royal Hotel 'went off alright'.

On 23 June Pennell formally turned the *Terra Nova* over to Teddy Evans and took the train to Exeter. He missed the last train to Honiton, but after a night at the Rougemont Hotel he caught the morning train. As he was walking from

Honiton station to his mother's home at Awliscombe, 'I passed the church just as Mother & Dorothy were going in (it being a saints day) & so we all went in & partook of the sacrament together.[18] Atkinson had come down on the Saturday & met us all on our way home.'

That afternoon Pennell played some tennis, went for a walk with his sister Dorothy and Atkinson (whom Mrs Pennell had 'taken straight to her heart') and embarked on a round of visits to relations and friends. Atkinson returned to London, so that Pennell could spend more time with his family before finding out what was expected of him in addition to completing his charts and other expedition paperwork.

Pennell's first job was to attend a meeting of a recently formed advisory committee which was in the process of winding up the expedition's business. This august body was chaired by Lord Curzon (in his capacity as president of the Royal Geographical Society) and included Sir Clements Markham, Reginald Smith (whose family publishing company would publish Scott's journals and other expedition records), Sir Edgar Speyer, Daniel Radcliffe (Cardiff's leading expedition supporter) and Admiral Sir Lewis Beaumont, an RGS council member who was also a long-standing naval colleague and friend of Scott. Pennell, as a member of Teddy Evans' hastily constituted *Terra Nova* committee, was happy to hand over his responsibilities, but Teddy Evans still seemed to regard himself as being in command of the expedition.

Atkinson, one of the few expedition members involved in the new structure, would be representing the scientists on a 'publications' sub-committee, which was run by Colonel Henry Lyons of the Royal Engineers, a widely travelled geologist and meteorologist.[19] Pennell joined Atkinson on a visit to Cambridge to meet the Master of Christ's College, Dr Arthur Shipley, an eminent parasitologist, who helped with arrangements for Lillie to complete his experiments in university laboratories.

At the end of June it was announced that Pennell, Campbell and Bruce were now promoted to the rank of commander (in the navy's main fleet, emergency list and Royal Naval Reserve respectively), Francis Davies was promoted to acting carpenter, and Rennick, Atkinson, Levick and Williams were noted for future accelerated advancement.[20]

Admiral Sir Lewis Beaumont invited Pennell to pay him a visit at his home near Brighton. Scott's old friend was 'very keen on the expedition & that things should run smoothly. Unfortunately he & Teddy do not see eye to eye; but the old gentleman is out for peace if possible. His position is not an easy one.'

Pennell soon fell in to a rhythm of working on his charts and records during the week and catching up with family and friends (usually outside London) at weekends.[21] In late July a state ball provided a change from his usual routine:[22]

Buckingham Palace ... is a very pretty sight but one wants a companion to appreciate it. Fortunately John Hughes came over. Also met ... Admiral Beaumont & saw a few other familiar faces but not many. At suppertime there was a good view of the King & Queen as they walked in – she was looking very nice.

A few days later Pennell and his sister Dorothy joined Atkinson on a visit to Scott's mother. Atkinson, whose only previous meeting with Mrs Scott had been when he had told her about her son's death, had been rather dreading the visit. Pennell and his sister enjoyed meeting the resilient old lady (who had now lost both her sons) and was glad that Atkinson had 'taken away a more cheerful memory' than he had from his earlier encounter.

In early August Pennell took his sisters Winifred and Dorothy on an evening out in London. After dinner they went to see Arnold Bennett's new play, *The Great Adventure*, which contained, Pennell thought, 'quite the best pieces of acting I have seen probably in my life'; in addition, 'Atkinson honoured us with his company & so made it a most successful evening.'[23]

Pennell spent the following weekend in the Cotswold village of Oddington, where the family of his HMS *Britannia* friend Gerry Hodson lived and where Gerry's father was vicar. Gerry was away on naval duties but his brothers Cyril, Reginald and Charlie were there, as was Katie, Gerry's younger and only sister. Pennell had first met Katie as a 16-year-old when Gerry and his family had been living in Charlton King's, near Cheltenham; Gerry and his brothers had all at one time attended Cheltenham College, Edward Wilson's old school. Over the years Pennell had gradually watched Katie become 'much older in manner' and less shy and self-conscious than she had been as a young girl. Of Gerry and Katie's other siblings, Tom was already married, Hubert was working in Canada and Harold was due to leave, with his twin brother Reginald, to spend time in the Antipodes.[24]

In London, Pennell and Atkinson became regular theatre-goers. Pennell found *Bunty Pulls the Strings*, *General John Regan* and *The Milestones* all 'entirely first class' but felt that, for acting, *The Great Adventure* could not be surpassed.

On 26 July Pennell and Atkinson donned dress uniform and went to join their *Terra Nova* companions at the expedition's office in Victoria Street. Rennick marched the seamen along the road to Buckingham Palace, where everyone was due to be presented with polar medals, or clasps in the case of those who had already had one from a previous expedition.[25] King George first presented insignia to Kathleen Scott, Oriana Wilson, Emily Bowers, Lois Evans and Rosa Brissenden, and to Evans on behalf of Mrs Oates.[26] Pennell and the officers and men were then introduced by First Sea Lord Admiral Prince

Louis of Battenberg to the king, who presented them all with medals or clasps. The king also presented Lashly and Crean with Albert Medals for their roles in saving Teddy Evans' life. Pennell was glad to hear the king also make 'a kindly and well deserved acknowledgement' of Atkinson's work following Scott's death. The king was clearly genuinely interested in the expedition and had, Pennell knew, already broken with royal precedent by attending the memorial service for Scott and other members of the South Pole party which had taken place in St Paul's Cathedral in February.[27]

Following the ceremony, everyone went along to Caxton Hall, where they drank toasts to the expedition, to each other and to absent friends. Francis Drake would be sending medals or clasps to Jim Dennistoun, Demitri Gerof and seven seamen who were all in New Zealand, to Bernard Day in Australia, George Simpson in India and Anton Omelchenko in Russia. He also had medals for Clissold, who was in England but apparently indisposed, and for Abbott, who was still under doctors' supervision.[28]

Pennell was glad to hear that a concluding meeting between Evans and the advisory committee had resulted in expedition matters being 'peaceful in every direction'. Atkinson would be taking a break from his report-writing and committee work to take a holiday with his sisters in the West Indies, where he had been born. While he was away Pennell would stay on in the house near Harley Street, where they both now had rooms:

It is very comfortable here at Queen Anne Street and being in the same house as Atkinson makes it most enjoyable. James Wyatt F.R.C.S. owns it & Miss Wyatt, lives here too, Atkinson, Treves, Senior & myself complete the household, while numerous [Wyatt] brothers drop in from time to time.[29] Wyatt & Miss Wyatt are exceedingly nice & considerably above the average.

Before Atkinson left Frankie Davies joined him, Pennell, Lillie and James Wyatt for an evening at the Trocadero grill and a variety show at the Tivoli theatre.[30] On 13 August Pennell went to see Atkinson and his three sisters, who were all 'in the highest spirits', off to the West Indies. Two days later Pennell's old friend Gerry Hodson passed through London on his way to Oddington for an extended home leave: 'It was our 1st meeting since the T.N. returned. He is looking well but is worried over his chances in the navy. At present he is in the *Blake* which is I am afraid a backwater, but he is trying hard for an independent command.'

Pennell spent the following two weekends with Gerry and his family in Oddington:[31]

It is lovely in the English country now. Mr Hodson is coming into his own now after a heart-breaking fight & the parish appreciate him at last. The old church has been done up and is now used again ... The wall opposite the door had a larger painting but this has been mainly obliterated; it must have been a startling picture when new as Hell obviously figures largely with devils & flames.

In a return visit, Gerry and Katie came to London to join Pennell for dinner and a performance of *The Great Adventure*, which, Pennell noted, Katie appeared to have enjoyed very much.

In early September Pennell visited a very different country residence, the Lamer Park estate which Cherry-Garrard had inherited whilst still a student:[32]

It is only 25 miles from town and yet in perfect country. The house is a large Georgian structure, ugly from the front but very comfortable inside. The front door opens straight onto the park ... [which] gives a curious sense of space & freedom. C.G. is the only son, but he has several sisters ... Mrs Cherry-Garrard (the mother) is most charming and delightful.

Cherry drove Pennell back to London on Monday, following a pleasant weekend of country pursuits. Cherry, Pennell and Atkinson would all be meeting up again in Scotland in a few days' time at an estate which Atkinson's aunt had recently inherited from her late husband, the eminent lawyer Sir Richard Nicholson. Pennell had agreed to wait and travel up to Scotland with James Wyatt and Atkinson, who was due back from the West Indies. On his return Atkinson, who appeared to have enjoyed his holiday, immediately 'fled off to Essex, where his lady love lives', but he was back in time to catch the following evening's night sleeper to Aberdeen. They arrived 'very hale and hearty & ready for great deeds' at Eden House, near Banff – on an estate which Pennell felt lived up to its name and where he thoroughly enjoyed himself:[33]

No salmon have been caught but there are always high hopes ... Fresh air, delightful company & most lovely country – well may this be called Eden ... The house is beautifully situated amongst the trees on the hillside near the river Deveron, a prettier spot could hardly have been chosen ... The land seems to be very good and the farmers are good at their work too.

Pennell was pleased that Oriana Wilson, whom he had seen recently when she had visited his mother in Awliscombe, was able to join them all for a few days.[34]

Pennell spent the following weekend in Colchester with his HMS *Britannia* friend, Edward Digby, whose father, Sir Kenelm Digby, was an eminent lawyer and civil servant who shared Pennell's liberal leanings. Sir Kenelm had recently been appointed to a Royal Commission on venereal disease and, as ever, Pennell found it 'a great treat to hear Sir Kenelm discuss matters of the day'.[35]

In October Pennell paid another visit to Oddington. He knew that Katie and her parents were due to leave for six months in Lausanne, Switzerland, and that, by the time they returned, he would probably be at sea. There was therefore something he felt he must say:[36]

> I proposed to Katie & dropped a bombshell in the vicarage. I know the poor girl had no idea either way but saw no other way to make her think of me. Mr & Mrs Hodson & all the family are delighted, the dear old Mum is delighted, all except poor Katie who is having rather a bad time.

Katie had clearly been taken aback at Pennell's proposal, but Pennell felt his cause was not lost. He certainly did not want Katie to 'jump at [him] without thorough thought', particularly as he would not be well off and knew that his long absences would mean she would 'have a hard life in some ways'.[37] But he was glad to have spoken out – and to be invited to join Katie and her parents in Lausanne for a week in January.

When Pennell returned to London, Atkinson took him to see *The Great Adventure* and for post-theatre dinner and a tête-à-tête about Pennell's news. Atkinson was wondering whether he might return to Antarctica in about four years' time 'to find out what is East of the Barrier' – the area which Campbell had left unexplored following the encounter with the *Fram*. Campbell was now back in London, ready to complete his charts, but Teddy Evans, with whom Pennell wanted to check some charts he had drafted based on Evans' notes, was 'still running about lecturing'.

Evans' lecturing career had begun at the Royal Albert Hall on 21 May 1913 when, shortly after returning to England, he had delivered only the sixth Royal Geographical Society lecture to be given by an explorer. The audience of 9,000 had included Lord Curzon, Prince Louis of Battenberg, General Sir Douglas Haig and Sir Robert Baden-Powell. Evans had been joined on the platform by Atkinson, Cherry-Garrard, Bruce, Drake, Meares, Taylor, Priestley, Gran and John Mather.[38] When Evans had spoken at the Queen's Hall the following month, Shackleton had been in the chair and Prime Minister Asquith and First Lord of the Admiralty Churchill had been in the audience.[39]

In September Evans was invited to speak in Scotland, where he and John Mather (by now working as Evans' assistant) stayed with Emily Bowers on Bute.[40] Evans began receiving invitations to give lectures on the Continent. He travelled to Antwerp, Belgium, where the British community was commissioning a memorial window to the South Pole party in St Boniface's Anglican church; he agreed to return the following year to inaugurate the window. When Evans lectured in Christiania, the Norwegian capital, he was presented to King Haakon and (courtesy of Gran) to Elsa Andvord, the strikingly attractive English-educated 'belle of Christiania'. Following a few more European lectures Evans embarked on a well-publicised sixty-lecture tour of Britain which would last from October almost to Christmas 1913.[41]

While Evans lectured, Pennell awaited Katie Hodson's response. His expedition work was tapering off, but he still had no news of a new naval posting. In the meantime, he contemplated national concerns, including the thorny 'Irish Question' which, he felt, hung 'like a cloud over the country'.

On 6 November, the charts on which Pennell had worked so hard and a report on the voyages of the *Terra Nova* which he had co-authored with Teddy Evans were finally published in *Scott's Last Expedition*. This two-volume publication, produced by Reginald Smith's publishing company, included Scott's edited journals, scientific reports and narratives about the Northern Party and other sub-expeditions. It was lavishly illustrated by watercolours and drawings by Edward Wilson and photographs by Ponting and others, including Scott, Bowers, Levick and Debenham, with whom 'Ponko' had shared his expertise.

A few days later Pennell, Atkinson, Evans, Meares, Levick and Lillie travelled to Oates' family home at Gestingthorpe, Essex, where a bronze memorial plaque in memory of their late friend, commissioned by his fellow-officers of the 6th Inniskilling Dragoons, was unveiled.[42]

On 10 November Lord Curzon presented Pennell, Atkinson and other officers and scientists with the Royal Geographical Society's Antarctic medal.[43] Evans was unable to attend due to a lecturing engagement in Cambridge; Victor Campbell had also given his apologies. Raymond Priestley, who had been invited to give a talk on the Northern Party's scientific work following the ceremony, took advantage of the opportunity to praise the 'unfailing cheerfulness and fertility of resource' of the notoriously shy and modest Campbell.

During the proceedings Lord Curzon read out a telegram of good wishes from Australia. It had been sent by Edgeworth David and Captain John Davis (of Mawson's *Aurora*) but also, thanks to the wireless link at Mawson's Cape Denison headquarters, included a message from the explorer himself. He was still on the ice: two members of his party had died earlier in the year and he and his companions would only be relieved when the *Aurora* returned in early 1914.[44]

Shackleton had recently let it be known that he was now contemplating another Antarctic expedition. This was not unexpected, but it was more of a surprise when J. Foster Stackhouse, a railways advertising agent from Kendal, announced that he was planning an expedition to King Edward VII Land, based on plans he had discussed with Scott. Stackhouse, who had part-sponsored a *Terra Nova* expedition pony, also claimed that he had raised further funds for Scott and only declined to join the expedition due to prior commitments.[45] Stackhouse's only previous experience of polar exploration had been a short expedition to Jan Mayen Island, off Greenland, but he persuaded Sir Clements Markham to write to *The Times* describing his plans as being 'in the best traditions of British discovery'. When one of Stackhouse's associates claimed (again through *The Times*) that Teddy Evans had also endorsed the expedition, Harry Pennell wrote his own letter to the editor:[46]

> Commanders Evans and Campbell, with Dr. Atkinson and other member of the expedition of 1910–1913, as well as Lady Scott, point out that, whatever the attractions of Mr. Stackhouse's enterprise, they know of no plans for exploration of this coast which were proposed by Captain Scott other than those to be undertaken by himself or by his lieutenants. The officers of the expedition of 1910–1913 protest against the use of their leader's name in a way for which they know of no authority given by Captain Scott.

Stackhouse, in response, maintained that he had discussed his project with Scott and was in the process of acquiring the *Discovery*, from which Scott had first seen King Edward VII Land. When Pennell declined to respond further the correspondence petered out.

On 22 November Pennell, Campbell, Levick and Meares joined other guests at the wedding of Wilfred Bruce and Dorothy, elder daughter of Sir Jesse Boot, the millionaire owner of a nationwide chain of some 500 pharmacies.[47] Henry Rennick, in his role as best man, and Bruce were both in full dress uniform, as were the members of a naval guard of honour. The reception took place at the Langham Hotel, where one of the highlights of the table displays was a wedding cake topped with a model of the *Terra Nova*.

On 27 November the postman delivered an envelope with a Swiss postal mark to Pennell:[48]

> Katie's letter came accepting me, which only needed a telegram to make us engaged. Dear little girl I am afraid it is a bigger step for her than for me. It's only on an occasion like this that one gets an idea of how ones messmates feel towards one, they have all written the most kind letters a man could receive.

On 11 December a notice in *The Times* confirmed that Harry Pennell and Katie Hodson were indeed engaged to be married.[49]

Katie and her parents were still in Switzerland, but Pennell was already looking forward to his visit to them early in the New Year. In the meantime, he kept busy. He took his sister Dorothy to see an exhibition of Edward Wilson's drawings and watercolours at the Alpine Club and Ponting's photographs at the Fine Art Society in Bond Street.[50] They also went to see a new production of *Quality Street*, an early play by Scott's friend J.M. Barrie. Pennell thought the production was 'very pretty' but found the story of two sisters running a school to be 'a little sad ... [and] for women between 30 & 40 almost distressing'. Dorothy, who was unmarried, was fortunately a nurse by profession.

Before the residents of 15 Queen Anne Street went their separate ways for Christmas, Atkinson and James Wyatt took Pennell out for dinner, a performance of *The Great Adventure* and post-theatre supper at the Piccadilly Restaurant.

Back in Awliscombe Pennell enjoyed his first 'home Christmas' for years. Gerry Hodson came down for a few days to join Pennell and his mother and sisters in the celebrations. Pennell felt that the 'Irish Question' cast something of a cloud over the New Year, but, with his engagement to Katie Hodson now confirmed and a holiday in Switzerland and a new naval posting in the offing, 1914 seemed full of promise.

Ring Out the Old, Ring In the New

On Saturday, 3 January 1914 Pennell and Atkinson marked the New Year with an outing to a performance of J.M. Barrie's *Peter Pan* – a work Pennell considered to be a 'real living masterpiece'.[1] Three days later Pennell tidied away his expedition papers, enjoyed 'a good solid meal' with Atkinson at Simpson's in the Strand, walked to Charing Cross station and boarded the night train. He arrived in Lausanne the following morning 'to the minute by the timetable'. At the 'comfortable, quiet & splendidly clean' hotel, he found his fiancée Katie and her parents, and her brothers Cyril and Charlie, who had joined them for a short holiday.

Pennell's first impressions of Lausanne were, with one exception, favourable:

1. Cleanliness
2. Good quality of shops & moderation in prices
3. Politeness & good humour of the shop attendants without servility
4. Absence of police
5. Irritating exactness of byelaws at railway stations & tramways, etc., which necessitate being very early to ensure catching a train or tram.

Pennell joined Katie and her brothers on day-long walks, during which they sustained themselves with picnic lunches supplemented by *cafés au lait* purchased from mountain cafés. After Cyril left for home, Pennell, Katie and Charlie continued to walk, ski, ride on mountain trams and take boat trips on the lake. They also visited Geneva and Les Avants, where there was a specially constructed *luge* course. After Charlie left, Pennell and Katie found themselves, for the first time in ten years of knowing each other, completely alone 'without brotherly support'. Pennell realised Katie was somewhat troubled by 'doubts & perplexities' regarding the physical side of marriage, but, having sisters, knew this was common amongst girls who, like Katie, had been 'brought up in complete ignorance of natural functions'.

On Pennell's last Saturday in Switzerland he and Katie made a return visit to Les Avants:

> it was gloriously sunny all day and few people were about. It was quite strange to have an extended view & to really see where we had been the first day. Caux was across the valley & we could make out the various details distinctly. It was in all respects a jolly day & Katie supremely happy.

On 26 January Pennell said goodbye to Katie and her parents and set off on the long journey, by train, steamer and foot, back to Awliscombe.

He returned to London in early February and dealt with a few tail ends of expedition work. Lady Nicholson, Atkinson's aunt, invited him and Atkinson for dinner and he had an evening out with Lillie (dinner at Les Gobelins and a performance of *The Great Adventure*). With little of his own work to do, he helped Atkinson with some of his work at the London School of Tropical Medicine, a favour he was happy to do for a friend who had been prepared to answer questions on 'aspects of the physical side of marriage', which Pennell felt he could only have raised with his late father.

When Pennell learned that he was to join HMS *Duke of Edinburgh* as navigator in about a month's time, he went to Awliscombe to spend some time with his mother and sisters. His new ship, the lead vessel of the 1st Battlecruiser Squadron of the Mediterranean Fleet, was commanded by Captain Cecil Prowse, whom Pennell had met in Lyttelton (when Prowse had been returning to England from the Australasian station). Prowse was known as an 'old school' sailor, but had been on training courses to prepare him for working on the new generation of battleships.

On 9 February Pennell travelled to London to attend a lecture at the Royal Geographical Society by Edgeworth David, who was visiting from Sydney. Pennell thought David's views on Antarctica were interesting but he found the eminent professor 'rather inclined to talk hot air!'[2] Shackleton, who was in the audience, spoke afterwards about his plans for a 1,700-mile trek across Antarctica which would, he estimated, take less than six months. For this expedition Shackleton would need two ships: one would sail from South America to the Weddell Sea, the other from New Zealand to the Ross Sea. The Weddell Sea party would cross the continent, while the smaller Ross Sea party would lay depots across the ice shelf to the Beardmore Glacier, which the Weddell Sea party would then use on the latter part of their journey.

Men were already signing up to join the expedition. Frank Wild (a *Discovery* and *Nimrod* veteran) would be Shackleton's second in command; Aeneas Mackintosh (a *Nimrod* veteran), Ernest Joyce (*Discovery* and *Nimrod*), Thomas Orde-Lees (an unsuccessful applicant to the *Terra Nova* expedition), and John Davis (a *Nimrod* veteran, still captaining the *Aurora* for Mawson) had also confirmed their interest in taking part. Alf Cheetham was also keen to take part in his fourth Antarctic expedition. Shackleton was keen to use aircraft during the expedition and had approached Tryggve Gran in London in May 1913, after hearing that Gran was planning to take up flying.[3] Gran had attended a dinner with some of Shackleton's potential backers but had not pursued the matter.

Pennell had intended to return to Awliscombe immediately after David's lecture but stayed in town for the following two weeks to help Rennick with some charting work. There would soon be a parting of the ways as Rennick was also expecting to hear about a new posting soon and Atkinson had recently committed to some work which would require him to travel to China.[4]

On Friday, 13 February, Pennell paid a visit on an old expedition associate:

> I went down to London Bridge to see George Wyatt about the disposal of the sledges & at the same time arranged with him to convert £200 in 100 shares in the original Northern Exploration Company that is working in Spitzbergen. It will be an interesting investment at any rate, even if not lucrative, but we have high hopes of the latter too. Spitzbergen is in a curious state as it is a No-man's Land, and is now proving to be full of mineral wealth.[5]

After completing his business Pennell returned to Queen Anne Street, where his sisters Dorothy and Winifred were due to arrive. Winifred would be leaving England the next day to take up a new post as a missionary with the Universities' Mission to Central Africa. With Pennell joining the *Duke of Edinburgh* and Atkinson going to China, it would be some time before they all saw each other or James Wyatt and his sister again.[6]

The next day Pennell and Dorothy waved Winifred off at Southampton on a journey which would eventually bring her to the island of Likoma on Lake Nyasa, where she would be based for the next few years. Pennell then went to Cambridge to see Wright, Debenham and Priestley. The *Terra Nova* scientists had always been close but the bonds had strengthened since Wright and Griff Taylor had visited Priestley's family home in Tewkesbury, Gloucestershire, and fallen in love with two of their friend's sisters.

Pennell returned to London for a farewell evening with Atkinson and Rennick – dinner at Les Gobelins, a performance of *The Great Adventure* and post-theatre supper at the Piccadilly Restaurant. The following day Pennell met up with Frankie Davies (now based in Devonport) to discuss a description of the structure of the *Terra Nova*, which was needed by the publications committee. In the evening James Wyatt joined Pennell and Davies for a light-hearted evening at the Oxford Music Halls.

On 20 February Atkinson and Cherry-Garrard left for China with Dr Robert Leiper. The eminent Scottish helminthologist, with whom Atkinson had previously worked, had travelled to Antarctica a decade earlier with William Speirs Bruce and knew of Edward Wilson's pre-*Terra Nova* work on parasites affecting Scottish grouse. Atkinson and Leiper were to be in the Far East for up to eighteen months, studying a waterborne parasite which caused bilharzia fever, which affected both locals and British troops working there.[7]

Cherry-Garrard was going to assist them for a few months, but would return in May to write an official narrative of the expedition. The publications sub-committee (on which Atkinson still served) had originally allocated this task to Teddy Evans but in his continuing absence had accepted Atkinson's suggestion that the task should be given to Cherry. Atkinson, who had kept a friendly professional eye on Cherry since his collapse in Antarctica, knew Cherry had no need to earn his living but needed to feel that he was 'playing his part'.

Teddy Evans was continuing to spread his wings on the lecturing front. He had been invited to give a lecture at the Sorbonne in Paris, so had taken himself off to France, taken a crash course in French and, on 27 January, addressed the French president and prime minister, explorer Jean-Baptiste Charcot and an audience of 5,000 in their own language.[8] His lectures in Rome, Vienna, Budapest and Berlin had been equally well received so, having decided that he enjoyed travelling and lecturing, he sought, and was granted, permission to remain on half-pay. He was now planning a lecture tour of North America.

By 22 February Pennell had completed his final expedition correspondence and had packed, ready to leave Queen Anne Street to return to Awliscombe, where he would stay until he was due to join the *Duke of Edinburgh*:[9]

> Mr [Reginald] Smith, Admiral Beaumont and Sir Edgar Speyer have all written very appreciative letters in reply to the letters of thanks written on behalf of the ship's party … The Wyatts are very sad at the breakup of the household. It has been the making … of the last 9 months having Wyatt's house to live in with [Atkinson] under the same roof. Old Mr Wyatt, James & Miss Wyatt are now friends I will try & keep in touch with.

On Tuesday, 24 February, Pennell wrote a long journal entry detailing the past fortnight's events. He closed the entry – and that volume of his journal –

with a poem by a young schoolgirl who had described, in her own words, the difficulties Wilson, Bowers and their companions had faced on their way to and from the South Pole:[10]

> The food was bad, their night bags froze
> They could not even blow their nose
> Because the drop upon it froze
> The heroes could not even doze.

* * *

On Friday, 23 January 1914, Herbert Ponting had showed a selection of his expedition photographs and cinematograph images to Ernest Shackleton and other invited guests at London's Philharmonic Hall in Great Portland Street. An article in the following day's *Times* praised both Ponting's work and Scott's foresight in appointing him as expedition photographer. The reviewer noted that, although some images had already been seen during lectures (notably that by Commander Evans at the Royal Albert Hall), Ponting's conversational style of commentary had added much to the audience's enjoyment.

Ponting had been unhappy for some time about the ways in which Teddy Evans and others used his work. On his return to England in 1912 he had written a long letter to Scott complaining about the use of his images for 'detestable advertisement work' by expedition sponsors and delays in reimbursing him for expenses. Following Scott's death Ponting's letter had been returned to him unopened.[11]

Almost as soon as Teddy Evans left for North America Ponting block-booked the Philharmonic Hall, which was conveniently close to the Oxford Mansions apartment he shared with his friend Meares. He placed advertisements in *The Times* with details of afternoon and evening performances and ticket prices. When he received enquiries for showings outside London, he passed them on to Meares.

While Ponting was attracting good houses to his film showings, people were also eager to see Scott's handwritten journals which, with Kathleen Scott's permission, had been put on display at the British Museum. In Cheltenham, Wilson's home town, thousands visited exhibitions of Ponting's photographs and of Wilson's drawings and watercolours.[12] One Cheltonian was so enthusiastic about Wilson's works that he suggested they should be permanently displayed in a new, purpose-built gallery adorned by 'a sculptured copy of a sledge drawn by a full team of Esquimaux dogs, accompanied by ski-shod explorers' and statues in the form of penguins.[13]

On 12 May Ponting had the honour of showing his photographs and films in the ballroom of Buckingham Palace to an audience including King George, Queen Mary, the King and Queen of Denmark, other members of the British royal family and numerous distinguished guests.[14] The king, who seemed to grasp the challenges Ponting had faced in capturing his striking images, expressed the hope that many of his subjects would have the opportunity to see the images in the future.

In early June Meares travelled to Cheltenham to give five lectures at the Town Hall. Audiences flocked to see Ponting's photographs and films and applause broke out whenever Edward Wilson appeared on screen. The following week *The Great White Silence*, a fictionalised but 'admiring tribute' to Wilson and his companions, ran for six performances at the town's Opera House.[15] Whether by coincidence or design, Oriana Wilson and other members of her husband's family left for holidays just before the play opened.[16]

* * *

By June 1914 Harry Pennell was some 1,500 miles south of London on the *Duke of Edinburgh*, which had a top speed almost four times that of the *Terra Nova* and a complement of almost 800; she was also armed with three torpedoes and thirty-six guns.[17] While Pennell had been in Valletta, Malta, he had written to Captain Ramsay of Oamaru, who had sent Pennell a photograph of his home as a souvenir of Pennell's visit in early 1913:[18]

> it brings to mind the typical New Zealand welcome we received in spite of arriving in the dead of night. I hope Mrs Ramsay appreciates the fact that we really were most comfortable despite the fact of choosing to sleep on the floor. It is all a matter of custom & if accustomed to sleeping on a board one gets to consider that the most comfortable form of couch.

In answer to Ramsay's enquiry after Atkinson, Pennell responded that his friend was now in the Far East.

Pennell was happy to be back at sea but he had already missed two important events in London. One was the presentation ceremony for a Murchison Grant (worth £40), which he had been awarded by the Royal Geographical Society for 'important services' to the expedition. The other was the wedding, on 25 April, of his friend Henry Rennick and his fiancée, Isabel Paterson of Dunedin.[19] There were now fewer 'Antarctics' in London than previously but Murray Levick had served as best man; Kathleen Scott had also arranged for the expedition pianola, which Rennick had so enjoyed playing, to be presented to the couple as a gift from the expedition.

Pennell had recently been concerned about the wedding gift he had sent to Silas Wright:[20]

> The parcel is a hearthrug & meant for your wedding present, why 'To be forwarded to Comd'r Pennell' should have been put on it I do not know at all …
>
> Life here is very pleasant. We are doing a 4 day stint at Trieste being entertained royally and soberly by the Austrians, [who] have too much sense to suppose that the only form of hospitality is to try and make a man drunk. On Saturday we go to Venice & then back to Malta where an Austrian squadron is visiting us. If the English must have *ententes* why not have them with either the Austrians or Germans, i.e. people it is a pleasure to meet.[21] We are hovering on the border of whites [summer uniform] now & as this ship refits at Malta in June & July will be pretty baked by the time it is over. Jane wrote very cheer-ho from Shanghai at the end of March.
>
> Give my chin-chin to Lillie, Deb & Priestley please.

Priestley's and Debenham's friend Douglas Mawson had recently arrived in England. Mawson had travelled to London with his new wife, Francesca 'Paquita' Delprat, whom he had wooed by wireless while marooned on Cape Denison, waiting for the *Aurora* to rescue him and his companions. Captain John Davis of the *Aurora* had served as Mawson's best man and guests including Edgeworth David had admired Antarctic-themed decorations in the form of penguins, icebergs, sledge dogs, snowy petrels and the *Aurora*. The visit to London was officially the couple's honeymoon, but Mawson and John Davis (who had sailed from Australia with the newly-weds) spent hours with Ernest Shackleton, discussing the role Davis and the *Aurora* would play in Shackleton's forthcoming Antarctic venture.

Priestley's 19-year-old sister Doris was due to travel in the opposite direction to the Mawsons, so she could be reunited with her fiancé 'Griff' Taylor.[22] After meeting Doris, Taylor had stayed on in England, writing up his scientific findings, drafting an Antarctic memoir and lecturing, including at the Royal Geographical Society. Before leaving England for Australia Taylor presented his fiancée with an engagement ring designed by Kathleen Scott and incorporating a piece of green marble Edgeworth David had gathered from the top of the Beardmore Glacier.

On Monday, 15 June, a few miles north of Cheltenham, Silas Wright married Priestley's sister Edith in Tewkesbury Abbey. Frank Debenham was best man;

guests with Antarctic connections included Oriana Wilson, Kathleen Scott, Wilfred and Dorothy Bruce, Murray Levick, Dennis Lillie, Edward Nelson and his new wife Violet and Frank Wild.[23]

Debenham returned immediately after the wedding to Cambridge to pack, as he was due to leave for Australia to attend, as a British delegate, the first overseas conference of the British Association for the Advancement of Science.[24]

Teddy Evans returned from the United States in June to fulfil a long-standing commitment. His North American lecture tour had gone well. In Washington he had stayed at the British Embassy as the guest of Ambassador Sir Cecil Spring-Rice, and lectured to 3,000 people, including the daughters of President Woodrow Wilson.[25] He had appeared in a weekly soap-opera-cum-documentary, *Our Mutual Girl*, clad in full dress uniform, playing himself.[26] He had also been forced to publicly deny rumours that he was engaged to be married to Kathleen Scott. On 22 June, in accordance with his promise to Antwerp's British community, Evans unveiled the new memorial window in St Boniface's church. The stained glass maker had ensured that the model ship held by St Nicholas, patron saint of seafarers, bore more than a passing resemblance to the *Terra Nova*.[27] Evans, having fulfilled his promise, returned to London and full-time naval duties.

On 28 June Archduke Franz Ferdinand, heir to the Austro-Hungarian Empire, was assassinated in Sarajevo, capital of Bosnia. The assassin had connections with Serbia, whose government Emperor Franz Joseph decided was responsible for his nephew's death.

In London, Cherry-Garrard was beginning to assemble material for his narrative history of the *Terra Nova* expedition. On his return from China he had met up with Colonel Lyons, secretary of the publications sub-committee, who assured him that, regardless of any differences of opinion about the exact causes of death of the South Pole party, Cherry would have a free hand in his narrative.[28]

On 9 July, on Cheltenham's Promenade, Cherry watched as Sir Clements Markham unveiled a bronze statue of Edward Wilson clad in sledging gear. Oriana Wilson, Wilson's parents, sisters and other family members were there, as were Joseph Kinsey and Reginald Smith and their wives and other representatives of the *Discovery* and *Terra Nova* expeditions. The statue had been sculpted by Kathleen Scott who had, as a young woman, studied in Paris with Auguste Rodin.[29] She was currently working on a sculpture of her late husband for a planned memorial, but had also been commissioned to create likenesses of Captain Smith of the *Titanic*, Prime Minister Asquith and explorer Fridtjof Nansen.[30] Following the unveiling ceremony Cherry joined other members of the platform party at Westal, the Wilsons' family home, which was close to Cheltenham College.

* * *

By the beginning of July, Tryggve Gran's plans for his attempt to break the record for the longest continuous flight over water were almost complete.[31] He had based himself at Cruden Bay, near Aberdeen, where he took delivery of his customised Bleriot monoplane *Ça Flotte* ('it floats') on a long beach suitable for take-offs. Once the aircraft was assembled, Gran had to wait for the weather to be right on both the Scottish and Norwegian coasts of the North Sea. He had done everything he could, including preparing for unexpected 'ditchings' by swimming fully clothed in the North Sea. But there was nothing he could do about the summer fog.

On the morning of Thursday, 30 July, the weather finally looked set fair. Gran took off to the east but was soon forced back by a dense bank of fog. He now only had one more chance at breaking the record. From 6 p.m. that evening all civil flights were banned due to the situation which was developing in Europe following the Archduke's assassination just over a month previously.

Just after 1 p.m. Gran was airborne again. This time the weather held and by 6 p.m. he had landed in Stavangar. His fuel tank was almost empty but he had broken the record for the longest-ever flight over open water.

Gran was received by King Haakon and Queen Maud and feted by his fellow-Norwegians. There were, however, disappointingly few reports in British newspapers about his achievement. One exception was the *Daily Mail*, whose proprietor, Alfred Harmsworth, Viscount Northcliffe, was a great flying enthusiast. Louis Blériot had received a £1,000 *Daily Mail* prize after crossing the Channel in 1909 – and Gran now had his eye on the £10,000 prize which would go to the first pilot (or pilots) to cross the Atlantic in less than seventy-two consecutive hours.

With aviation there would always be something new to strive for. Gran was glad he had decided not to travel to Antarctica with Shackleton.

* * *

On Friday, 1 August, Germany (an ally of Austria-Hungary) declared war on Russia (an ally of Serbia). France (an ally of Russia) began mobilising troops; Britain (linked to France by the *Entente Cordiale*) put her navy on alert; Italy and Belgium reiterated their neutrality.

As Britain put her navy on a war footing Ernest Shackleton contacted the Admiralty. Although J. Foster Stackhouse was still fundraising for his planned purchase of Scott's *Discovery*, Shackleton was all prepared to sail on his third Antarctic expedition. He had his two ships, the *Endurance* and the *Aurora*, the blessing of the RGS and, thanks to the generosity of Dundee jute mill owner and philanthropist Sir James Caird, a fully financed expedition.[32] He had an experienced crew: Alf Cheetham was third mate and Tom Crean was boatswain, in charge of sledges for the trans–Antarctic crossing.

Shackleton was relieved to receive Admiralty clearance to leave Britain with a ship and several naval officers and seamen at a time of national crisis. An Admiralty official sent him a one-word telegram ('Proceed') and First Lord of the Admiralty Churchill sent a longer message, thanking him for offering to forego his expedition.[33] Shackleton then gave his men the option of leaving the ship, in case they wanted to rejoin or join the armed forces. Frank Bickerton, who had been working on a propeller-driven 'air tractor' (based on one he had developed for Mawson's expedition), decided to leave the expedition; Alf Cheetham and Tom Crean stayed on board the *Endurance*.[34]

* * *

On 3 August, Bank Holiday Monday, the sun shone in Cheltenham as a motor vehicle decorated as the *Terra Nova* joined a procession heading north to Prestbury, where crowds had already gathered to enjoy the village fair. The day's proceedings ended with rousing renditions of *Rule Britannia* and the national anthem and a firework display, a highlight of which was a 'fire portrait' of the town's Member of Parliament, James Agg-Gardner. He had hoped to be present, but had been detained in London for an emergency sitting of the House of Commons.

The following day, 4 August, Germany invaded Belgium. As this was in direct violation of the 1839 Treaty of London (of which both Britain and Germany were signatories), the British government issued an ultimatum to Germany requiring her to withdraw from Belgian soil by 11 p.m. Greenwich Mean Time, midnight in Berlin. The deadline passed with no response from Germany.

By 11.01 p.m. Greenwich Mean Time on Tuesday, 4 August 1914, Britain was at war with Germany.

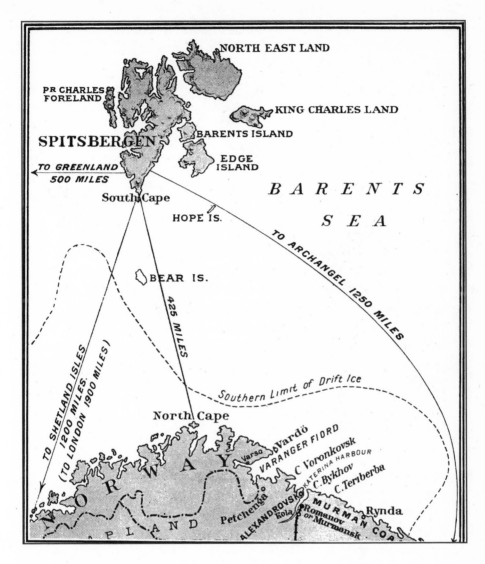

Spitsbergen, showing distances from Norway, North Russia and Britain. Map from *The Sphere*, 9 November 1918; Image © private.

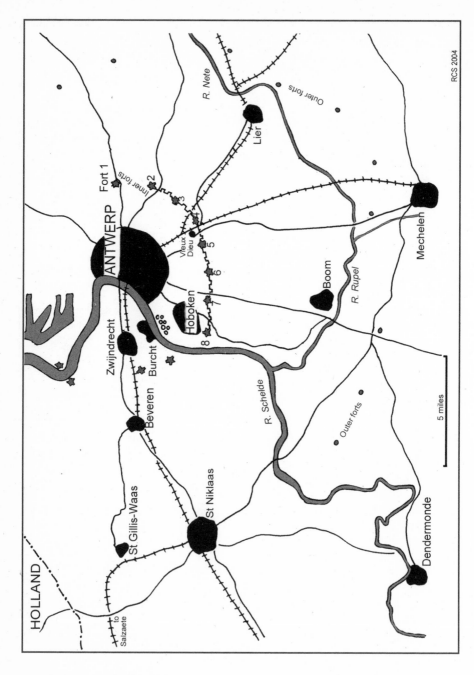

Antwerp, showing forts, railway lines, River Schelde and Dutch border. Map © and courtesy of Roy C. Swales.

HOLLAND

to Salzaete

St Gillis-Waas

St Niklaas

Beveren

Zwijndrecht

Burcht

ANTWERP

Fort 1

Inner forts

2

3

Vieux Dieu

5

6

7

8

Hoboken

R. Schelde

Boom

R. Rupel

Dendermonde

Outer forts

5 miles

Mechelen

Lier

R. Nete

Outer forts

RCS 2004

From Arctic to Antwerp

On 4 August 1914, Victor Campbell sailed the *Willem Barents* into Grønfjorden, the main Norwegian settlement on Spitsbergen. When he disembarked he found British, Norwegian, Swedish and Russian mariners and prospectors huddled around the settlement radio or discussing the news that Austria-Hungary had declared war on Serbia.[1] Campbell was coming to the end of his second visit to Spitsbergen on behalf of the Northern Exploration Company, for whom he had been carrying out work since returning to England in early 1913. Campbell and his wife had, over the years, become accustomed to long separations and short periods together with their young son.[2]

For this voyage, Campbell had recruited his long-standing friend Michael Barne (a *Discovery* veteran) and *Terra Nova* helmsman Mortimer McCarthy; Wilfred Bruce had accompanied him on his first voyage, but had since married.[3] The *Willem Barents* had been refitted in Tromsø and, apart from some difficulties in persuading NEC's London office to send money to pay for the repairs, things had gone well. Late pack-ice had sometimes hampered their progress but by the end of July they had delivered food supplies to encampments, loaded coal to take back for analysis, built a new settlement and checked that NEC's land claim signs had not been removed.

After digesting the latest news about the situation in the Balkans, Campbell set out to visit NEC's marble quarry and the last few sites he had yet to visit. On 7 August the *Willem Barents* arrived at Krossfjorden, where the Germans had built a meteorological station which, Campbell knew, had a two-way radio. The station leader told him that France and Germany were also now at war. When the *Willem Barents* arrived at Grønfjorden the following day, Campbell found out that Britain had declared war on Germany.

Campbell immediately set sail for Aberdeen, but when, two days out from Spitsbergen, a propeller blade broke, he changed course for Tromsø. He, Barne and McCarthy put the *Willem Barents* in dock, signed themselves off from their duties with NEC and went to find a ship which would take them back to Britain.

They arrived back in England on 28 August; by mid-September Campbell had been appointed as No. 2 in Drake Battalion, part of the 1st Brigade of the newly formed Royal Naval Division.

The RND had been formed, largely at the instigation of Winston Churchill, First Lord of the Admiralty, soon after the outbreak of war. It had three brigades. Its 1st and 2nd (Naval) Brigades were largely made up of naval reservists, serving men currently not attached to a ship and volunteers from all backgrounds. Each brigade had four battalions, named for famous admirals: 1st Brigade was made up of Drake, Benbow, Hawke and Collingwood battalions; 2nd Brigade of Nelson, Howe, Hood and Anson. The 3rd (Marine) Brigade was drawn from shore-based mariners from Chatham, Portsmouth, Plymouth and Deal (for which its battalions were named).

As the RND would need to fight alongside army units, some senior army officers had been drafted into the Division. Under this hybrid command structure, Campbell's brigade commander, Commodore Henderson, reported to Major-General Paris, the Division's commanding officer.

Within a few weeks of joining, Campbell was appointed commander of Drake Battalion. After four years of working with small groups of skilled men, he was now in charge of 1,000 men, including about thirty full-time naval officers, several hundred below-decks seamen, reservists and raw recruits.[4] But Campbell's time on the *Terra Nova* expedition had taught him to expect and deal with the unexpected.

* * *

The week before Campbell arrived back in Britain the Germans had attacked and occupied Brussels. The Belgian government, royal family and army senior command retreated to Antwerp. The fortified port was, in effect, the last bastion between the German army and the Channel ports.

In Britain, newspapers were full of reports based on official government announcements, army dispatches and cables sent from the front by newspaper correspondents who were following British and Allied troops as they moved round Europe. One byline which appeared regularly above first-hand accounts was that of Central New Agency's 'B.J.' Hodson. Since leaving Akaroa in 1912, Hodson had spent most of his time in Eastern Europe, reporting on the Balkan Wars. As an ex-soldier, he was accustomed to being on the front line and had, when based at a gun emplacement near Constantinople, lyrically described 'missiles singing across the valley, raising clouds of earth as they plunged into the hill around the battery'.

By September 1914 Hodson was in Antwerp, where he travelled to the city's outer ring of fortifications to report on a visit by the King of Belgium to his troops. He was greeted as a comrade by Belgian soldiers, who had been fighting since early August and were already exhausted:[5]

> My lieutenant was a Brussels man. He married on 8 July, and his wife was still at Brussels, only 12 miles distant. This he told me while now and then rifle fire rattled viciously behind us. Four black-frocked priests dug a large hole, where, just as the sun set, they placed four bodies of brave Belgian soldiers, and read a brief burial service … The eager question was asked, 'Are any British troops coming?'

When Hodson went to see the German defences around Brussels and Louvain he found them 'characterised by German thoroughness [and] … well furnished with machine guns, field pieces and howitzers of considerable calibre'. Any frontal attack on them would, he decided, be 'a very serious proposition'. He was equally impressed at the resilience of Belgian troops who tried to hold Termonde, south-west of Antwerp, against the Germans:

> … one company was cut off … others hid in the ruins of the burned streets until the Germans retreated … The Germans burned the fine old Town Hall … The scene presents itself to the imagination as one rivalling Dante's 'Inferno'. Overhead shells screamed … in the outer darkness stood the silent charred skeletons of twelve hundred once happy homesteads.

When he arrived in Antwerp on 26 September, Hodson was somewhat surprised to find locals going about their business 'in placid Belgian style'. American reporters began to leave town in search of 'war atmosphere' for their dispatches. Hodson headed for a village south of Antwerp where he found that houses had been gutted and the streets were littered with shattered glass:

> My chauffeur pulls up close to an arch, which is barricaded by railway trucks … I produce my papers and am informed that the Germans are in a coppice some 300 metres further on, and that I had better have the car turned round. This done, I mount the railway embankment cautiously … the scene before me is … a far, smiling prospect of flat meadows broken up by woodland – mustard and cress beds broken up by broad beans.

He learned that only recently the apparent calm had been broken by the 'harsh clack-clack-clack of a German machine gun', which had resulted in the deaths of two locals and the wounding of two of their companions.

On 28 September Hodson reported from the fortified settlements south of Antwerp:

Shells followed a survey of the town by a German aeroplane. The first fell into a cemetery where a company of soldiers were burying a popular comrade … The second projectile struck the Barracks and the third the Red Cross Hospital … All around the horizon there were clouds of smoke from burning villages.

Hodson noticed some large craters near the town's waterworks; he was told they had been caused by German 11-inch shells, but:

[a] few seconds' delay would have saved us the trouble of inquiry, for, singing overhead, there came another, which likewise exploded in the field, about 200 metres away … [I] awaited events with a London photographer, who was desirous of obtaining 'front seat' pictures of shells bursting … The fourteenth projectile … whined, as it seemed, up into our very faces, and dropped into the garden of a cottage nearby … This satisfied the photographer, and was quite enough for me.

As the bombardment continued, Zeppelins and aircraft from both sides regularly flew above the city. On 1 October crowds gathered to watch an aerial battle between a Belgian biplane and a German Taube monoplane:

The Taube had chased the biplane …, the Belgian pilot not being averse to persuading the Taube to come within the range of the forts. The Taube's armament included a *mitrailleuse* and the Belgian pilot, armed only with an automatic pistol, found himself unable to cope effectively with his foe … the Belgian pilot began to descend, and the Taube, greatly daring, followed him down until he found himself ringed around with bursting shrapnel. Promptly he rose again and flew away to the south-east … The thrilling encounter was witnessed by practically the whole population, who crowded the streets and house-roofs when they heard the sound of the guns.

That night, another Taube dropped leaflets suggesting that the Belgians should consider surrendering to the Germans rather than fight in the interests of Britain and Russia.

On 3 October Churchill arrived in Antwerp, where he tried to persuade the Belgian king and army commanders to stay and defend the city rather than retreat to Ostend. To encourage them he offered to send reinforcements in the form of the 1st and 2nd Naval Brigades of the Royal Naval Division.

* * *

On 4 October, Campbell and his fellow officers were told that they would be crossing the Channel and joining Belgian and other troops in Antwerp, in an effort to hold the city.[6] Training exercises were halted, firearms and ammunition issued from naval stockpiles and naval sweaters and trousers handed out to volunteers; necessities such as water-bottles, food-containers, haversacks, winter-weight outer garments and first aid supplies were procured from wherever they could be found.

Campbell and his men marched to Dover, where ships were waiting to carry them across the Channel in convoy. The vessels were so crowded that few managed to sleep during the crossing. It was still dark when they reached Ostend, where they unloaded their kit and gulped down some food. Some men scribbled letters home to go back with the ship. Campbell and his men piled into the trains and requisitioned London buses which were waiting to take them to Antwerp. The men were ordered to stay awake in case the Germans attacked the trains or convoys of buses, but few managed to do so.

In the small hours of 6 October 8,000 exhausted RND officers and men arrived in Antwerp. As they marched through the city they were greeted by flag-waving, cheering crowds who proffered beer and coffee. But they continued to the outer ring of fortifications, where Belgian troops were waiting to be relieved after days of being pounded by German 'Big Bertha' howitzers and heavy artillery.

Sir John French, Commander-in-Chief of the British Expeditionary Force, considered the situation at Antwerp to be so serious that he sent Colonel John Seely, one of his senior staff officers (a personal friend of Churchill and a former Secretary of State for War), to assess the situation. If Seely reported back that there was a chance the city could be held for a few days more 20,000 men of the BEF's 7th Division would come to Antwerp; if not, French would deploy the 7th Division elsewhere.

On 7 October Campbell and other RND battalion commanders were ordered to retire from the outer ring of fortifications to Antwerp's inner ring of forts. Once there, Campbell and his men began sinking additional trenches between forts 4 and 5, which defended the roads and railway lines running south to Brussels. With Brussels already in German hands the only main means of escape from Antwerp was to the west, where the railway line to Ghent and the coast was still open. But to reach the railway line Campbell and his men would need to cross the River Scheldt on a pontoon bridge. The bridge and the roads leading down to it were already packed with Antwerp residents who were fleeing their homes, rather than risk being killed in the bombardment or taken prisoner by German soldiers. That night the Germans stepped up their bombardment.

By dawn on 8 October much of Antwerp was ablaze or in ruins. During the day rumours began circulating that some forts had already been taken by the

Germans and, as darkness began to fall, Seely and another staff officer came to Campbell and told him to retire his men as the RND was about to withdraw from Antwerp.

Campbell, reluctant to accept orders from a staff officer, told Seely he needed to confirm the order with Commodore Henderson. Seely assured Campbell that everyone was retiring, heading for nearby stations, where trains were waiting to take them to Ostend and British ships. He gave Campbell a map and explained where he would find the trains and, in all probability, the other RND battalions.

Campbell sent a runner to the neighbouring forts to double-check for other RND men who might still be there, but was assured that there were none in sight. He led his men out of the trenches and, following 2nd Brigade, entered the city, keeping his machine-gunners at the back of the column to act as rear-guard and disguise the retreat. Seely, who was by now driving around in a car, came up to Campbell twice to make sure he knew where he was going.

Campbell led his men through the crowded streets of a city none of them had seen in daylight. Smoke and dust from burning and collapsing buildings swirled around them and, as they headed downhill towards the river and the pontoon bridge, fumes and smoke from blazing petrol tankers on the river bank made it hard to breathe. Moving with the crowds, they eventually made it across the bridge and, in company of Plymouth Marine Battalion, tried to find a station and a train heading towards Ostend.

Campbell kept hoping to meet up with the other three 1st Naval Brigade battalions but there was still no sign of them. He asked several brigade and divisional senior officers, but they had not seen them either. All Campbell could do was to try to get his own men away and safely to Ostend. He eventually managed to get all of his men, some of whom were wounded or on the point of collapse, onto one of the trains heading towards the coast. When it stopped about 10 miles short of Ostend, at Blankenberge, an officer from Chatham Marine Battalion managed, against the odds, to find a billet for Campbell and his men. In the morning one of the light trams which usually carried holiday-makers along the sea-front brought them to Ostend.

On 10 October the Military Governor of Antwerp surrendered his city to the Germans.

When Campbell returned to England he discovered his battalion was the only one from 1st Brigade to have escaped from Antwerp and that almost 2,000 men from Benbow, Hawke and Collingwood were missing. It seemed that they had not, as Seely had suggested, left their positions ahead of Campbell's battalion but that, due to a misunderstanding, had received their orders to retire too late. Over the coming days and weeks it became clear that most of the men in Campbell's brigade had either been taken prisoner by the Germans or fled into neutral Holland, where, in accordance with the rules of war, they had been interned.

B.J. Hodson had stayed to the bitter end; he had sent a cable describing the fall of Antwerp, but, thanks to the censor, readers only saw a truncated version:

> We hear our guns crashing out loud defiance to the enemy in a persistent roar. We hear the enemy's reply almost as distinctly. (The message here breaks off, the remaining portion having been stopped by the censor.) (Signed) B.J. Hodson (Central News).

Some people suggested that the RND men at Antwerp had not been sufficiently well trained and equipped for their task. When a letter from one of them, Mr F.B. Hulke, was published in *The Times* of 16 October and in regional newspapers, Bertie Hodson felt he should let people know what he had seen at Antwerp:

> Many of the [RND] men lacked overcoats, but their fighting equipment was efficient … If these men were 'practically untrained,' they must have had an abnormally high standard of training in naval brigades. The way they set about improving the Belgian trenches was a revelation to the Belgian sappers … If [their] parade drill was weak they showed no weakness in field work … The handy way in which the men handled their rifles left me no ground for questions … Mr F.B. Hulke's tale may be told to the Marines. It will not be believed by anyone who saw the naval men in the trenches around Antwerp.

While Campbell had been at Antwerp a steady stream of new recruits had joined the RND and begun their training. One of those assigned to Drake Battalion was Frederick Septimus Kelly (usually known as 'Sep').[7] Kelly, who was 33, had been born in Australia to an Anglo-Irish family. After Eton (where Campbell had also been educated), he had gone on to Balliol College, Oxford. The fact he had been awarded a fourth-class honours degree did not signify a lack of intelligence, rather that he had spent much of his time rowing. This had paid dividends when, in 1908, he had won an Olympic gold for Britain. Kelly had also studied music, including in Germany, and had just been beginning to make his mark as a pianist and composer in London when war had been declared.

Campbell, who had spent all his working life in the navy, had no particular reason to know anything about Kelly. But Kelly knew who Campbell was, as he had responded to a 1909 appeal for donations towards the costs of the *Terra Nova* expedition.[8]

Campbell, who was impressed by Kelly's evident organisational skills, offered him the post of deputy assistant quartermaster-general. Kelly initially accepted, but, when he realised that his new duties might require him to stay in Britain rather than fight overseas, he requested a transfer to Hood Battalion, which his friend and fellow-musician Denis Browne had already joined.

On 15 February 1915, at Blandford Camp, near Salisbury, the usually reticent Campbell showed Kelly and three other officers his photographs from the *Terra Nova* expedition; Kelly found Campbell's description of his winter in the 'igloo' particularly interesting. Ten days later Kelly joined his friends in Hood Battalion and prepared to sail east.

8

'Antarctics' on the Seven Seas

—◦◦◦—

At 1 a.m. on 5 August 1914, commanders of the British navy's Mediterranean Fleet received signals confirming that Britain had declared war on Germany. By then Harry Pennell's ship, the *Duke of Edinburgh*, had been on a war footing for a week. On the morning of 30 July Pennell and his shipmates helped erect a boom defence across Malta's harbour. That afternoon their commanding officer, Captain Prowse, was recalled to England and replaced by Captain Henry Blackett, son-in-law of Churchill's former First Sea Lord and close associate of Admiral 'Jackie' Fisher. On 2 August all leave was cancelled and all men recalled from shore or other leave. At 1.30 a.m. on 3 August Blackett opened 'secret package A' and gave orders to sail eastwards. On 4 August the only two German ships in the Mediterranean, *Goeben* and *Breslau*, began bombarding the North African coast, from where French ships, escorted by members of the British fleet, were bringing soldiers from their colonies in North Africa to fight in Europe. British battleships challenged and began pursuing the *Goeben* and *Breslau*; the German ships, although heavily outnumbered, used their superior speed to escape to the east, towards neutral Turkish waters.

On 12 August, following a week of patrolling the Mediterranean, the *Duke of Edinburgh* was ordered to Aden. She would be based there for several months, escorting troopships carrying thousands of soldiers from India and other parts of Britain's eastern empire to and from the Suez Canal. Two of the first troopships Pennell escorted were the *Northbrook* and the *Dufferin*, on which his friend Birdie Bowers had served during his time in the Royal Indian Marine.[1]

* * *

On 13 August 1914 Britain claimed her first naval victory of the war. This morale-boosting engagement did not, as might have been expected, take place in the Mediterranean or the North Sea, but on Lake Nyasa, in Central Africa – where Harry Pennell's sister Winifred was working at the missionary post on the island of Likoma.[2]

As Lake Nyasa was bounded by both British and German East African territories, both countries maintained a naval presence on its waters. The British ship, HMS *Gwendolen*, was named for a daughter of the 3rd Marquess of Salisbury; the German ship, SS *Hermann von Wissmann*, for a famous German explorer and slave-trade abolitionist. The two ships had, for many years, co-existed happily and efficiently, patrolling the lake for illegal slave-traders and collaborating in naval exercises – which usually involved one captain trying to catch the other unawares around the islands and inlets of the lake.

When, in early August, Captain Rhoades of the *Gwendolen* learned that Britain and Germany were at war, he felt it was his duty to try to put the *Hermann von Wissmann* out of action. He entered the harbour where the German ship was being repaired and fired sufficient shots to ensure she would remain out of the water for some time. During the 'attack' his regular drinking companion Captain Berndt arrived to find out what was happening and was informed of Britain's declaration of war. Rhoades sent a cable to the Admiralty in London, where newspapers, eager for good news, reported that Britain had won a small, but significant, naval victory in Africa.

* * *

Back in Britain, the Grand Fleet had established its main base at Scapa Flow, Orkney, near where the North Sea meets the Atlantic Ocean. Other British squadrons were based further south on the east coast or at Channel ports. The German High Seas Fleet, based at Jade Bay, off Heligoland Bight, was now effectively trapped within the confines of the North Sea.

William Williams, Pennell's stalwart of the *Terra Nova* engine room, had joined the battleship *Lord Nelson*, flagship of Vice-Admiral Sir Cecil Burney, commander of the newly formed Channel Fleet. The Channel Fleet's first operation had been to escort the British Expeditionary Force safely to French and Belgian Channel ports. Now they were charged with keeping the BEF supplied with equipment, ammunition, provisions and reinforcements.

During the early months of the war the world's two greatest navies played 'cat and mouse' across the North Sea. On 28 August a decoy force of British destroyers and cruisers put out from Scapa Flow with the aim of drawing their German opposite numbers into Heligoland Bight, where British submarines and battlecruisers were waiting. By the end of the day, thanks to battlecruisers HMS *Lion*, HMS *Queen Mary* and HMS *Princess Royal*, four German ships had been sunk and three more badly damaged. Three British ships had also been sunk and one damaged, but casualties had been well under a hundred; the Germans had lost considerably more men, including many who had been taken prisoner.[3]

A second wave of Grand Fleet vessels had stood in reserve during the engagement. Bill Burton, a bastion of the Pennell's *Terra Nova* engine room, had been on HMS *Lowestoft*.[4] Henry Rennick and Murray Levick had been with the 7th Cruiser Squadron: Rennick, on the *Hogue*, had seen no action, but Levick, on the *Bacchante*, had been called on to treat injured sailors, including by amputating shell-damaged limbs.[5]

* * *

On 22 September Henry Rennick's ship, the *Hogue*, and two sister ships, the *Cressy* and *Aboukir*, set out on one of their regular morning patrols of the southern area of the North Sea. There was no sign of enemy ships.

Suddenly the *Aboukir* was struck by a torpedo from an unseen German submarine.[6] British cruisers had, in order to deter submarines, been ordered to zig-zag rather than sail straight courses, but the age and slowness of the *Cressy* class ships made it difficult for them to follow this command. When the *Aboukir* began to list, it became increasingly difficult, then impossible, to launch lifeboats. As it became clear that she was going to go under, the captain gave orders to abandon ship.

The *Hogue* and the *Cressy* were already steaming towards their stricken sister-ship. Admiralty officials knew that such rescue attempts risked making ships a sitting target for the next torpedo, but to forbid them would run counter to the instincts of most mariners. As the *Hogue* and the *Cressy* lowered their lifeboats, those on deck threw lifebelts and anything buoyant they could find into the water, where men were struggling to keep afloat.

At about 7 a.m. the *Aboukir* rolled over and began sinking. Minutes later the *Hogue*, which had by now brought aboard several *Aboukir* survivors, was hit by two torpedoes. As water flooded into the *Hogue*'s engine room, her gunners spotted a periscope above the waves. They and gunners on the *Cressy* opened fire but made no impact on their unseen target.

By 7.15 a.m. the *Hogue* was sinking. Within minutes the *Cressy*, which had already picked up survivors from both her sister ships, was hit by two torpedoes.

By 8 a.m. all three ships had sunk. Thousands of men were now swimming or floundering in the cold North Sea, trying to save themselves and help injured men; all around were floating bodies and wreckage from their vessels.[7] Henry Rennick, who was a strong swimmer, began steering planks, oars and anything buoyant he could find towards those who seemed most at risk of drowning.

When British fishing trawlers and naval vessels arrived at the scene a few hours later they found that most of the crew members of the *Hogue*, *Cressy* and *Aboukir* had died in explosions, drowned or died from exposure in the chill

waters of the North Sea. Henry Rennick's name appeared in the lists of those
who were presumed to have died in the disaster.[8] According to the Admiralty's
official report the long firing range of the German submarines and the age and
slowness of the *Hogue* and her sister ships had contributed to the disaster.

One survivor, Petty Officer Alfred Renwick, gave an interview in which he
described what had happened as his ship began to go down:[9]

> Before the ship turned turtle the captain told us that it was a case of each one for
> himself and that we must take to the water. Being a good swimmer, I dived and
> caught hold of a piece of wreckage, with which I swam about for nearly four
> hours …
>
> One of the tars shouted out 'Are we downhearted?' and there was a chorus of
> 'No's', followed by the lustiest singing of 'God Save the King' that I have heard for
> a long time.
>
> I saw Lieutenant-Commander Rennick, one of Captain Scott's heroes, hand his
> lifebelt to an exhausted comrade, and shortly afterwards a huge wave swept him
> away. Such self-sacrifice I have never seen. All did their best to help one another.

When Wilfred Bruce wrote to friends in New Zealand, he told them of the
death of his friend, who had, earlier in the year, married a New Zealand girl:[10]

> You will have heard by now that poor Parny is gone. I lost my very best pal, and
> you will all be sorry, I know, but he finished splendidly… His wife will have
> something to look back to with pride. Of course, there's practically no mourning
> here, but there are many heavy hearts, and I'm afraid we've barely started yet.

Wilfred Bruce had news of other 'Antarctics' to pass on to his New Zealand
friends:[11]

> Commander Evans is commanding the *Mohawk* destroyer, and was missed by
> 10yds by a torpedo from a German submarine one night last week. Commander
> Pennell is in the *Duke of Edinburgh* … Dr Atkinson is in the *Saint Vincent*, a first
> liner, somewhere in the North Sea. Dr Levick is on the *Bacchante*, whereabouts also
> vague. Staff-Paymaster Drake is in the new light cruiser [*Undaunted*]. Lieutenant
> Campbell is serving in the Naval Brigade, and was adjutant of the battalion that
> was interned in Holland; but I heard yesterday that somehow or other he was
> back in England.

Evans' ship, the *Mohawk*, was one of the 'Tribal' class fast destroyers which
made up the majority of the Patrol Flotilla of the Dover Strait Fleet.[12] When

Campbell had been crossing the Channel on his way to Antwerp Teddy Evans had been on an escort vessel: as he watched his charges sail safely into harbour Evans felt envious of Campbell and also thought of Hood Battalion, named for the famous ancestor of Evans' commanding officer, Rear Admiral Horace Hood.

Bruce himself was serving on the minesweeper *Halcyon*, based at Lowestoft on the Suffolk coast. In the early hours of 3 November the *Halcyon* had challenged the German battlecruiser *Seydlitz*, one of several German ships which had weaved through the Great Yarmouth night fishing fleet and were fast approaching Lowestoft. As the two ships traded fire the *Halcyon* suffered some slight damage but was at more serious risk of being swamped by cascades of water raised by German shells over- or under-shooting their mark.

By 8.30 a.m. the *Seydlitz* and several German ships were within firing range of Lowestoft. Four British destroyers and three submarines based in Yarmouth put out to try to chase the intruders away. As a North Sea fog descended, the Germans took advantage of the cover to head back to their base at Jade Bay. Reinforcements summoned from the Grand Fleet's Scottish bases could do nothing but turn back. Casualties on the *Halcyon* were light but several submariners and fishermen died when their vessels hit mines left by the retreating German fleet.

The Times reported that Yarmouth residents had felt the 'reverberation of the guns and the clattering of windows and shaking of houses'.[13] Several fishermen, assuming (in the absence of flags on the German destroyers) that the large ships passing through their midst were British vessels, had waved and saluted; they had been surprised when those on board the larger ships had responded by shaking their fists.

* * *

In London, First Lord of the Admiralty Churchill had recently suffered a different kind of set-back. His First Sea Lord, Admiral Prince Louis of Battenberg, was German-born but a naturalised British citizen and a friend of Prime Minister Asquith. Those who had always felt that Battenberg's family ties made him unsuitable to hold high-ranking naval office could now point to recent demonstrations against Germans living in Britain and the fact that Sir Edgar Speyer, another naturalised citizen, had been forced to resign from family businesses in the United States which traded with Germany.

After Battenberg resigned, Churchill publicly thanked him for his long and valued service. He also mentioned that Battenberg's son was serving in the navy and that his nephew had recently died in Belgium fighting the Germans.

Churchill announced that Battenberg's successor as First Sea Lord would be Admiral 'Jackie' Fisher. Although the vigorous septuagenarian and Churchill did not always see eye to eye, Fisher had helped shape the modern British navy on which the country now depended.

* * *

On 7 November it was announced that German ships had sunk two British armoured cruisers off Coronel in central Chile. The engagement had involved only nine vessels but more than 1,000 British seamen had died in what was Britain's first defeat at sea for over a century.

Following the German victory, battlecruisers *Invincible* and *Inflexible* and armoured cruiser *Carnarvon* (on which Browning of the Northern Party now served) set sail across the Atlantic to reinforce Britain's naval presence in southern waters.

On 8 December they arrived at the British supply port of Stanley in the Falklands, where they had planned to refuel. While they were in harbour they became aware that a German squadron, which clearly did not expect to find British ships so far south, was heading for the Falklands. The German ships, which were outnumbered, turned back. The British squadron gave chase and succeeded in sinking, capturing or scuttling six German ships for no losses.

* * *

As the first year of the war drew to a close, Harry Pennell's ship, the *Duke of Edinburgh*, was transferred to the British Grand Fleet at Orkney. Pennell's final voyage on troop convoy duty had been the most eventful by some margin.

The *Duke of Edinburgh* had left Aden for Karachi in late October, leaving again on 3 November followed by ten troopships carrying men of the 11th Indian Division to Suez. They would be assisting with the defence of the canal which linked the Mediterranean to Aden, India and points east.

During the first few days of her voyage the *Duke of Edinburgh* stopped briefly to rescue a man who had fallen overboard from a troopship and to take part in a target practice exercise. When she arrived in Aden on 9 November, Brigadier-General Cox, commander of the 29th Indian Infantry, came aboard to explain the situation following Britain's declaration of war on Turkey four days previously.

Much had changed since the *Duke of Edinburgh* had left the Mediterranean in August. The *Breslau* and *Goeben*, which had been absorbed into the Turkish navy, now guarded the Dardanelles and bombarded Russia's Black Sea settlements.[14]

Turkish troops had now moved south through Yemen and taken Turba Fort at Sheikh Said, near the southern entrance of the Red Sea. If they could not be dislodged there was a risk that troop and supply ships from India, other parts of Asia, New Zealand and Australia might need to sail around Africa on their way to Europe.

After Captain Blackett and Major-General Cox had conferred at length orders were issued. At 3 a.m. on 10 November, under cover of darkness, the *Duke of Edinburgh* moved into firing range of Turba Fort and dropped anchor. At 6 a.m., she began bombarding the Turkish garrison fort, at a distance of 2 to 3 miles. When no response was forthcoming she stopped firing and moved inshore, followed by the ten-ship convoy and several tugs which had joined them at Aden. Over the next few hours almost 3,000 Indian soldiers piled into small boats, which were then pulled to shore by tug. As they rushed up the hill towards the Turkish stronghold the *Duke of Edinburgh*'s gunners provided cover and returned Turkish fire. By mid-afternoon Turba Fort had been taken with minimal casualties.[15]

The next morning, the *Duke of Edinburgh* continued on her way to Suez. After a brief stop at Port Said she arrived in Malta on 21 November, where three British ships, nine French ships and four submarines were in harbour. She left Malta on 25 November and, after recoaling at Queenstown, Ireland, arrived at Scapa Flow on 8 December.

Harry Pennell spent Christmas Day 1914 at sea with other members of 1st and 2nd Cruiser Squadrons. Over the past five years, no two Christmases had been the same. Who knew what the following year might bring?

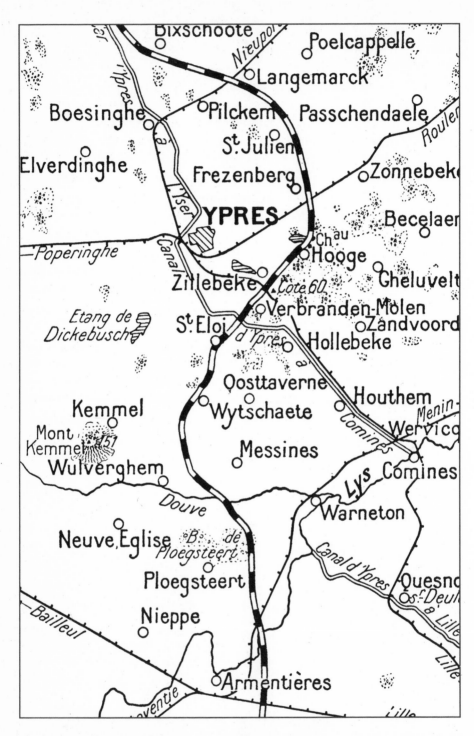

Map showing Ypres, the 'salient' and surrounding area; Hooge is to the east of Ypres, just south of the Ypres–Menin road. From 1919 Michelin guide to Ypres. Image © private.

9

Cavalry Officers, Chateaux and Censors

In the early hours of 6 October 1914 the Northumberland Hussars arrived in Zeebrugge. The regiment, the first territorials to be called to serve overseas, had travelled to Belgium as part of the 7th Division of the 4th Corps of the British Expeditionary Force.

Cecil Meares, who had served as a cavalry officer in the Boer War, was pleased to have been accepted for a regiment in which Sir Robert Baden-Powell and Sir John French (the BEF's Commander-in-Chief) had also served. Since returning from Antarctica in 1912 Meares had spent most of his time in London but occasionally visited Scotland (where his father, stepmother and other family members lived) or travelled to give lectures and show his friend Herbert Ponting's films of Antarctica.

When the Hussars reached Bruges Meares sent some postcards to Annie Spengler, a lady friend with whom he was on nickname terms (she was 'Spuffy' or 'Lola', he was 'Lobby'). Meares had left money with her so she could purchase and send him items such as his favourite make of puttees and a dictionary of military expressions in French and German.[1] Since arriving in Belgium, Meares and other linguists had already been pressed into service, thanking people for gifts and explaining to pretty girls that many of the soldiers were already spoken for.

On the way to Ostend it became clear that hard *pavé* roads were not really suitable for thoroughbred cavalry horses. After a night in some barns on the sand dunes outside Ostend, Meares and his comrades entered town. The station was packed with refugees fleeing from the advancing German army and the trains which would take the Hussars and other troops to Ghent had been delayed, so Meares took himself off to the Hotel de L'Espérance, which was just opposite the station. When he found some notepaper there he started writing a letter to Annie Spengler. He knew his letter would be scrutinised by the regimental censor for anything which might give away the location or tactics of the BEF:[2]

We started from Southampton to a certain new port where we landed and went inland to another large town where I had a busy time arranging quarters for the horses & men as about 20,000 men were in the town. Next day we returned to another large place on the sea which is simply filled with refugees[,] wounded and troops of all kinds. Tomorrow we expect to go off to a very hot corner ... I don't know if this letter or the postcards will ever reach you.

When the Hussars arrived in Ghent they received a rousing welcome and were showered with gifts and refreshments. As Ghent was now under threat from the Germans, people were busy blowing up bridges, digging trenches and putting up barbed wire defences to deter them. From time to time Belgian and French soldiers would arrive on bicycles with reports of encounters with Germans.

The Hussars left Ghent on 12 October, heading for Ypres. By that time, everyone knew that Antwerp had fallen. As Meares and his fellow Hussars rode along the sound of horses' hooves clattering over cobbled *pavés* mingled with the noise of distant rapid rifle and machine-gun fire. When they slept under canvas in fields and woods, they were woken by the sound of low-flying German aircraft. As the rain poured down they, their horses, their kit and their possessions became soaked through. Men and horses alike became increasingly exhausted and tense from being on constant alert for possible ambushes by lance-wielding German 'Uhlan' cavalry.[3]

The Hussars rode into Ypres on 14 October. The Germans had recently passed through the city but stayed only long enough to help themselves to provisions and fodder. The cavalry barracks and parts of the medieval Cloth Hall were now at the disposal of the 7th Division. The following day the Hussars made their first strike against a group of Uhlans they encountered during a reconnaissance and had the satisfaction of chasing another group at a break-neck gallop through the cobbled streets of Zillebeke, to the east of Ypres.

The Hussars were to join the front line which bulged out of the main north to south Western Front, around the east of Ypres, from Zonnebeke, through Gheluvelt to Zanvoorde. As the prospect of the forthcoming clash between two mighty armies loomed, local residents fled their homes, carrying what they could carry in small carts or on their backs.

On Monday, 19 October, the 7th Division moved forward to attack German-held Menin (which Sir John French regarded as a key strategic point) but German resistance soon drove them back. During the day the Hussars came under fire from a German cycle battalion but, thanks to prompt relief from other divisional troops, made it back to Zonnebeke with few casualties.

But it was not long before word had spread that British infantry regiments had suffered huge losses in the face of incessant German artillery fire. When

Meares wrote to Annie Spengler that night, he tried not to worry her too much – or incur the wrath of the censor:

> Many thanks for your sweet letter … we have had a very strenuous time, marching all the time and in some rather tight places. Now we are in a certain town and have been out hunting Uhlans this morning[;] we shot one and I had a shot at some at about 50 yds in a thick wood but did not get them … The country here is very beautiful, rolling wooded country and very pretty villages; the people are very glad to see us and bring out fruit, coffee etc and think that we will help them, but I am sorry to say we have not been able to do much for them.
>
> This is a beautiful town and is full of troops of all kinds. I expect that there will be a big fight here soon, of course I can't say where we are or have been but you will be surprised when you do hear. We have shot down 3 of their aeroplanes already …
>
> It seems to me that the war will last a long time. I am longing to see you again but I will have to be patient … we are up about 3 or 4 marching & fighting all day. Luckily I don't have to go on guard at night. Now I am very tired so must say goodbye.

The next morning Meares and his companions woke to the sound of heavy artillery and the buzz of German reconnaissance aircraft overhead. German reinforcements were now heading towards them, flanked and screened by Uhlans and armed cyclists.

Cavalry officers riding out on patrol or surveillance duties (their usual role in a battle zone) were at risk of being mown down if they ventured beyond their own front line. There was also little cavalry officers could do in terms of fighting in an area which was becoming increasing scored by deep trenches. Meares and the Hussars effectively became support troops, helping out General Lawford's 22nd Infantry Brigade with trench-building.[4] After a hard day's work in the salient bulge they were glad to return to Ypres for a night's rest out of earshot of constant shell fire.

One evening, just after they had tethered their horses and begun cooking, the Hussars were ordered out to a new billet at Hooge (Hooghe to Flemish-speaking locals), near Zillebeke, off the Ypres–Menin road. As the rain lashed down they struggled (in pitch darkness) to find their mud-spattered mounts and then to strap sopping saddles and blankets onto them. As they rode over to Hooge, they were suddenly ordered off to the front line trenches, where they had their first sight of German 'Black Marias'.[5]

When they arrived at Hooge, they met exhausted but stoical survivors of the 20th and 21st Infantry Brigades, which had been under heavy German artillery fire for several days. But, before they had time to settle into their new billet, they were ordered out to the now-deserted village of Klein Zillebeke, where they helped build trenches and barricades in anticipation of a German attack. Finally, after being relieved by the 6th Cavalry, they returned to Hooge for the night. As they passed through the wrought-iron gates and entered the grounds a loud burst of shrapnel announced that the Germans were not far away.

Hooge chateau had been built in the turreted Normandy style and was surrounded by formal and landscape gardens. It had recently been used by General Haig and other high-ranking British officers as a headquarters, but Haig had since moved on. Meares tried to describe to Annie Spengler what his new surroundings were like and what had been happening:[6]

I am writing to you in the drawing room of a beautiful chateau & the horses are all on the lawns in front; the big 4.7 guns are making a great din all round. At intervals the Germans drop big shells on this house which is very annoying. We have had a very hot time here lately, the 7th division has been holding up a whole German Army Corps for about 5 days and has had a rough time but now other troops & guns are coming up to help, so I hope it will be alright.

Yesterday the regiment was in a very hot corner indeed but the men were splendid and we were very fortunate, not a man killed, but some wounded; the shrapnel fire was very heavy & lots of the very big shells; we were making some soup in a farm when 5 big ones dropped around it, but we & all the horses got away.

My major with whom I mess was shot thro the lungs, I did not think he would pull thro, as we could not get a stretcher or ambulance to take him away, after a long time we got a motor ambulance but it was wrecked about a mile away. The doctor & I stayed with him all night and got him into a motor car and away just as the shells were beginning to fall again … I do hope that Major Johnstone [sic] will recover he was an awfully nice man.

I do hope that we will get a few days rest soon as everyone is worn out & of the regiments which left Lyndhurst only fragments remain. Today lots of French soldiers have come & I hear that the Indian troops are not far away. It is difficult to realise how bad this war is till one sees the thousands of refugees & hundreds of burning houses all around.

You might lend this letter to Ponting to read … Could you send by post some chewing gum & some meat extract lozenges.

Major Lawrence Johnston was, like Meares, a life-long traveller.[7] The son of a wealthy, devoted mother, he had moved around the United States, England and France before studying at Cambridge and becoming a naturalised British citizen.

After joining the Hussars and fighting for his adopted country in the Boer War, he had now more or less settled on an estate at Hidcote Barton in the Cotswolds (some 25 miles north of Cheltenham) where he was creating a large garden.

On 24 October the Hussars rode over to what was usually referred to as 'Polygon Wood', where they helped the 2nd Royal Warwickshires consolidate their line. That done, they and some Divisional HQ staff galloped down the Menin Road and over a muddy turnip field towards what they thought was their new front line. But when several officers riding at the front of the group were shot down, they flung themselves off their mounts to the ground, ready to return fire.

When French cavalry and Welsh Fusiliers joined them they mounted a counter-attack but by the afternoon the Germans looked like breaking through a weak spot in the Allied line. Finally, after some Grenadier Guards arrived, they managed to hold their position. But it had been a close thing. When reinforcements finally arrived the Hussars and others who had been fighting all day broke into cheers.

That night, despite being exhausted, Meares and others found it hard to sleep while shells were exploding all around Hooge. Gradually the German bombardment became less intensive and the number of engagements up and down the line began to taper off. There were rumours and counter-rumours of victories and defeats but some men suspected they were in the midst of a lull before a storm. Meares and the Hussars, who were now billeted in farm buildings around Hooge, spent most days saddled up in reserve, ready to reconnoitre in the woods or do whatever was required of them.

On 29 October, the day the Germans launched their anticipated attack, Meares and his regiment were in reserve – which meant he had time to write a letter to Annie Spengler:[8]

Since I wrote last we have had a terrible time. A number of our officers have been wounded & gone home but this regiment has been very fortunate compared with the others. At present we are having a few days rest, but even now the guns are going hard all round & shrapnel is bursting fairly near. Fortunately crowds of soldiers have arrived here and the place is full of English & French troops so I hope that things will not be so strenuous.

This regiment has done splendid work. There is so much that I would like to tell you but cannot do so. I hope that I will get back some day & tell you about it[;] no-one can have any idea how terrible this war is and this seems to be the very hottest corner. … The weather here is splendid, I am glad to say.

Some of those small very strong peppermints would be welcome & a knitted Balaclava cap.

Over the next few days the Germans pushed the British back from Zanvoorde Ridge and Gheluvelt. The Royal Welsh Fusiliers were virtually wiped out. As soon as the Hussars received orders to move forward to the line they mounted up in a clump of bare, splintered stumps which had once been a leafy wood and galloped across shell-strewn fields to Polygon Wood. All day they charged and recharged, attacked and counter-attacked. By night-fall the Germans had gained Messines, south of Ypres, but lost Gheluvelt. The salient around Ypres seemed to be holding.

On 31 October a large group of commanding, senior and staff officers from the British 1st and 2nd Divisions gathered in a large room overlooking the gardens at Hooge chateau.[9] The Germans, who had recently broken through parts of the Allied front line, were only two miles away; they also held several of the ridges overlooking the chateau – where the cars of visiting officers were parked in the gardens. During the bombardment of Hooge six senior officers were killed by shrapnel and glass which ripped across the garden room; several others were badly injured and were evacuated to casualty clearing stations. Fortunately some of the officers had withdrawn from the garden room into an interior room and were not injured.

Back in London, Herbert Ponting was glad to hear from his old friend and travelling companion:[10]

> Dear Miss Spengler
>
> I was glad to get your letter and hear from Meares, and I want you to read & send enclosed out to him. He is sure in the midst of it, and in some respects I really envy him, but what an awful business it all is, and how totally unnecessary, but for the real necessity of removing this menace once and for all. I only hope that Meares will come back safe and sound. Anything I can get for him I will gladly do so.

The byline 'B.J. Hodson' was now appearing regularly on reports from northern France and around Ypres. Hodson was full of praise of the men who had travelled thousands of miles to fight with the Allied forces:[11]

> the Germans gained the briefest victory of the war last week in the neighbourhood of Lille ... and then they met ... the Indian troops ... I hope the Censor will now permit the fact to become public that the Eastern contingent is at the front ... The Sikhs and the Ghurkas gave the enemy a few rounds 'rapid' and then swung into them with the utmost fervour. Back past our own evacuated trenches ... went the grey-coated Teutons while Sikh bayonet and Ghurkha kukri played havoc among their disordered ranks ...

> At Ypres the Germans have suffered severely, an unsuccessful attack resulting in
> 3,000 casualties ... The German artillery fire is still good, and the Belgians, before
> giving way on the Yser, suffered severely from shrapnel. Should the Germans
> pursue their advantage in force they (i.e. the enemy) are likely to have a very
> awkward time –

The main part of Hodson's report came to an abrupt end with the words
'lengthy excision', although the censor allowed his comments on the weather
('continues bad'), food supply chain ('remains good') and troop morale ('bearing
the conditions well') to stand.

On 7 November, during a break from front-line duties, Meares tried to
summarise the situation for Annie Spengler:[12]

> We have come back from the firing line for a few days rest; there are very very
> few left of the splendid 7th Division, the fighting has been beyond anything in the
> history of the world and we have had to bear the brunt of it. Lately the Germans
> have been pouring hundreds of shells into the town, huge shells 16 inches across
> which they used at Antwerp & they make holes in the ground big enough to hold
> a house and even during the night they drop close all round us. [I]t gets on ones
> nerves and we get very little sleep[;] it is fine to be out of reach if only for a day
> or two ...
>
> I am glad to say we are having lovely weather, the wet days are terrible. There are
> crowds of soldiers everywhere French, Arabs, Indians, etc. The muffler is splendid I
> am keeping it till it gets cold at present it is quite warm ... it would be nice to see
> you again in a little time but I am afraid the war will go on for a long time.

After his letter was returned by the censor, Meares tried to provide a less graphic
picture of events:[13]

> We have another day's holiday today so I will write a few lines ... You can have no
> idea what a relief it is to be away from the constant stream of shells for a little time.
> Some new officers arrived here yesterday to replace those who were damaged,
> they seem very nice fellows.
>
> The weather has been rather depressing lately, foggy & damp & all the leaves
> falling off the trees, I wonder what we were doing this time last year. I am so glad
> that I have this nice photograph of you. I want so badly to get back and see you
> again; heaps of new soldiers are coming up so I hope things will begin to move
> soon; today the Artists [Rifles] arrived, we saw them one day at Oxford Circus
> [trenches].[14]

On 13 November, as the Hussars prepared to move to another sector of the front line, an important visitor arrived:[15]

> This afternoon General French arrived here suddenly in the rain, and congratulated the regiment on the splendid work they had done under very difficult circumstances, and made a very flattering & rousing speech.
>
> Please write soon. You might look round & see if you can find one of those little muff manner things; they would be useful for winter.

On 16 November the Hussars moved to Le Mortier, about 15 miles south of Ypres, where they were billeted with Indian troops. Meares was glad of the warm scarf and peppermints Annie Spengler sent him, but, as winter set in, he was clearly not happy with his lot:[16]

> we are having a cold spell now there was snow this morning & the country is feet deep in mud. We have moved back to the fighting line but it seems fairly quiet especially after Ypres. I am glad we have left that spot. I am afraid you have not had all my letters as I wrote a good many lately …
>
> We are here in rather a dirty little farm mostly manure heaps … and one scratches as well … we are back in the fighting line but in a rather quiet place & there are lots of troops so we dont have much to do at present. Poor Lord Roberts died near here a few days ago.[17] I am afraid that the war will not finish by this Xmas but perhaps I may be back by the spring time if all goes well. I have had very unpleasant work of late, turning all the French farm people out of their houses behind the trenches; it is heart breaking work but necessary as people in the pay of the Germans have been cutting our wires & shooting the soldiers, so the only thing is to clear all civilians from the fighting area. It is beginning to get cold now frost ice & snow, getting up at 5am is rather chilly work.
>
> … Everything for the present depends on the success of the Russians in Poland … The people in England seem to be really nervous from all accounts in the papers … we are short of coal & oil & candles but we hope to get supplies soon. We had a good spell of frost but now it has begun to thaw again and everything is covered with deep mud.

A postscript to one letter gave Annie Spengler a clue as to why Meares was sometimes able to be more open in his letters than on other occasions: 'I am the censor so I pass my own letters.'

When Meares was awarded a short period of home leave in early December, he went to London so he could spend time with Annie Spengler. While there, he made enquiries regarding other opportunities for war service which might make better use of his linguistic and other skills.

When Meares returned to the front he discovered he had missed a royal visit – and that his Colonel had his own ideas regarding Meares' future:[18]

> Things here are just the same as when I left; but they had terrible storms of wind and rain and tonight is one of the worst nights I have known … The King came here and the regiment acted as guard of honour; the king went near the trenches and the Staff were very worried as he insisted on going along a road which is constantly shelled. I dont know what I will do, as the Colonel has written to the War Office saying that he wants me to stay on here.

After spending some time in London, it was difficult to be out of contact again:

> I wrote you a long letter and sent it to you by an officer who was returning on leave … [but] havent had a line from you since I came back … The weather has been terrible since I came back, simply pouring with rain all the time and the mud is a foot deep. Today we had a game of football and it was terribly dirty work. There is nothing happening here it is very dull indeed, a little shooting goes on all the time.

Just as Annie Spengler's latest letter caught up with Meares, he learned he would be moving on:

> Thank you very much for your nice letter I was very glad to get it … We have had pouring rain all the time lately, this afternoon we had a football match against the Scots Grays officers, it was very hard work and we all feel very stiff. There is a rumour that we are going to advance in a few days. I am sorry as we are very comfortable here and dont want to move into country that has been desolated by the Germans.

All in all, however, despite everything, Meares was proud of what had been achieved at Ypres and of the Hussars:

> Will you get the Evening Standard of Nov 25th and keep the article called the Immortal [7th] Division … I am glad you like the photographs. Please send one to Mrs MacDougall, 23 Park Circus, Ayr, Scotland & Mrs Meares, Acharra, Colinton Edinburgh.[19] And you might send one to Ponting …

On 18 December the Hussars moved southwest to Fleurbaix, where General Lawson and his 22nd Brigade were attempting to break through a German front near 'Well Farm', La Boutillerie. The brigade's pre-assault bombardment made little impact on German defences and Lawson's men suffered heavy casualties. By late afternoon the mud of no-man's-land was strewn with dead and badly injured British soldiers, some of whom were lying up against parapets of the front rows of German trenches. As darkness fell, Lawson called off the attack and ordered the uninjured and walking wounded to retire to their own trenches.

During December every British soldier on the Western Front received a Christmas card from King George and, in the name of his daughter Princess Mary, a little brass box containing tobacco or a writing-set. Parcels began arriving from home, filled with favourite delicacies and warm items of clothing. Across no-man's-land, on a clear night, British soldiers could see candles flickering on small Christmas trees which appeared to have mysteriously sprung up from the mud.

At La Boutillerie German officers signalled that they would not fire on British soldiers who entered no-man's-land to retrieve their dead and wounded. As the Hussars moved forward to help Lawson's men German soldiers clambered out of their own trenches and started walking across the mud. When Harold Robson, a Hussars officer, brought out his camera men from both sides stood together, smiling. At one point Robson handed his camera to a fellow Hussar who took a photograph with Robson in it.[20]

The officer responsible for maintaining the Hussars' regimental diary took the precaution of not recording what those further up the command chain might regard as fraternisation.

It was not long before fighting resumed, but during January, as far as the Hussars were concerned, it remained spasmodic and casualties were light. But several men were suffering from typhoid and scarlet fever and others had 'trench foot', of which the symptoms were very similar to those of frostbite.

Early in 1915 Cecil Meares returned to London, where, on 6 February, he married Annie Spengler at St Andrew's Church, Marylebone. By 30 March Meares had resigned his Hussars commission, sat and passed proficiency tests in French, German and Russian and joined the Royal Naval Air Service. He would initially be working in Dunkirk, where he would be considerably nearer to London and his new wife than he had been on the Western Front.[21]

10

Your Country Needs You!

When war was declared in August 1914, Apsley Cherry-Garrard knew immediately that he wanted to play his part. But despite being only 28 years old and strong enough to haul a laden sledge for miles across snow and ice, Cherry found it difficult to prove that he was 'fit for service'. He was short-sighted and had, since returning from Antarctica, suffered occasional but debilitating bouts of colitis.[1]

Cherry did not have any immediate entrée to the armed forces. Of the other scientists, Debenham was a voluntary trooper with King Edward's Horse and Priestley and Wright were both members of the Wireless Section of Cambridge University's Signal Company Officers Training Corps.[2] Cecil Meares had previously served in a cavalry regiment in the Boer War. Ponting, although well above the age limit for volunteering, had not hesitated to approach the War Office about the possibility of serving as a war photographer.

In terms of skills, Cherry had his degree in biology and his expedition experience; he spent much of his time running the Lamer estate, but, having never needed to earn his living, had no employment record. He had joined the *Terra Nova* expedition due to a chance meeting with Edward Wilson at the Scottish holiday home of Reginald Smith, Cherry's cousin, whose publishing company had compiled and published Scott's *Discovery* papers. Wilson had encouraged Cherry to apply to join Scott's second expedition, but that had not been a straightforward process, even after Scott had appointed Wilson as his chief of scientific staff. Knowing competition for places on the expedition was fierce, Cherry had offered to make a £1,000 donation towards the costs of the expedition (as, it had been hinted, another comfortably off applicant had done) but Scott had still turned him down.[3] It had only been when Cherry had offered to make his donation unconditional, and Wilson had told Scott that he needed more scientific staff, that Cherry had been accepted for the expedition.

When Cherry had returned from China in May 1914 he had started working in earnest on his narrative of the expedition. He and Lyons of the publishing sub-committee had made contact with the scientists and others from whom

Cherry needed information but as naval reservists were called to serve and Atkinson, Debenham and others rushed back from overseas to join ships and regiments, it was clear (and right) that Cherry's need for information would be low amongst his friends' priorities. Even the demands of the Suffragettes and attempts to solve the 'Irish Question' had now taken a back seat.

There was, however, one thing which Cherry could do immediately. He and his mother offered Lamer, their family home, for use as a hospital for wounded soldiers. Sir Frederick Treves, the eminent surgeon, came to Lamer with representatives of the Red Cross to discuss what adaptations might be required to make the building suitable for its new purpose. Treves had come to discuss how Lamer might serve in the war, but when he saw Kris, the sledge-dog Cherry had 'adopted' after the expedition, he suggested a way in which Cherry's experience with working dogs could help the war effort.

By 17 August Cherry was sailing across the Channel with Major Edwin Richardson and a pack of specially trained dogs. Richardson, a Scotsman, had devoted years to training dogs to track down people (alive or dead). His work was well regarded by dog experts overseas and he regularly acted as a judge at military dog trials in Russia and elsewhere. Richardson also knew that the German army had the most advanced training system and that their dog-handlers regularly visited England to purchase collies to work alongside their native breeds.

But Richardson's efforts to convince the British army that dogs could serve as sentries and in other roles had so far met with little success.[4] As the Germans began to bombard Belgian cities Richardson saw his opportunity to demonstrate what his dogs could do. He decided to transport some bloodhounds across the Channel at his own expense and take them to Belgian cities where they could help sniff out injured soldiers or civilians who might be lying hidden under rubble.[5] Richardson needed someone who knew how to handle working dogs in difficult conditions.

Cherry did not expect his first trip with Richardson to last for long. Richardson would simply establish what the dogs could do in the current conditions, then return to Britain and train more dogs to take out to France and Belgium. While Cherry was away, his mother and sisters would oversee the conversion of Lamer into a hospital.

Cherry, Richardson and the bloodhounds made it safely across the Channel, but by the time they reached Brussels the Belgian government, royal family and army were in retreat to Antwerp. With German forces about to enter the city and the British Expeditionary Force several days away, Brussels was a dangerous place to be.

When Richardson learned that German soldiers had been shooting French army 'sniffer' dogs wearing coats emblazoned with a Red Cross, he decided he must also retreat and return to Scotland, where he could think about what to do next.

Within a week of leaving England Cherry was back at Lamer, from where he wrote to Arthur Farrer, his family's lawyer:[6]

> It was an awful wild goose chase. From an early stage it was obvious that it could be impossible to work dogs. Then communications were cut by the Germans … The Red Cross Staff came in by car & told us we had better get back – which we did. We might have as well run a confectioner's shop as try & work dogs. It is most disappointing, but there it is …
>
> I would like to keep my power of attorney intact in case anything which really seems useful turns up. But I will never be hurried into another job of this kind again – by Treves or anybody. And I expect to get a considerable sum back from the Life Insurance, to whom you sent a cheque for £315.0.0.
>
> It was a horrid business.

It was not long, however, before Cherry wrote to Farrer with news about another possible opportunity for war service:[7]

> I am not sure if I am going to take a job helping to run a converted yacht with wounded etc. I want a job if possible, but the doctor here refuses me medically – however I think something will turn up. But I won't be hurried – once bit twice shy …

When the idea of working on the hospital ship came to nothing, Treves offered to provide a car so Cherry could transport injured soldiers for the Royal Army Medical Corps. When that opportunity failed to materialise, Cherry purchased a motor bike, enlisted as a private in the Royal Engineers and went to Aldershot army camp to train as a dispatch rider. It did not take Cherry long to settle down into being a 'Tommy' (as opposed to an 'Officer Boy') and to become accustomed to working with 'rough but very good diamonds'.

But one day he received an unexpected telegram from the Admiralty. Would Mr Cherry-Garrard consider joining the Royal Naval Air Service's new armoured car division? The Admiralty's approach resulted from a long chain of coincidences which began with Farrer. He had met Lady Boothby, whose RNAS officer husband had worked with Captain Murray Sueter, who was a former shipmate of Captain Scott. Sueter, who had provided Scott with advice on his motor-sledges, was now (with encouragement from First Lord of the Admiralty Churchill) establishing a new armoured car division within the RNAS. When Boothby had mentioned Cherry-Garrard's name to Sueter, wheels had soon been set in motion.

By the middle of October Cherry's commanding officer in the Royal Engineers had reluctantly agreed to release him from duty. Cherry was appointed as a Lieutenant in the RNVR and sent to join the RNAS's Armoured Car Division. Within three weeks he had been promoted to Lieutenant-Commander and put in command of the Division's No. 5 Squadron.

When Cherry realised that his squadron had no headquarters and few staff, he cleared out garages and other outbuildings at Lamer and found places where his men could be billeted. He contacted George Abbott, who was now sufficiently recovered from his breakdown to sign up with Cherry; he also managed to recruit several other drivers and mechanics locally.

As Cherry prepared his unit for action, Lamer's spacious rooms were already filling up with wounded soldiers returning from the front. Cherry's sisters had now, like Pennell's sister Dorothy and Edie Bowers, sister of Cherry's friend Birdie, joined the ranks of nurses, whose services would be much needed in the months to come.

* * *

Soon after war had broken out Edie Bowers, a full-time nursing sister, had answered an appeal for nurses to join a mission to Serbia led by Lady Paget, wife of Britain's former ambassador to Serbia. Lady Paget had previously helped establish a military hospital in Belgrade during the Balkan wars and now wanted to provide a 250-bed facility in Nish (Niš), where wounded Serbian soldiers could be treated.

When Edie passed through London on her way to Southampton to catch her ship, George Wyatt, the expedition agent who had helped her brother reload the *Terra Nova* in Lyttelton, met her and escorted her across the city and onto the boat train to Southampton.

Edie and her fellow-nurses boarded the troopship SS *Dongola*, which would carry them east; it was, as she told her mother, 'quite a sight':[8]

all the Serbian Legation & a hundred other Lady's, Lord's & Sir's arrived to shake hands, & promised us the dinner of our lives when we all returned. We were all bundled into a first class saloon carriage; the reporters from the *Sphere, Mirror* & *Sketch* were trying to take photos, notes, etc. . . .

We have about 1,000 Tommies on board & a couple of hundred officers. We are the only ones of the opposite sex, one of the officers told me they were not expecting any Ladies & were highly pleased to see us arrive.....We are one of about thirteen or fourteen ships, P & O & all sorts of transport lines & we are being convoyed by several cruisers & two boats with search lights ... we are fifty miles away from the ordinary trade route [and] we can also see French gun boats & English torpedoes.

For Edie, the least-travelled member of Bowers family, being sea-sick in the Bay of Biscay was a small price to pay for such an adventure:

we are going to such funny places ... it really is an experience that I am very glad to get ...You will be greatly relieved to know that we are not going up the Adriatic but going through Greece instead to Salonika ... I believe we have been through one mine-field after we left Southampton; at any rate we got through alright.

As the *Dongola* entered the Mediterranean and temperatures soared, nurses were barred from certain areas of the ship whilst soldiers were taking their baths. When news reached the ship that Turkey had entered the war Edie's soldier companions began joking about having to rescue her and the other nurses from 'hamans'. The closing of the Dardanelles to British and Allied shipping also meant that Lady Paget and her nurses would no longer be able to travel to Serbia via Salonika.

But Edie did not mind the delay:

We really are having an awfully good time ... there is a regular scramble amongst the men to take us out & it is so funny to see how jealous some of them are when they get left behind without anybody. I am afraid I see many difficulties ahead which will make trouble ... It seems so funny to think of the cold & wet in this hot climate with everybody wearing the thinnest of clothing & solar topees.

One of the doctors on the ship turned out to be on his way to join the troopship *Northbrook*, on which Edie's brother Henry had served before leaving the Royal Indian Marine and joining the *Terra Nova* expedition.

When the *Dongola* docked in Malta, Edie, her fellow nurses, Lady Paget and the other medical staff travelling to Serbia disembarked. While they waited to find out how they would be travelling to Nish, Edie and her new friends visited the catacombs and '100 other places' in and around Valletta. Within a few days transport for the next leg of their journey had been organised:

we are being shipped in a coal barge for a bit, after that I don't know where we shall go ... what it may be in the future I don't know but up to the present it is like a holiday with plenty of nice men to help do things for us … I wonder how I will get on 'In Service'. I am sure it will not be all plain sailing by all means. Still I am not meeting trouble half-way.

Conscious that her mother had been outwardly stoical but distraught about what had happened to her only son on his great Antarctic adventure just over two years previously, she added, 'Now dearest don't worry about me, I am afraid I am not one to die an untimely death, if so we would have been shipwrecked in that awful storm …'

Although Edie made light of the situation, Lady Paget and her nurses were now entering dangerous waters.[9]

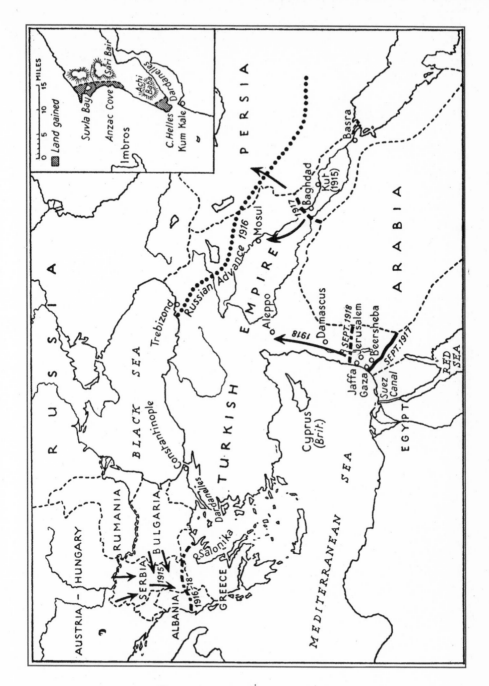

Turkey and surrounding area and Gallipoli (inset), showing Allied gains during the Gallipoli campaign (1915) and (on main map) other major fronts and advances in subsequent years. Map originally published by Carter and Mears. Image © private.

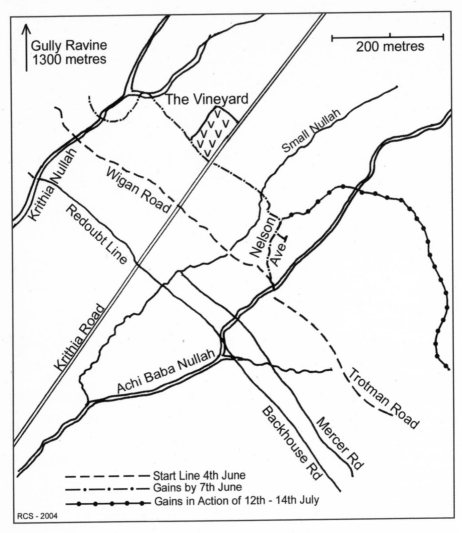

↑ Gully Ravine
1300 metres

200 metres

The Vineyard

Small Nullah

Krithia Nullah

Redoubt Line

Wigan Road

Nelson Ave

Krithia Road

Achi Baba Nullah

Trotman Road

Backhouse Rd

Mercer Rd

‒ ‒ ‒ ‒ ‒ Start Line 4th June
‒·‒·‒·‒ Gains by 7th June
•‒•‒•‒•‒ Gains in Action of 12th - 14th July

RCS - 2004

Helles Sector, Gallipoli, showing starting position of Allied front (including Royal
Naval Division sector) and gains made during June and July 1915 during advances on
Krithia and Achi Bula. Map © and courtesy of Roy C. Swales.

11

From Blandford Camp Towards Byzantium

━━⊰∂∕∂∂⊱━━

Within a month of war breaking out Edward Nelson left his work at the Plymouth Marine Laboratory to join the Royal Naval Division. He had not yet completed his training when the Division was called to serve at Antwerp, but he had since been allocated to Hood Battalion, part of the Division's 2nd Naval Brigade. In November 1914 all the Naval Brigade battalions moved en masse to a new base and training camp near Blandford Forum. Nelson's new base was about 20 miles from Salisbury and 35 miles from Beckington, near Bath, where his parents lived.

Christmas at Blandford had been a fairly rowdy 'all ranks' affair, following which Nelson and his fellow-officers were awarded a week's home leave. Nelson had by then been allocated to Hood's 'A' Company, serving under Lieutenant-Commander Bernard Freyberg.

Freyberg, who was almost six years younger than Nelson, was an imposing young man.[1] He had been born in England, raised and educated in New Zealand, swum for his adopted country at national level and worked as a dentist, territorial army officer and special constable. He had arrived in England in autumn 1914, via Tahiti, other Pacific Ocean islands, the United States (where he had abandoned a planned advanced dentistry course) and Mexico, where he had worked as an armed guard during the country's civil war. When Freyberg heard that war had broken out in Europe he walked to the Mexican coast (some 300 miles away) and took a steamer to Britain. After he arrived in London, a chance encounter with Colonel George Richardson, with whom he had served in the New Zealand territorials, and a meeting with Winston Churchill had resulted in his present appointment. When Freyberg realised Nelson had taken part in the *Terra Nova* expedition, he admitted that he regretted not having applied to join the expedition for at least a season.

Of Hood's other senior officers, Commanding Officer Lieutenant-Commander Quilter was a Grenadier Guard, Lieutenant-Commander Parsons was a career naval officer and Adjutant Alexander Graham had worked as a soldier-cum-war-correspondent in the Boer War and a stockbroker. Most of Hood's junior officers were, like Graham and Nelson, volunteers. Most had, like Nelson, been educated at public schools and Oxbridge colleges, but others also had connections with the navy or with Churchill.

Rupert Brooke (Rugby, Cambridge), a charismatically handsome, sensitive young man, had joined the RND not long after returning from an extensive tour of North America and the Pacific Ocean islands. Brooke had served at Antwerp in Anson Battalion but had requested a transfer to Hood so he could be with friends already serving with the battalion.[2] Brooke was also a literary protégé of Churchill's private secretary Edward Marsh and had been working on his latest collection of poems while at Blandford.

Denis Browne (Rugby, Cambridge organ scholar) was a school-friend of Brooke; Arthur Asquith (Winchester, New College) was the third son of the prime minister; Johnnie Dodge, an American, was a cousin of Churchill on his mother's side; Maurice Hood, son and heir of Viscount Bridport, was related to Admirals Nelson and Hood; William Egerton's father was Vice-Admiral Egerton (a friend of Scott and recipient of one of his final letters); Scotsman Hew Hedderwick (Fettes College) was a chartered accountant with RNVR experience.[3] By February Brooke had added to his Hood 'circle' Patrick Shaw-Stewart (Eton, Oxford), a banker (Baring's) who was, like Brooke, a member of the 'Coterie' of Lady Diana Manners.[4] Around the same time musician and Olympic oarsman Frederick Septimus Kelly (Eton, Oxford) arrived from Victor Campbell's Drake Battalion to join his friend Denis Browne.

On 17 February Churchill arrived at Blandford to inspect what was sometimes referred to as 'Winston's Army'. Three days later Quilter announced that the RND's Naval Brigades would be sailing east to join the RND's Marine Brigade in a short campaign in Turkey. The aim was to break through the straits of the Dardanelles to Constantinople, force Turkey out of the war and thus reopen Russia's route from the Black Sea to the Mediterranean.

On 25 February King George, accompanied by Churchill, arrived at Blandford for a final pre-departure inspection. The day was clear and bright and the sun glinted on the instruments of Hood Battalion's Silver Band as they played the national anthem.

Two days later, following final kit inspections and farewells, Nelson and his fellow-officers marched their men 10 miles from Blandford to Shillingstone station; from there trains took them to Avonmouth, where they boarded the *Grantully Castle*, which would take them, their mules, equipment and stores to Turkey.

While Brooke and his more romantically inclined friends talked of 'sailing to Byzantium', another (anonymous) Hood poet had a less romantic view:[5]

> We've a rather mixed collection in the Blandford RND
> For we've got 5,000 sailors who have never seen the sea,
> And we've got a naval transport of 500 horse-marines,
> The express design of Winston to supply the Turks with beans.

As the *Grantully Castle* sailed east non-sailors tried to find their 'sea legs' and long-serving seamen groused about being forced to wear army-style khaki uniforms, rather than navy blue. But sing-songs organised by Kelly and Browne raised spirits and passed the time. They followed a course west of the Scillies (to avoid German submarines), through the Straits of Gibraltar and along the North African coast before docking in Malta. Whilst in port, Brooke and Shaw-Stewart met up with Charles Lister, a friend and Divisional HQ linguist who had applied to transfer to Hood. As they pulled out of harbour Browne conducted the battalion band in a surprise performance of the 'Marseillaise' which was duly acknowledged by cheers from sailors in French ships which were moored nearby.[6]

On 11 March the *Grantully Castle* sailed into the already crowded harbour in Mudros Bay on the Greek island of Lemnos. For the next week Nelson and his companions explored the island, carried out training exercises and practised rowing in the ocean and landing on the beach from tenders. Nelson also gave a lecture on the use of the prismatic compass, an instrument he had, thanks to Pennell, learned to use during the *Terra Nova* expedition.[7] They were told they were leaving for Turkish waters, but after packing up, re-embarking and setting sail, they were soon back in Mudros Bay.[8]

On 24 March they were transferred to Port Said, outside Cairo, where RND men were billeted in tents near the docks. Nelson initially shared a tent with Freyberg, Brooke and Dodge, but Brooke and Dodge left after two nights to join Asquith on a tour of Cairo's 'sights'.

On 2 April the RND's new Commander-in-Chief, Sir Ian Hamilton, came to inspect his men. By now Brooke was felling unwell due, he suspected, to sunstroke. Hamilton visited him in his tent where, according to Brooke, they discussed poetry, which they had discovered was a shared interest.[9] Soon afterwards Brooke took a taxi to Cairo, where he joined fellow-invalid Patrick Shaw-Stewart at the latter's hotel. By now Brooke was suffering from acute diarrhoea and a swollen sore had appeared on his upper lip.

On 10 April the Grantully Castle left Port Said for Lemnos, towing an auxiliary vessel which would be used for troop disembarkation. As Mudros Bay was now completely full of ships the Grantully Castle continued to Trebuki Bay, on Skyros. Over the next week Nelson and his companions practised semaphore by sending messages to each other, improved their fitness by doing Swedish exercises and honed their machine-gun handling and firing skills.

Brooke was up and about again and enjoying discussions with the 'Latin Club' (Brooke, Kelly, Dodge, Browne, Lister, Asquith and Shaw-Stewart) about the parallels between their current situation and ancient Greek and Roman wars. Brooke also began taking photographs of his friends and their surroundings and jotting down fragments of verse:[10]

> I strayed about the deck, an hour, to-night
> Under a cloudy moonless sky; and peeped
> In at the windows, watched my friends at table,
> Or playing cards, or standing in the doorway,
> Or coming out into the darkness. Still
> No one could see me.

A highlight of the week in Skyros was the all-ranks fancy dress ball: prizes were awarded for the best costumes – many of which had been fashioned from cabin curtains – and Kelly and Browne took turns at playing the saloon piano. Another evening Nelson took Kelly on at chess, but lost two games to one.[11] When ships transporting other RND battalions arrived at Trebuki Bay, Johnnie Dodge, along with a group of officers and 300 stokers, returned to Lemnos to be trained on the tugs and trawlers which would ferry men from troop carriers to the beaches of the Gallipoli peninsula.

On 20 April everyone joined in a divisional sports day. Brooke, who had been on watch the night before, was feeling tired, but took part in a few events. During a lull between races he, Browne, Shaw-Stewart and Lister went exploring and found a quiet little olive grove where they rested for a while. When it was time to leave the island Lister and Freyberg suggested they should all swim back to the ship, but Brooke did not feel up to joining them.

The following morning Asquith and Lister found Brooke in his cabin, complaining of pains in his head and back; by now his upper lip was very swollen. Edward Marsh had recently sent Brooke a copy of The Times in which 'The Soldier', one of the poems Brooke had been working on at Blandford, had been published. Dean Inge of St Paul's Cathedral had, it appeared, read it out during his Easter Sunday sermon:[12]

If I should die, think only this of me:
That there's some corner of a foreign field
That is for ever England. There shall be
In that rich earth a richer dust concealed;
A dust whom England bore, shaped, made aware,
Gave, once, her flowers to love, her ways to roam,
A body of England's, breathing English air,
Washed by the rivers, blest by suns of home.
And think, this heart, all evil shed away,
A pulse in the eternal mind, no less
Gives somewhere back the thoughts by England given;
Her sights and sounds; dreams happy as her day;
And laughter, learnt of friends; and gentleness,
In hearts at peace, under an English heaven.

'The Soldier' had already, according to the article, been reviewed in *The Times Literary Supplement* after appearing in *New Numbers*, a poetry journal published by Brooke's friends and fellow poets Lascelles Abercrombie and Wilfred Gibson. Brooke, who had visited them at their home in Dymock, Gloucestershire, after returning from North America, had sent them the poems before leaving Blandford in February.[13]

On the *Grantully Castle*, Brooke's friends were becoming concerned for his health. When William McCracken, Hood's Medical Officer, examined Brooke he found his patient had a temperature of 101°F.[14] McCracken ordered poultices to be applied to the swelling on Brooke's lip, but when Brooke's temperature continued to rise, he began considering the possibility of pneumonia, something he felt Brooke was in no state to resist. Over the next twenty-four hours, as Brooke lapsed in and out of consciousness, McCracken summoned additional medical assistance from Divisional HQ. Eventually Brooke's temperature reached 104°F; by this time the swelling had spread across his face and when a bacteriologist took a swab he found there was infection in Brooke's bloodstream. McCracken insisted, despite Brooke's drowsy protests, that Brooke should be evacuated to the nearest hospital ship, which was the French Navy's *Duguy Trouin*. Browne and Asquith went with him in the tender and returned in the evening with the news that Brooke was the only patient on the ship and was being well looked after, including by an English-speaking nurse.

On the morning of 23 April (St George's Day and Asquith's 32nd birthday) Asquith and Browne returned to the *Duguy Trouin*, where French surgeons were operating on the now comatose Brooke in the hope of drawing out the infection which was poisoning his blood. But by 2 p.m. Brooke's temperature had risen to 106°F. He died at 4.45 p.m. with his old schoolmate Denis Browne at his bedside. He was 27 years old.

When Asquith returned to the hospital ship he told Browne that the *Grantully Castle* was due to leave for the Dardanelles at 5 a.m. the following morning.[15] As Browne was sure that Brooke would not have wanted to be buried at sea, Freyberg, Browne, Lister and other members of the 'Latin Club' went over to Skyros and began digging a grave in the olive grove Brooke had enjoyed visiting three days earlier. By mid-evening everything was ready for the burial. Hood officers, seamen who would act as pall-bearers and Divisional and Brigade senior officers crossed to the *Duguy Trouin* on a pinnace to collect Brooke's body and some French officers who would attend the ceremony. Brooke's body had been dressed in full uniform; his coffin was covered by a Union Jack and topped by his pith helmet and holstered pistol. It was dark, but a lantern-bearer and a partially clouded half-moon lit the pathway up the rocky hillside to the grave. By 11 p.m. everyone had arrived at the grove.

After the 1st Brigade's Chaplain had performed the burial service, Shaw-Stewart ordered the guard of honour to fire a three-volley salute. The grave had been lined with flowering sage and sweet-smelling olive sprigs and marked by two white crosses. After the Last Post had been played, most of the funeral party made their way slowly down the rocky path, leaving Asquith, Browne, Kelly, Lister and Freyberg to cover the grave with lumps of pink and white marble they found lying around the grove.

When Kelly returned to the ship he copied out the contents of Brooke's notebook to cover against the eventuality of it going astray when it was sent back to England with his other effects.

It had, everyone agreed, been a sad day, but Brooke was now lying in the 'corner of a foreign field' he had already envisaged in his mind's eye.

∗ ∗ ∗

By 5.30 a.m. on 24 April the *Grantully Castle* was steaming towards Gallipoli. While the main body of troops landed on beaches in the south of the peninsula (between Sulva Bay and Cape Helles), Hood and other RND Battalions were to mount a series of feints and diversions in the north of the peninsula, in the hope of diverting the Turks' attention and firepower. Quilter had considered several options in terms of Hood's contribution to this effort but eventually agreed that Freyberg, the former champion swimmer, should go ashore alone under cover of darkness, create a diversion and spy out the land. Nelson was put in charge of a cutter which would keep track of Freyberg's progress and, when he returned from his mission, help him out of the water and bring him back to the ship. The exercise would take place during the night of 25–26 April.

Freyberg, protected from the cold and camouflaged by a thick layer of dark grease, jumped into Nelson's cutter. By midnight, when they were about 2 miles offshore, he slipped into the water and began swimming to shore, dragging behind him a canvas bag-cum-raft loaded with flares, lights, a knife and a revolver.[16] An hour later he clambered up the beach and lit his first flare. He returned to the water, swam along the shoreline and repeated the exercise. He hid in some bushes to see if there would be a reaction from the Turks, but none was forthcoming. He crept further inland and found some trenches which, on inspection, turned to be newly dug and empty. He started heading towards some lights on nearby hilltops, but could see no sign of movement. He returned to the beach, lit his final flare and waded back into the water with his raft.

Around 3 a.m. Nelson, peering into the darkness, saw Freyberg swimming slowly in his direction, apparently suffering from cramp. Nelson brought the cutter over and hauled his exhausted commanding officer out of the water. After Nelson and Freyberg and others in the cutter had reboarded their ship, the *Grantully Castle*'s gunners made a 'sweep' of the shore, but there was no response from the hillsides.

After being held offshore for several days Hood Battalion landed on the beaches below Cape Helles, on the southern tip of the peninsula, on the night of 29 April.[17] Under a full moon and clear sky, Nelson and his companions could see that the beach was strewn with bodies from earlier landings; as they moved up the beach constant fire from the heights made it impossible to help their own wounded or others who had been left behind by other units.

By the beginning of May Hood Battalion had taken their place in the line of troops which stretched for miles on either side of the road leading to Krithia and Achi Baba, the main Turkish positions in the Cape Hellas sector. Prior to the Hood's arrival a first attempt to take these positions had resulted in some 3,000 casualties.

After Hood Battalion had 'settled in', Kelly, Lister and Browne went on a reconnaissance; on their return they reported that the countryside was pretty and covered with small orchards, wild flowers and herbs.

On 4 May Hood embarked on a major 'push' across a 400yd front during which, it was hoped, they would advance 2,000yds. The plan was then for them to hold their position while other British and French units swept past them and surrounded Achi Baba and Krithia. By 6 May, following some apparent miscommunication with French troops on their flank, Hood companies found themselves too far ahead of the overall line. As the Turks opened fire on their unprotected flanks Kelly and his platoon became isolated but after he found Nelson and his men they consolidated and dug in together.[18] They spent that night and the following day and night under heavy fire before finally being relieved early on 8 May.

When Nelson and Kelly returned to their original line they learned that Quilter, their popular and well-respected Commander, had been killed in the advance, Freyberg had been shot in the stomach, Asquith had received a bullet wound in the knee and Dodge had been shot in both arms. Lister had also been wounded and Browne had been shot by a sniper after the battle. Shaw-Stewart had enjoyed a lucky escape when a bullet bounced off the Asprey's mirror he carried in his breast pocket.[19]

Over a few days Hood's fighting strength had been reduced from thirty officers and 800 men to ten officers and under 400 men. The next few days were spent tending to injured men and carrying them down to the beaches, from where they would be taken to hospital ships or evacuated to hospital in Egypt. During the post-battle lull a Hood officer summarised the sorry state of some fellow officers in verse:[20]

> **A** is for Asquith, Arthur or 'Oc',
> Who's winged by a bullet just now and a crock.
> **B** is for Burnett, a scout bred and born;
> Both bullets and snipers he treats with mere scorn.
> **C** stands for Chalmers, who grouses all day,
> But works like a Trojan, as all of us say.
> **D** denotes Daglish, who's positive quite,
> That one's view's either wrong, or else perfectly right.
> Egerton's **E**, and my very good friend,
> Who has read through this trash and helped me no end.
> **F** is for Fergie, and Freyberg as well,
> Both jolly good fellows, but different as h★★l.
> Graham is **G**, or adjutant really:
> His arm's in a sling and he's doing but queerly.
> **H** is for Hedderwick, Hood and the rest
> Who've been into action and well stood the test.
> **I**'s for ideas that we all of us hold,
> That to get through the straits would be better than gold.
> **J** stands for Johnny [Dodge], unselfish and kind;
> He's hit in both arms, but pretends he don't mind.
> **K** stands for Kelly, that oarsman of fame,
> Who's now lending a hand at a different game.

L is the line of the trenches we hold:

Hot and dusty all day – at night terribly cold.

M stands for Maxim [gun], with Martin and crew;

Without their stout help, I don't know what we'd do.

Nobb knows the drill-book from first page to last,

While Nelson at scouting cannot be surpassed.

O is the orders that must be obeyed,

Though one's dying for sleep and one's nerves are all frayed.

P is for Parsons, as calm as can be,

Though I fancy he'd rather be fighting at sea.

Q is for Quilter – he's now laid to rest:

A leader of men, he was one of the best.

R for recruits who have stuck it A1,

And are proving a thorn in the flesh of the Hun.

Shaw-Stewart and Shadbolt both start with an **S**;

One excels at finance, and the other at chess.

T is for Trimmer, who's hit in the head;

He's now convalescent, but ought to be dead.

U is unselfishness shown by our Doc [McCracken];

He's one in a million and stands like a rock.

V's for these verses – they're awful, it's true;

But I'm not a born poet – that's evident too!

Waller is **W**, small but replete

With good stories and jests from his head to his feet.

For **X**, **Y** and **Z** there are no words I know

That fit into this rhyme, so I'll just let them go.

By the end of May nearly half a mile had been gained for 'only' fifty casualties and in early June reinforcements arrived in the shape of the 'new' (post-Antwerp) Hawke, Benbow and Collingwood Battalions. Freyberg's younger brother Oscar, who had recently joined Collingwood, found that his elder brother had just been evacuated to Egypt for hospital treatment.[21]

On 4 June, Hood and other RND battalions took part in another major advance on Krithia and Achi Baba.[22] By 8.15 a.m., following a preliminary bombardment, Hood's company commanders prepared to give the order to advance. Parsons (who had taken over 'B' Company from the injured Asquith) climbed up a short ladder propped against his trench wall and asked his men if they were ready. Within minutes of shouting 'Come on, then, follow me!', he and a large number of his men were killed by a volley of Turkish rapid rifle and machine-gun fire. Hood men who made it through the hail of Turkish bullets to the front-line Turkish trenches found that their bombardment had done its work, but they and RND battalions who followed in their wake were also cut down in their droves.

By 3 p.m. the remnants of Hood, Howe and Collingwood were being withdrawn from battle. Collingwood had been virtually wiped out and Hood had lost another twelve officers and about 300 men. Denis Browne had reached the Turkish trenches, where he bayoneted two soldiers before being mortally wounded by two bullets, one of which drove his belt-buckle into his body. Johnny Dodge and Maurice Hood were also killed, as was Lieutenant-Colonel Crawford-Stuart, Quilter's replacement.[23] Kelly, Hedderwick and Surgeon McCracken had all been injured.

After the battle Edward Nelson was promoted to Lieutenant-Commander and put in temporary command of Hood Battalion, a position he would, snipers permitting, retain until Freyberg returned from hospital in Egypt.

Freyberg returned the following week and resumed command of Hood Battalion. In Egypt he had learned that he had been awarded a Distinguished Service Order in recognition of his midnight swim; now he was told that his brother and many of his Hood friends had died on the third unsuccessful attack on Krithia. He also brought news of events in Britain: Asquith's father, the prime minister, was now the leader of a wartime coalition government, which included Lord Kitchener and representatives of the Labour and Unionist parties. Churchill had, following criticism of his handling of the Gallipoli campaign, been moved from the post of First Lord of the Admiralty to the less important role of Chancellor of the Duchy of Lancaster. Some of Brooke's poems, including 'The Soldier' and other poems he had worked on at Blandford, had recently been published in London in a volume entitled *1914*, which was selling so well that it was being reprinted.

By the middle of July, Asquith, Kelly, Egerton and most of the other injured Hood officers were back. Hood was not involved in any major offensives during July, but on 20 July Freyberg was again badly wounded in the stomach and invalided out. Nelson was once more in command of Hood Battalion. By August the heat was intense, flies were everywhere and water was in short supply – a situation exacerbated by the poison the Turks had poured down some wells near British positions. More men were now falling prey to dysentery than to Turkish bullets or shells.

Freyberg returned from Egypt in mid-August to resume command of Hood. Towards the end of the month Brooke's friend Charles Lister was injured by shellfire (for the third time); he was evacuated to a hospital ship but died of his wounds a few days later and was buried on Lemnos.

By now most of the RND battalions were well below fighting strength and, weakened by injury and disease, only able to hold defensive positions. As summer heat gave way to autumn gales and rain, Edward Nelson succumbed to jaundice and was evacuated to hospital ship *Harapar*. That month his wife Violet gave birth to their first child, a daughter.

In mid-November Lord Kitchener came to Gallipoli to review the situation. In the weeks following his visit the Allies' landing piers were almost destroyed by gales and storms. As temperatures plunged below freezing and lashing rain turned to blizzards, men (who were still sleeping in the open) began suffering from exposure and frostbite.

On the night of 18 December 1915 the evacuation from Gallipoli began.

12

Crossing Paths and Keeping in Touch

William Lashly arrived in Turkish waters on HMS *Irresistible* in February 1915. He had been 'discharged to pension' after arriving back from Antarctica, but had joined the Royal Fleet Reserve.[1] On 1 September 1914, at the age of 46, he had been posted to HMS *Irresistible*. Since then he had carried out patrol and escort duties in the Channel, and taken part in a bombardment of the Belgian coast. During February and early March 1915 Lashly and his shipmates swept for mines, took part in several bombardments of the forts guarding the Dardanelles and assisted with troop landings on the peninsula.

On 18 March 1915 the *Irresistible* joined seventeen other ships in a three-wave attack on the forts guarding the Dardanelles. During the early stages of the engagement one ship hit a mine, exploded and sank and others were damaged by mines, but the *Irresistible* and other members of the squadron kept their guns blazing.

Shortly after 4 p.m. the *Irresistible* struck a mine. An explosion ripped through her engine-rooms, killing most of the below-deck crew. As water flooded the holds, she began to list, making it impossible to launch lifeboats. With no engine power and most of the crew still on board, she began to drift helplessly into range of Turkish guns; as shells exploded all around, the *Irresistible* became engulfed in smoke and spray. When orders to abandon ship were issued HMS *Wear* came alongside and managed to take over 600 men aboard. HMS *Ocean* sailed across to take the *Irresistible* in tow but struck a mine and was forced to withdraw.

As evening approached, the *Irresistible* drifted helplessly towards shore. By nightfall, still being pounded by Turkish guns, she disappeared beneath the waters of the Dardanelles.

William Lashly, who had survived a 50ft fall into a crevasse on Christmas Day 1911 (his 44th birthday), marched for longer than anyone else on the South

Pole journey and come close to starvation whilst saving Teddy Evans' life, was again lucky and was taken off the *Irresistible* before she sank.

* * *

Murray Levick's ship, the *Bacchante*, had been transferred from the North Sea Fleet to assist with landing British troops on the Gallipoli beaches. The *Bacchante* had remained offshore to provide fire cover for troops and to bombard Turkish positions during Allied offensives. During early summer Levick had helped treated Allied casualties and in August the *Bacchante* had supported Australian troops during attacks on Turkish positions.

The *Bacchante* had been recalled to the Mediterranean before the evacuation of Gallipoli, but Levick and his ship's captain had remained behind to provide assistance at ANZAC Cove.[2] Following the evacuation, Levick's efforts at Gallipoli were recognised with a promotion to the rank of surgeon-commander.

* * *

Edward Atkinson had arrived on the Gallipoli peninsula in late August 1915, when temperatures in the Mediterranean were at their height. On 12 August, the day before he left England, Atkinson married his 'lady love', Jessie Hamilton, at the registry office in Rochford, Essex.

Atkinson had been sent to Gallipoli to investigate and suggest measures to contain outbreaks of dysentery and other fly-borne diseases which were cutting a swathe through British and Allied troops. His daily work involved exhuming and inspecting fly-covered, decomposing bodies and spraying them with large quantities of 'Liquid C' (for chlorine). He would then return over the next few days – often in the face of enemy sniper fire – to check and re-examine the bodies, before retiring to relative safety to record his findings.[3]

The results of Atkinson's work were gratifyingly immediate: overpowering stenches abated, bodies became less swollen, swarms of flies disappeared and the few remaining flies appeared to be deterred from alighting on bodies. 'Liquid C' also proved effective in killing flies and reducing larvae infestations in and around dug-outs, latrines, dung heaps and in men's quarters. The fact that Liquid C was highly inflammable, greasy, staining and irritated skin and eyes was, Atkinson concluded, a small price to pay given the potential improvements in men's health.

While in Gallipoli, Atkinson received a letter from Cherry-Garrard; his friend had, since collapsing in July, been diagnosed with a severe, possibly long-term, case of colitis. To add to Cherry's woes, his armoured car division had been disbanded. Atkinson was sympathetic:[4]

You poor old thing your luck seems dead out and I am sorry to have such a bad report of you … [I] have been sniped and that sort of thing and it really is queer how callous one gets … Now buck up and get well quick … [Turkey] is not such a bad country after all. It is very sweet with wild thyme and sage and rosemary but they are all getting pounded to dust[;] the flies are going rapidly and the sickness dropped over a 1/3 last week.

By early December Atkinson had left Gallipoli, but not of his own volition. He wrote to Cherry from Malta's Tigore Hospital:[5]

I have come through paratyphoid and double pneumonia and am now being bothered by successive attacks of pleurisy but I am gradually getting on top of them. They refuse to send me back before I have been to England and so I shall return and apply immediately to go out again. I have been badly bitten by the life and my work was going along splendidly when this d…..d thing happened …

Hope you are fit and well.

By the time Atkinson was in a fit state to return to Gallipoli, the evacuation had begun.

* * *

Frank Debenham's younger brother had been killed on Gallipoli shortly before Atkinson arrived there. Herbert Debenham, a Lieutenant in the East Lancashire regiment had died while leading his men in a charge on a Turkish position.[6] Herbert had, like his elder brother, left Australia to further his studies and had won the Gladstone Prize during his first year at London University's School of Economics. In the army, his evident leadership abilities had resulted in his being promoted to acting company commander; he had already been mentioned in despatches for 'gallant and distinguished service in the field'.[7]

Frank Debenham, who was now a Major with 'D' Company of the 7th Battalion Oxfordshire & Buckinghamshire Light Infantry, arrived in France a month after his brother's death. After a short spell fighting alongside French regiments at Loos, he and his men had been sent to Marseilles, from where they would sail to Salonika.

The Greek prime minister had requested assistance from British troops to help defend Greece's north-western borders against possible attacks by Bulgarian troops. Salonika was not known territory to most of the British troops arriving there, but life promised to be less dangerous than it was on the Western Front or in Gallipoli.

The fighting at Loos dragged on into November, by which time heavy rains had reduced the battlefields to mud. The casualty lists, which grew by the day, included John Kipling, the 18-year-old son of Rudyard Kipling, and William Brooke, younger brother of Rupert Brooke.

* * *

Victor Campbell's Drake Battalion had sailed to Gallipoli with the RND's 2nd Naval Brigade. Like other RND units, it had suffered heavy losses at Krithia, but Campbell had been awarded a Distinguished Service Order for:[8]

> conspicuous ability and initiative during operations between May 5th and 10th, near Krithia, Cape Helles; owing to his judgment and skill as Officer Commanding the forward line, losses, though heavy, were less severe than they would otherwise have been.

In August Campbell had returned to London, where he resigned from the RND and rejoined the navy. He enrolled in a gunnery training course, following which he would be qualified and eligible to command armed vessels. He spent Christmas Day 1915 in Dover in the company of Teddy Evans, Francis Drake and Thomas Williamson.[9] The news in London was that General Sir John French, who had been Commander-in-Chief of the British Expeditionary Force since the beginning of the war, would be replaced by his deputy, General Sir Douglas Haig. French, who had been suffering from ill health, would remain in Britain, in charge of home-based troops.

Teddy Evans had spent most of 1915 on the destroyer HMS *Viking* (where he kept a toy penguin mascot on the bridge) but was in the process of exchanging commands with Commander Williams of HMS *Crusader*. As the latter ship was currently in dock undergoing repairs, Evans was able to take the 'rest cure' which had been prescribed in an effort to bring an end to a recent series of migraines.

Francis Drake, who had come out of retirement to join the *Terra Nova* expedition, came out of retirement again to serve as a paymaster. Williamson (now a chief petty officer), who had recently transferred to the *Viking* from another ship, would remain there under Williams.

On Saturday, 22 January 1916, Campbell and Drake were guests at Teddy Evans' wedding at Christ Church, Broadway (which lay a few hundred yards from the expedition's Victoria Street office), and a reception at St Ermin's Hotel.[10] North Sea storms had almost caused Evans' bride, Elsa Andvord, to miss her wedding. Her preparations in London had been rushed, but newspaper reports confirmed that she looked elegant in an ankle-length ivory-white silk taffeta dress with chiffon sleeves, small plumed hat and white fox fur neck-stole. Evans had presented the bridesmaids with *Terra Nova* cap-ribbons to tie round their wrists and brooches in the form of Norway's Order of St Olaf.

Other guests with Antarctic connections who attended the wedding and reception included Kathleen Scott, Mrs Oates, Lady Shackleton, French explorer Jean-Baptiste Charcot and John Mather; Birdie Bowers' mother had sent a gift from Scotland.[11]

On 29 January, exactly a week after Evans' wedding, HMS *Viking* hit a mine in the Channel. The explosion ripped through the mess quarters of the ship killing Evans' successor, Commander Williams, and most of the officers, who had been in the midst of eating their lunch. Thomas Williamson survived but was badly injured.

The following day, 30 January, Sir Clements Markham died in a fire at his home, which had started after the cigarette he had been smoking in bed set fire to his bedclothes. Markham, who had been Scott's constant supporter, had travelled the world and championed the exploration of Antarctica, but had never seen the frozen continent.

* * *

Edward Atkinson saw in New Year 1916 in the infectious diseases wing of Haslar naval hospital. With time on his hands for letter writing, he began the first of a stream of letters to Cherry-Garrard:[12]

> A very happy New Year to you and to your people. They have sent me here for 3 weeks isolation. I have been so sorry to hear of your illness and I hope that things are going better ... the Dardanelles ... has been the most damnable affair that we have ever had and the Public have not the smallest inkling of what happened ...
>
> What I hope is that they send me out to the [Royal Naval] Division if they are going to Serbia or Egypt as I think there will be some fairly tough work there and I should like to be in at a fairly open scrap as this Trench warfare is the most ungentlemanly game ever invented.
>
> The sickness from Gallipoli is absolutely appalling and the hospital ships come rolling home absolutely full.

By the first week in January, the Gallipoli adventure was clearly at an end:[13]

> The troops that came from Suvla have recently gone to ... Lemnos and Alexandria ... and Salonica. The Australians are going temporarily to Tripoli but I expect

Harry Pennell and members of his 'afterguard' on board the *Terra Nova* near Akaroa, April 1912. Left to right: Jim Dennistoun, Alfred Cheetham, Henry Rennick, Francis Drake, William Williams, Harry Pennell, Wilfred Bruce, Dennis Lillie. Photograph: Herbert Ponting; from *Scott's Last Expedition*, Vol. II © private

Scott and members of the expedition landing party, January 1911. Left to right: Tom Crean, Edward Wilson (sitting), Patrick Keohane, Henry 'Birdie' Bowers (sitting), Tryggve Gran, Captain Robert Scott, Robert Forde, Cecil Meares, Apsley Cherry-Garrard, Lawrence Oates, Edward Atkinson. Photograph: Herbert Ponting; image © Mary Evans/Epic/Tallandier

Left: *Terra Nova* in a storm in the Southern Ocean, March 1912. Photograph: Herbert Ponting; from *Scott's Last Expedition*, Vol. I © private

Below left: *Terra Nova* in the Ross Sea ice pack, with its sails being furled. Photograph: Herbert Ponting; from *Scott's Last Expedition*, Vol. I © private

Below right: Teddy Evans in the crow's nest. Photograph: Herbert Ponting; from *Scott's Last Expedition*, Vol. I © private

Opposite: All photographs from *Scott's Last Expedition*, Vol. II © private
Top: The Northern Party in November 1912, after returning to Cape Evans: left to right, Dickason, Abbott, Browning, Campbell, Priestley, Levick. Photograph: Debenham
Centre left: Winter work at Cape Evans: left to right, Debenham, Cherry-Garrard, Bowers, Teddy Evans, Taylor. Photograph: Ponting
Centre right: Lillie with sponges from a record 'trawl' from the ship. Photograph: Ponting
Bottom left: Tom Crean shouldering his skis. Photograph: Ponting
Bottom centre: Nelson with the Nansen–Petersen insulated water bottle used to take water samples. Photograph: Ponting
Bottom right: Pennell using a prismatic compass. Photograph: Ponting

All photographs from *Scott's Last Expedition*, Vol. I © private

Top: Lashly, Day, Teddy Evans, Hooper (left to right) with a motor sledge. Photograph: Ponting

Centre left: Rennick meets a friendly Adélie penguin. Photograph: Ponting

Centre middle: Meares with Osman, the lead sledging dog. Photograph: Ponting

Centre right: Edgar 'Taff' Evans binds the badly frostbitten hand of Edward Atkinson, the only doctor then at Cape Evans. Photograph: Ponting

Bottom left: Tryggve Gran skiing. Photograph: Ponting

Bottom right: Ponting filming the ice from the *Terra Nova*. Photographer unknown.

Right: Terra Nova officers in New Zealand, February 1913. Left to right: front row: Bruce, Joseph Kinsey (expedition agent), Teddy Evans, Atkinson, Lillie; middle row: Levick, Gran, Campbell, Pennell; back row: Cherry-Garrard, Rennick, Cheetham, Williams, Nelson. © Illustrated London News Ltd/Mary Evans

Left: Many British newspapers published special editions on the *Terra Nova* expedition in February 1913; in the *Daily Mirror*'s special edition (12 February), an article about Lord Roberts's efforts to recruit men for the army was placed alongside one about Scott's heroism and sacrifice. Image © private

Right: Harry Pennell so enjoyed *The Great Adventure* (opened March 1913) that he went to at least six performance between August 1913 and early 1914; well-known artists and art collectors, including Roger Fry, Duncan Grant and Sir William Nicholson, loaned or created works for the play. Image © private

Wilfred Bruce married Dorothy Boot, daughter of millionaire Sir Jesse Boot (who owned over 500 pharmacies) in November 1913. Bruce and his best man, Henry Rennick, stand on either side of the bride; the other uniformed officer may be Francis Drake. Sir Jesse Boot sits on the right. Photographer: unknown; image © and courtesy The Alliance Boots Archive and Museum

Major Edwin Richardson, a specialist military dog trainer, and Cherry-Garrard (who may be behind the policeman in the photograph) just before leaving London for Belgium in August 1914. © Illustrated London News Ltd/Mary Evans

Men of the Royal Naval Division arriving (many on double-decker London buses) in Antwerp in October 1914. Victor Campbell arrived with the RND's Drake Battalion; Rupert Brooke and several of his friends were with other battalions. Image from contemporary French magazine © private

During October 1914 inhabitants of Antwerp fled as the German army approached; the pontoon bridge in the background was the only means of escape to the coast. © Mary Evans Picture Library

HMS *Hogue*, on which Henry Rennick served, was torpedoed on 22 September 1914 while assisting the *Aboukir*; HMS *Cressy* then tried to rescue men from both ships. The dotted lines to the *Hogue* indicate the trajectory of the torpedoes. Picture from *The Great War* magazine, image © private

HMS *Irresistible*, on which William Lashly served, sank after hitting a mine whilst bombarding the forts around the Dardanelles on 28 March 1915. Photograph © and courtesy of Stephen Chambers

Left: Cecil Meares in the uniform of the Northumberland Hussars, with whom he served at Ypres and neighbouring areas of the Western Front. Photograph (J-00279) courtesy of the Royal BC Museum, BC Archives, Vancouver, Canada

Below: Hooge chateau, near Ypres, before the war; its formal gardens may have inspired Major Lawrence Johnston (who was billeted there with Meares) to plant an alley of stilted hornbeams at Hidcote, his Cotswolds garden. 1910s postcard, image © private

Christmas truce near La Boutillerie (Rouge-Banc sector), December 1914, with officers of the Northumberland Hussars; the photograph was probably taken by Hussars officer, Lieutenant Robson. © Mary Evans/Robert Hunt Collection/Imperial War Museum

Rupert Brooke took this photograph of Edward Nelson, Bernard Freyberg and other comrades from Hood Battalion (Royal Naval Division) during training exercises on the way to Gallipoli in March 1915; he wrote on the reverse: 'Lemnos. 'A' Company with Freyberg (left) + Nelson (right) Windmills in distance.' Photograph (RCB/Ph/267k) © and courtesy of King's College Library, Cambridge

Above left: Royal Naval Division men charging from a trench; the photograph, described as 'Charge in Gallipoli' was probably taken during training in Lemnos, Greece. © Illustrated London News Ltd/Mary Evans

Above right: When visiting America in 1913 Rupert Brooke had a studio session with Sherril Schell, whose photographs were later engraved and widely circulated by Emery Walker. Image from Marsh (see bibliography) © private

Right: Harry Pennell married Katie Hodson in Oddington, Gloucestershire, on 15 April 1915. Contemporary postcard (photographer unknown), image © and courtesy of David Wilson

Below left: Harry Pennell's medals: China 1900; British War and Victory Medals; Polar Medal (silver), Antarctic 1910–13, George V; Royal Geographical Society medal (for *Terra Nova* expedition); image © and courtesy of Spink, www.spink.com.

Below right: The first news of Shackleton's *Endurance* expedition (which left Britain in August 1914) reached Britain in early 1916. This *Daily Mirror* front page of 10 July 1916 shows the ice-bound ship and expedition members including *Terra Nova* veteran Tom Crean (lower right). Image © John Frost Newspapers/Mary Evans Picture Library

THE MARRIAGE OF MISS KATHRINE HODSON AND COMMANDER HARRY PENNELL AT ODDINGTON — APRIL 18TH 1915 —

Left: HMS *Queen Mary*, on which Harry Pennell served, was hit and almost immediately exploded and sank during the Battle of Jutland on 31 May 1916. Photograph (taken from another ship) © Mary Evans/ *Süddeutsche Zeitung* Photo

Below: Victor Campbell in uniform, date unknown; image courtesy of David Parsons and Newfoundland Museum.

Above: Vincent Campbell's medals, left to right: DSO and bar; OBE; 1914 Star and clasp; War Medal; Victory Medal; Canadian Volunteer Service Medal and War Medal (both 1939–45); Polar Medal (silver), Antarctic 1910–13, George V; George V Jubilee medal (1937); Croix de Guerre 1914–18. Image © and courtesy of David Parsons

Above: Gran with members of Royal Flying Corps No. 44 (Home Defence) Squadron at Hainault Farm, 1917; Gran (wearing light-coloured flying suit) lies on the grass, awaiting orders to jump into his Sopwith Camel. Photographer unknown: image © and courtesy of Trevor Henshaw

Below left: Portsmouth Naval Memorial, where about 10,000 First World War sailors (including Harry Pennell) are commemorated; other sailors are commemorated on identical memorials at Plymouth and Chatham (where Henry Rennick is commemorated). Photograph © Anne Strathie

Below right: War memorial, Oddington, Gloucestershire, where Harry Pennell's name is listed just below that of his brother-in-law Hubert Hodson. Photograph © Anne Strathie

Above left: Hooge chateau after the war; contemporary postcard, image © private

Above right: The ruins of Ypres seen from the Hooge–Menin road after the war. Image, from Michelin's guidebook to Ypres (published in English in 1920 for British visitors to the battlefields), © private

Left: The Menin Gate memorial, Ypres, commemorates almost 55,000 soldiers with no known grave (including Hubert Hodson, Harry Pennell's brother-in-law). Photograph © Anne Strathie

Above left: Tyne Cot memorial and cemetery, near Ypres, where 50,000 men (including Raymond Priestley's brother Donald) are commemorated; the candles on gravestones were lit during 'Light Front', a centenary event on 17 October 2014. Photograph © Anne Strathie

Above right: Edward Nelson's fellow RND officer, Frederick 'Sep' Kelly (grave in foreground), is buried at Martinsart, near Beaucourt-sur-Ancre. Photograph © Anne Strathie

J.M. Barrie, Scott's friend and godfather to Scott's son Peter, was installed as rector of St Andrews University on 3 May 1922. Here he sits between Field Marshall Earl Haig (Chancellor of St Andrews) and actress Ellen Terry; Bernard Freyberg, VC, stands behind Barrie and Haig. Freyberg, Terry, Thomas Hardy, John Galsworthy (bareheaded, beside pillar on left) and others had been nominated by Barrie to receive honorary degrees. During his rectorial address Barrie read from Scott's last letter to him. Photographer unknown: image (Group 1922-2) © and courtesy of the University of St Andrews Library (Special Collections Division).

An early remembrance poppy; the first British 'Poppy Day' was on 11 November 1921; by the following year poppies were being made by Field Marshall Earl Haig's British Legion. Image © and courtesy of The Wilson, Cheltenham (which holds a large collection of Edward Wilson's work)

Left: Part of 'Blood Swept Lands and Seas of Red' (original concept and poppies by ceramic artist Paul Cummins, installation designed by Tom Piper) which was on display at the Tower of London during 2014. The 888,246 ceramic poppies (the number of British and Commonwealth soldiers who died in the war) filled the moat and structures including (as shown here) 'Over the Top'. Photograph (taken soon after 11 a.m. on 11 November 2014) © Anne Strathie

Above: The Tower Hill Memorial commemorates 12,000 sailors of Britain's merchant and fishing fleets (such as Alf Cheetham) who died during the First World War; the memorial, designed by Lutyens, was unveiled in 1928. Photograph © Anne Strathie.

after a while they will all be collected again in Egypt for I think the big show will come off there at first and Serbia afterwards. I am longing to get back to it and to some work … The Lord keep me from the Grand Fleet again.

[Edward] Nelson is well and so far has come through without a scratch. He has come out well in this show.

Atkinson was also thinking about Cherry-Garrard's health:[14]

Look here old chap in my usual interfering way I have been worrying around. I believe a change of scene and taking your mind off things completely would very likely benefit you … with your motor [car] … you could plan out a tour or something like it. With this in mind I wrote to Lillie at Cambridge and he would be willing to help as far as he could … I would like to see you well and about again and am certain some such change would hurry it. If you think fit write to Lillie at St John's College Cambridge. I expect you will be angry at this but I can only urge that I think it right and I want to see you better again. If it will relieve you, write and tell me to be damned.

As his own health improved, Atkinson began considering his options. He could return to the Admiralty's laboratories as a bacteriologist or accept command of a new RND hospital ship.[15] But he was reluctant to miss 'the naval affair' which he was sure was imminent, so decided to wait until Haslar hospital doctors signed him off for active duty.[16]

After that happened, Atkinson had to decide between going to France 'with the Heavy battalions' or waiting for a suitable opening at sea.[17] He initially turned down the French option, but then changed his mind and decided he would be 'happy as a peacock' just to be back on active service. He had some news (or in some cases rumours) for Cherry-Garrard about 'Antarctics': 'Silas came to [London] after I had left. I had an idea that he had been wounded but apparently not. Also Williamson tells me that Nelson was reported killed but I do not lend any credence to this.'

Atkinson would, he admitted to Cherry, be in 'a devil of a state' until he knew when he might be going to France and when the 'big show' might happen.

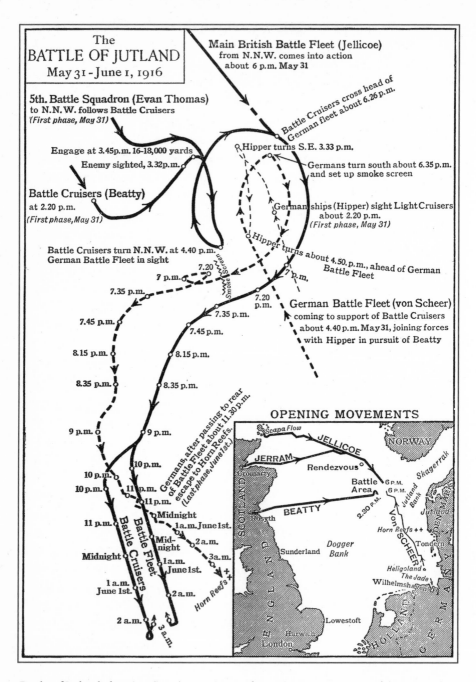

The Battle of Jutland, showing (inset) overview and opening movements and (main map) progress of battle. Map originally published in *Gresham Compact Encyclopedia*, 1928; image © private.

13

The 'Big Show' – and a Great Loss

On Friday, 17 December 1915, Harry Pennell settled down to write some Christmas letters from his cabin on HMS *Queen Mary*. Since the previous Christmas Henry Rennick's widow had given birth to a son; no other members of Pennell's afterguard or close friends had died, but some had been injured or had lucky escapes.[1] The 'Antarctics' were by now scattered all over the world and Alf Cheetham and Tom Crean had not yet emerged from Antarctica.

But Pennell knew that a letter addressed to Lamer would always find Cherry-Garrard:[2]

> Dear Cherry
> It is ages since I heard of you this is to prove that I am still alive and kicking.
>
> The war from a naval (big ship) point of view is about as dull as it could be. However this fleet is the advance face of the Grand Fleet & so if & when the Huns come out, we ought to be there.
>
> Jane [Atkinson] is 'seriously' ill at Malta. He had a fever & then got pleurisy. I understand that he is better & likely to come home, but my news only comes through my wife, who heard from Mrs Kinsey who heard from Lady Nicholson [Atkinson's aunt]. After Jane left the Grand Fleet the only one of the expedition I've seen has been [Frankie] Davies who is on the *Blanche* and as merry as usual … Burton is in one of the Light Cruisers based south & occasionally sees a German. He has a son & heir (some 5 or 6 months old now) & is as proud as Lucifer in consequence.

William Burton, in appreciation of the kindness Pennell had shown him following Brissenden's death at French Pass in 1912, had named his son Lewin (one of Pennell's middle names); he had also asked Pennell to be the boy's godfather.[3]

Pennell had news of several other 'Antarctics', some of which he suspected Cherry already knew:[4]

Drake is in the *Undaunted* & safely married to a very charming girl … Mather is (or was) at Crystal Palace instructing recruits. He is a Lieut R.N.V.R. I believe. Ponting is still in town & very sad that the War Office couldn't make use of him as a photographer. He volunteered but was refused as being not required. He is 46 & so cannot do anything in the military line …

It is very unfortunate about Jane. Luck of war of course, but one hoped he might escape … There is no news from the fleet & if there were it would be taboo. The men are absolute gold, they all seem to realise what is at stake & keep their spirits up & try to keep efficient; at it does require some patience.

Well so long, my dear, I do hope you are getting better luck than you had at first …

Pennell had kept in touch with Emily Bowers, with whose son he had spent an ice-bound Christmas in the Ross Sea five years previously:[5]

Dear Mrs Bowers

A short note to send you the season's greetings. 'Hope for the present & Peace & Happiness in the future' is the nicest motto I have seen in the cards.

It is a time when it is necessary for the British Public to keep their heads & they are not assisted much by the great London Daily newspapers except the Telegraph. The position though dangerous is not unfavourable & it seems likely that during 1916 the Germans will make a bid for an inconclusive peace, which for us would be no peace but only a truce. The more the war drags on the more plain becomes the enemy we are fighting against & the fact that we can no more make a truce than we can between wrong & right in one's own life.

All the family are scattered now, the old home having broken up at my mother's death early this year. My eldest sister [Winifred] is in Nyasaland teaching natives the rudiments of Christianity … The youngest [Nesta] is married & gone to Australia, her husband having been invalided out of the Army … & blown up by a bomb after he got back again … two brothers are in Egypt & Burma & Dorothy is joining the Canterbury hospital this month. Ann, married to a clergyman, is safely settled down at Wool & is the only one who has resisted the 'call of the wild'.

I myself was married last April, but of course can as yet see nothing of my wife. That good time will come when the business in hand is settled. I much hope then that she may have the pleasure of meeting you.

With all good wishes to you & the Misses Bowers

Pennell had married Katie Hodson on 15 April 1915 during a short spell of home leave. The couple had been married at Oddington parish church by

Katie's father; Cyril Hodson, Katie's vicar brother (whose profession exempted him from military service), had served as best man. Atkinson had been sorry to miss the wedding, but Pennell had introduced him to Katie in London a few weeks before the wedding. (Atkinson later told Cherry-Garrard that Pennell's 'Missus' was 'nice and pretty'.[6])

The *Cheltenham & Gloucester Graphic* had devoted several column inches to Pennell's 'very pretty' wedding.[7] Oddington's streets had been festooned with flags and other decorations. Katie Hodson wore a white satin dress trimmed with Honiton lace (made near Awliscombe) and carried a bouquet of orchids and lilies of the valley. She wore an antique pearl and diamond necklace around her neck which Pennell had given her as a wedding present. Pennell wore full dress uniform. The wedding was very much a family affair: one of Katie's bridesmaids, 'Maynie' Hedderwick, would soon be marrying Pennell's friend, Katie's brother Gerry, and three of Pennell's sisters had travelled to Gloucestershire for the wedding. After the ceremony there had been a wedding tea at the vicarage: the cake, decorated by Cheltenham's Oriental Café with models of penguins, seals, lifebelts, anchors and a model ship, had been much admired.

It had been a happy day, but since then Katie Pennell had lost her father and her brother Hubert. The latter had been killed near Ypres whilst serving with his Canadian regiment.[8] Another of Katie's brothers, Francis, had been wounded while serving with the 7th Gloucestershire Regiment at Gallipoli.

* * *

Although Pennell sometimes found life on the *Queen Mary* rather dull, the appointment of Captain Prowse to command of a large modern battlecruiser had not been without controversy.

Prowse's predecessor, William Hall (the *Queen Mary*'s first captain) had been a 'moderniser' who had insisted his ship should be fitted out with all modern conveniences, including a hot water system, laundry, bookstall, cinema and chapel. After Hall moved to his next command one of his protégés, Commander William James, requested a transfer from the *Queen Mary* rather than serve under an 'old school' captain like Prowse.[9] James was regarded as exceptionally bright but not as hardworking as ambitious young commanders were expected to be.[10] 'Bubbles', as James was known (from a painting of him, by his grandfather Sir John Everett Millais, which had been used to advertise Pears soap) had left the *Queen Mary* early in 1916.

After Gallipoli, the British press and public had become increasingly impatient for Britain's navy to deal a knock-out blow to the enemy. It was not only Edward Atkinson who was waiting for the 'big show'.

On Sunday, 24 April 1916, ships from the German High Seas Fleet emerged from Jade Bay, crossed the North Sea and began bombarding Lowestoft and Yarmouth. The German ships were on their way back to Jade Bay long before any Grand Fleet ships arrived from Scapa Flow. Soon afterwards the Battlecruiser Fleet, including the *Queen Mary*, was relocated to Rosyth, near Edinburgh; the 5th Battle Squadron was moved south to the Cromarty Firth.

In early May ships from the British Grand Fleet crossed the North Sea to Jutland Bank, from where seaplanes attacked the German Zeppelin base at Tondern. Some damage was done, but the raid failed to lure the High Seas Fleet out of Jade Bay.

In mid-May cryptographers working at the navy's Intelligence Division intercepted German wireless signals which suggested that the High Seas Fleet was preparing for a major offensive.

On the afternoon of Tuesday, 30 May, after it was confirmed that the German fleet was about to put out from Jade Bay, captains of coal-fired Dreadnoughts were ordered to raise steam. That evening Admiral Jellicoe's flagship, *King George V*, led a convoy of Dreadnoughts, destroyers and smaller ships out of Scapa Flow.

Jellicoe had issued a seventy-page battle-plan which outlined his strategy and provided instructions for almost every eventuality. Pennell and his fellow officers were confident that, with fifty more ships than the Germans and, on average, newer and better equipped vessels, the odds were in favour of the Grand Fleet.

The Battlecruiser Fleet which emerged from Rosyth consisted of HMS *Lion* (Beatty's flagship), *Queen Mary*, *Princess Royal*, *Tiger*, *New Zealand* and *Indefatigable*. They would engage directly with five German battlecruisers: SMS *Lützow* (the German flagship), *Seydlitz*, *Derfflinger*, *Von der Tann* and *Moltke*. Well before any German ships were in sight, everything was ready on the *Queen Mary* and her sister ships: decks were clear, gunners on alert, ammunition piles to hand and sickbays clean and ready to receive any casualties.

Just before 3.30 p.m. *New Zealand* and *Princess Royal* signalled that they could see the German battlecruisers. The *Queen Mary*'s guns, like those of the other five battlecruisers, had a range of almost 14 miles – although accuracy could not be guaranteed when firing at grey-painted German battlecruisers through North Sea mists.

The Germans opened fire first and by 3.50 p.m. the eleven ships were engaged in battle. The *Lützow* began firing on the *Lion*, *Derfflinger* on *Princess Royal*, *Seydlitz* on *Queen Mary*, *Moltke* on *Tiger* and *Von der Tann* on *Indefatigable*. As the Germans had one less ship, the *New Zealand* was unmarked. The *Indefatigable* returned fire on the *Von der Tann*, while the *Lion* and *Princess Royal* both fired on the *Lützow*. The *New Zealand* began firing at *Moltke*, but there appeared to be some signalling or other confusion as the *Queen Mary*, which had been ordered to fire at the *Derfflinger*, spent the first half-hour firing at the *Seydlitz*. Meanwhile the *Tiger*, which should have been firing at the *Seydlitz*, was aiming at the *Moltke*.

Waterspouts shot into the air as shells landed over or under target, but eventually gunners on both sides began to find their range. From the British side, the *Queen Mary* and *Lion* scored two hits each on the *Seydlitz* and *Lützow* respectively. But before *Princess Royal*, *Tiger*, *New Zealand* and *Indefatigable* scored their first hits, all the British battlecruisers except *New Zealand* had been struck by shells. Beatty withdrew *Lion* from the line, to allow his men to deal with fires which had broken out and assess the damage.

Around 4 p.m., as the *Indefatigable* and the *Von der Tann* traded salvoes, a shell from the *Von der Tann* hit one of the *Indefatigable*'s magazines. In the explosion which followed, turrets, funnels and debris shot 200ft into the air, followed by a huge column of flames and smoke. Within minutes the stricken ship keeled over and began to sink. From what those on the *Queen Mary* and other ships could see, it seemed unlikely than anyone could have survived the explosions or escaped before the ship sank.[11]

Just before 4.10 p.m. the ships of the 5th Battle Squadron arrived on the scene and began firing on the German battlecruisers. They inflicted some damage on *Von der Tann* and *Moltke*, but with the *Lion* still out of the fighting line, the *Queen Mary*, *Princess Royal*, *Tiger* and *New Zealand* were now outnumbered five to four.

A few minutes later *Seydlitz* and *Derfflinger* both turned their guns on the *Queen Mary*. Her gunners managed to score four hits on the *Seydlitz* but just after 4.20 p.m. one of the *Queen Mary*'s gun turrets was hit. Most of the gunners in the turret were killed instantly. As unloaded shells exploded, toxic gases began spreading around the ship. Suddenly a second huge explosion almost broke the *Queen Mary* in two. Her bow section, including the bridge, lifted clean out of the water, then plunged downwards and sank beneath the waves. As the now-detached stern tilted forward into the water, it became impossible for survivors to launch life-boats or drop ladders into the sea. Those who had been blown or jumped into the water now risked being pulled down with the remaining part of their ship.

When the *Queen Mary* had been hit the *Tiger* and *New Zealand* had been forced to swerve to avoid ramming into her. By the time they emerged from the smoke all that remained of the *Queen Mary* was a partial skeleton, some floating chunks of debris and a few oil slicks. In the sky, a huge tower of black smoke floated upwards above where the *Queen Mary* had been. There were less than twenty survivors in the water waiting to be rescued.

Beatty had entered battle with the odds 6–5 in his favour; they were now 5–4 against him. If he chased his assailants he risked finding himself against the full force of the German fleet. He ordered the *Lion*, *Princess Royal*, *Tiger* and *New Zealand* to swing round and rejoin the rest of the Grand Fleet. The 'run south' was over.

The sea-battle continued into the evening and the short night. By 3 a.m. on 1 June (by which time the sky was becoming light again) *Lion*, *Princess Royal*, *Tiger* and *New Zealand* had joined other ships of the Grand Fleet in battle line. But as the High Seas Fleet retreated to Jade Bay, it was clear that the 'big show' was over.

* * *

On 2 June 1916 *The Times* reported that Sir Ernest Shackleton had rescued members of his expedition from Elephant Island and brought them safely to Port Stanley in the Falkland Islands. Raymond Priestley, who was working the army's Wireless Training Centre in Worcester, was puzzled that no official communiqué had been published in *The Times* or elsewhere about the major naval engagement which he knew from wireless messages had taken place in the North Sea two days previously.

On 3 June *The Times* published an official announcement which the Admiralty had issued at 7 p.m. the previous evening.

On the afternoon of Wednesday May 31, a naval engagement took place off the coast of Jutland. The British ships on which the brunt of the fighting fell were the Battle Cruiser Fleet and some cruisers and light cruisers, supported by four fast battle ships. Amongst those the losses were heavy.

The German Battle Fleet, aided by low visibility, avoided prolonged action with our main forces, and soon after these appeared on the scene the enemy returned to port, though not before receiving severe damage from our battle-ships.

The battle-cruisers, *Queen Mary*, *Indefatigable*, *Invincible*, and the cruisers *Defence* and *Black Prince* were sunk … the destroyers *Tipperary*, *Turbulent*, *Fortune*, *Sparrowhawk*, and *Ardent* were lost, and others are not yet accounted for …

The enemy's losses were serious.

On 5 June *The Times* listed the names of over 300 officers known to have died during the engagement. The third name on the list of the officers who had died on HMS *Queen Mary* was that of its navigator, Harry Pennell. Edward Atkinson wrote immediately to Cherry-Garrard:[12]

Penelope has gone and I am very sore at his loss as I know you will be too …
Our fellows did splendidly, outnumbered as they were … and made the Germans

suffer even more than they did. I am so sorry for [Pennell's] poor little wife ...
I hope soon the tide will turn and we shall wipe the scum still further from
France ... Apparently Crean was with S[hackleton] and got through again. I don't
believe you could kill old Crean he is wonderful.

Atkinson was doubly relieved that Shackleton's Weddell Sea party were safe as
he had been approached about joining a relief party to assist Shackleton but
been reluctant to do so, given his war service duties.[13]

Over the next week Atkinson received several letters about Pennell's death.
There was one from Sir Lewis Beaumont which he told Cherry he would like
to show to Katie Pennell at the appropriate time.[14]

Atkinson, who was now in France, could not disclose his current location to
Cherry, but assured him it was 'all pretty interesting, very much more peaceful
than Gallipoli and much more comfortable'. He was, he could reveal, under
canvas, in weather which was 'beastly cold and wet with hailstones and thunder'.
In closing, Atkinson, who knew Cherry would be deeply affected by Pennell's
death and worry about his own limited war service, assured his friend he had
already done 'far more than most' and must concentrate on getting better.

William Burton, father of Pennell's godson Lewin, had been at Jutland on
HMS *Midge* of the Fourth Destroyer Flotilla; his squadron had lost five of its
nineteen ships but, happily, the *Midge* was not among them. Campbell had also
been there, but had also returned unscathed.

The 'big show' was over. But one of the most admired and popular 'Antarctics'
had not survived it.

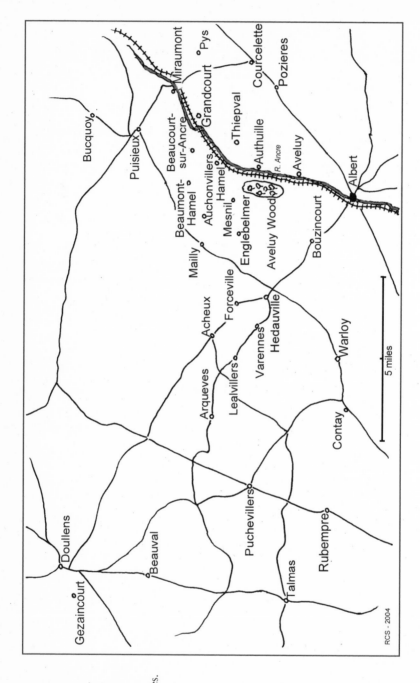

Ancre area of operation, showing Beaucourt and Thiepval. Map © and courtesy of Roy C. Swales.

RCS - 2004

5 miles

Doullens
Gezaincourt
Beauval
Puchevillers
Talmas
Rubempre
Contay
Warloy
Arqueves
Lealvillers
Acheux
Varennes
Hedauville
Forceville
Mailly
Bucquoy
Puisieux
Beaumont-Hamel
Mesnil
Auchonvillers
Hamel
Englebelmer
Aveluy Wood
Aveluy
Bouzincourt
Beaucourt-sur-Ancre
Miraumont
Grandcourt
Pys
Thiepval
Authuille
Courcelette
Pozieres
Albert
R. Ancre

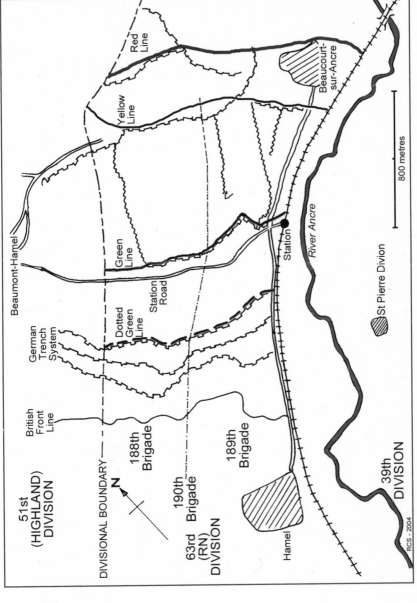

Beaucourt-sur-Ancre area, showing trenches and overview of Royal Naval Division to plan to take Beaucourt. Map © and courtesy of Roy C. Swales.

51st (HIGHLAND) DIVISION

DIVISIONAL BOUNDARY

N

63rd (RN) DIVISION

188th Brigade

190th Brigade

189th Brigade

Hamel

39th DIVISION

British Front Line

German Trench System

Dotted Green Line

Station Road

Green Line

Yellow Line

Red Line

Beaumont-Hamel

Beaucourt-sur-Ancre

Station

River Ancre

St Pierre Divion

800 metres

RCS - 2004

14

Deaths on the Western Front

━━◦◦◦◦━━

In February 1916 Edward Nelson and other RND officers who had served continuously on Gallipoli were given a period of home leave (other ranks were sent to Malta). Nelson, Freyberg, Asquith and Kelly travelled on the troop-ship *Olympic* to France. Before they disembarked Kelly gave his friends a private performance (on the ship's saloon piano) of the elegy he was composing in memory of Rupert Brooke.[1] They broke their train journey to the Channel in Paris, where the four of them, together with some other friends, enjoyed a delicious lunch at a restaurant in the Place de la Madeleine. Afterwards they all jumped into a car and drove to the Louvre in the hope of seeing Leonardo's famous portrait *La Giaconda* (also known as Mona Lisa), but the galleries turned out to be closed.[2]

In early March 1916, over a year after leaving Blandford, Nelson returned to England; now, at last, he would be reunited with his wife and family and see his baby daughter. Nelson was now in command of the RND battalion with which he shared a name; he did not, however, lay claim to be descended from the famous Admiral.[3] He had originally been 'loaned' to Nelson in late 1915, after its commander, Lieutenant-Colonel Norman Burge, had fallen sick and been evacuated from Gallipoli. The transfer had been made permanent, but, soon after Nelson had been promoted to temporary commander, he succumbed to a fever and was evacuated to Malta's naval hospital. By the time he was well enough to return to duty his battalion had been evacuated from Gallipoli to Lemnos and Burge was back in post. Nelson was duly confirmed as second in command to Burge; his new commanding officer was a well-respected leader who was known for looking after his men well and trying to keep them cheerful in trying conditions.

In early May, at the end of his leave, Nelson met up with Freyberg, Asquith and Kelly at Charing Cross station, from where they were waved off by, inter alia, the prime minister's wife, Margot Asquith. Nelson shared a cabin with Kelly on the crossing and joined him, Freyberg and Asquith for a drive to Wimereaux before joining the Boulogne–Marseilles P&O Express. When they reached Marseilles they found that the ships bringing their men from Malta had not yet arrived, so had time for a good meal, fine wine and lively discussions at the Hotel Splendide and a stroll around the crowded town before taking a late supper.[4]

On 24 May, having bade his Hood Battalion companions farewell, Edward Nelson rejoined Nelson Battalion after six months away from the front line. An 8-mile march through streaming rain brought them to a village far enough from the front line to have sufficient intact buildings to shelter them for the night.

In Nelson's absence the RND had been reorganised into the 63rd (Royal Naval) Division of the British Expeditionary Force which consisted of the 188th Infantry Brigade (Anson, Howe and RND Marine Battalions), 189th Infantry Brigade (Nelson, Drake, Hawke and Hood Battalions) and 190th Brigade of four army battalions.

During June the Nelsons and other RND battalions carried out exercises and trained for a planned 'big push' along a 20-mile front around the River Ancre. The Germans had captured most of the area in 1914, since when tens of thousands of Allied troops had been killed and injured in attempts to take German positions. Although the Allies had made some progress in the south of the area, they had been unable to break through in the north. The Allies' efforts were currently concentrated on trying to capture Thiepval ridge and plateau, a strategic high point overlooking and commanding several crossing points on the Ancre, a railway line and the villages of Beaumont-Hamel and Beaucourt.

On 1 July 1916 the Nelsons received their first taste of British Expeditionary Force style trench warfare. Although the 'new' RND Division was now supported by machine-gun units, field artillery and trench mortar companies, five men from Nelson died (three in action, one from battle wounds, one in an accident) and seventeen were wounded during their first seventy-two hours on active duty.

By mid-July Nelson and his men had completed their initial BEF induction and training and were deemed ready to begin trench 'rotations' at a safe distance from the main front line. Over the next three months they moved around the area, fighting in trenches, joining working parties and undergoing further training in preparation for moving up to the main battle area on the Ancre.

On Saturday, 16 September Edward Nelson rode over to see his friends in Hood Battalion. It was a special occasion, as, following dinner with Kelly, Freyberg and Asquith, he would join them and the rest of the battalion for a special performance of Tchaikovsky's *1812* Overture by the Hood's Silver Band.[5] This was the fulfilment of Kelly's long-cherished ambition to conduct this stirring work in the open air to the accompaniment of 'live' battle sounds provided by Hood's artillery and mortar cannons. The triumphant performance, which they all enjoyed, was the result of long hours of work by Kelly and rehearsing by the band – all of which had been fitted in between battle training and fighting duties.

Within a few days of the concert Asquith learned that his elder brother Raymond had died after being shot in the chest while leading his company of Grenadier Guards into battle.[6] A married man with three children, Raymond had studied at Balliol, Oxford; he had then moved to London, where he trained as a barrister and worked on the investigation into the sinking of the *Titanic*. He had, like Brooke and Patrick Shaw-Stewart, been a member of the 'Coterie' of Lady Diana Manners – and had also, like his brother Arthur, refused to be relegated to 'staff duties' simply because he was a son of the prime minister. Within a few days of Raymond Asquith's death, that suggestion was put again to Arthur Asquith – who again refused to consider it.

During the second part of September Nelson and his men were moved, in stages, towards the front line. At Acheux station they had their first glimpse of the tanks which Churchill and others hoped would transform trench warfare. At their new billets they cleaned camp, bathed and enjoyed a film show at the YMCA before continuing their training. On 8 October, they moved to Englebelmer, where they received instruction on aircraft-to-infantry communication; they also joined working parties which had been instructed to keep waterlogged trenches in working, habitable order.

On 14 October, RND's long-standing and popular commander, Major-General Archibald Paris, was badly wounded in the leg and invalided home. His replacement, Major-General Cameron Shute, had little time for what remained of the RND's navel ethos and traditions. After Sub-Lieutenant Alan Herbert penned a satirical poem about him, he became known as 'that shit Shute'.[7]

Trench life, already cold, damp and uncomfortable, became increasingly unpleasant and dangerous after the Germans began attacking RND positions with tear gas shells. By early November everyone was waiting for their orders for the forthcoming 'big push'. Asquith, much to his annoyance but the relief of his superiors, would not be taking part; he had recently been badly injured by a 'Minnie' (*minenwerfer*) mortar and invalided home to England.

On 27 October the Nelsons moved to new billets 12 miles from the front line, where they were told that Shute would inspect his division on 2 November. Everyone assembled on the appointed day but after they had been standing in pouring rain for several hours it was announced that Shute would now arrive the following day – which he duly did.

On 1 November the *London Gazette* listed men who had been mentioned in dispatches 'for distinguished and gallant service' at Gallipoli: amongst the names were those of Nelson, Kelly and Egerton.[8]

On 8 November Nelson and his men arrived at Hamel. While Burge and Nelson waited for their final orders, 21-year-old Sub-Lieutenant Edwin Dyett approached Nelson with the latest of several requests to be reassigned to sea duties due to the state of his nerves.[9] Nelson considered his request sympathetically but, given that everyone was suffering under the same conditions, he did not feel he could make an exception for Dyett.

On 10 November Nelson received his final battle orders. The aim was to capture German trenches and other lines of defence designated as the 'Dotted Green Line' (German front-line trenches), 'Green Line' (a fortified line near Beaucourt railway station), 'Yellow Line' (a fortified trench defending Beaucourt village) and 'Red Line' (German position on the far side of Beaucourt). This would be achieved through a series of 'leap-frog' movements, whereby Hood, Howe, Hawke and 1st Royal Marine Light Infantry would take the Dotted Green and Yellow Lines, and Nelson, Drake, Anson and a light infantry unit would take the Green and Red Lines.

Edward Nelson would be based at Hédeauville (some 4 miles from the front line), from where he would dispatch reserve RND troops to Divisional and Brigade HQ and the front line, based on messages and orders passed back from HQ and the front line.

On paper, it all seemed understandable, but the appearance, in the early hours of 13 November, of a blanket of thick, freezing mist over the still-dark battleground threatened to complicate matters.

During the day Nelson dispatched men forward as required. When it came for Edwin Dyett to move forward, Nelson sent him in a car to Brigade HQ, together with Lieutenant Cyril Truscott, a more experienced officer who had served at Gallipoli. He told them that they would be given further orders when they arrived at Brigade HQ.

The following day Nelson learned that Beaucourt had been captured but that, of the senior officers, Burge (Edward Nelson's CO) had been killed and Freyberg had been seriously injured. 'Sep' Kelly had also been killed whilst attacking a bombing post on the German third line of trenches.

It had become apparent to Freyberg quite early in the day that, with hundreds of RND men being mown down by German machine guns and artillery, the 'leap-frogging' was unlikely to work. Casualties apart, the dense fog and the damage done to German trenches by the British pre-assault bombardment meant that it was almost impossible to get a sense of direction without using a compass.

After Freyberg and his men reached the Dotted Green Line, he decided not to wait for the next group of men to 'leapfrog' them but to continue forward, gathering men as he went. At dusk Freyberg and the 800 men with him (largely from Hood and Drake) dug in and waited for water, rations and reinforcements to be brought forward. Freyberg then received a message telling him to hold his ground until the following morning when everyone who had reached the Yellow Line in front of Beaucourt would join in an attack on the village.[10]

Nelson Battalion had, it appeared, suffered particularly badly. Burge, nine sub-lieutenants and twenty-four other ranks had been killed; a lieutenant-commander, two lieutenants, six sub-lieutenants and 200 other ranks had been wounded; over 100 men were reported missing.

On the morning of 14 November, following an all-night bombardment, Freyberg led his men towards Beaucourt. When they entered the village they found it was already in ruins. Large numbers of Germans were ready to surrender, but it was not long before a German bombardment sent everyone scuttling into trenches. Freyberg had been hit and badly wounded. While he took some morphine (which he carried for just such eventualities), a Hood fellow-officer, Captain Montagu, dressed his wounds. Montagu offered to run for assistance so that Freyberg (who weighed 16 stone) could be stretchered to a casualty station but Freyberg refused to let him leave the trench. As the morphia began to take effect Freyberg stood up and, and, with Montagu's assistance, staggered to the nearest first-aid post. The regimental doctor applied some temporary dressings and prepared to evacuate Freyberg back down the line.

The day after the battle Edward Nelson was appointed as temporary commander of Nelson, replacing Burge. The following day, two days after Nelson had ordered him report for duty at the front, Edwin Dyett was found wandering around aimlessly, far from the field of battle; he was immediately placed under arrest.[11] Sir Douglas Haig came to congratulate the Division on their efforts in capturing Beaucourt and to advise them that Freyberg was now out of danger and had been recommended for a Victoria Cross.

On 2 December, Nelson was placed in temporary command of a much depleted 189th Infantry Brigade when his brigade commander left for England on ten days' leave. On 19 December he signed a charge sheet on which Dyett was accused of one of two alternative offences: desertion 'when it was his duty to join his battalion, which was engaged in operations against the Enemy' or 'conduct to the prejudice of good order and Military discipline'. General Haig gave his approval for the convening of a court martial.

On 26 December, Boxing Day, Dyett was brought from the prison cell where he had been detained since his arrest. The prosecutor was Sub-Lieutenant Herbert Strickland of Nelson Battalion; Dyett's defence counsel was (in the absence of a suitable Nelson Battalion officer) Sub-Lieutenant Cecil Trevanion of Hawke, who had practised briefly as a solicitor before the war. Dyett pleaded 'not guilty' to both charges.

Edward Nelson was the first to give his evidence:

> On 13 November, 1916, I was in command of the officers of the Nelson Battalion who were not taken into action with the Battalion at the commencement of operations. We were then stationed at Hédauville. In consequence of orders I received that day from the 63rd RN Divisional Headquarters I detailed Lieutenant Truscott and the accused to report to Brigade Headquarters. I personally gave these orders to both these officers and told them that a car was waiting to take them up at Divisional Headquarters. I saw both these officers leave in this car. The accused appeared to be quite nervous when I gave him these orders.

Under cross-examination from Trevanion, Nelson expanded on what he had said about Dyett:

> I have known the accused since about June last ... My opinion of the accused's capabilities as an officer up to 13 November 1916 was that he was a very poor one. His authority in command over men was not good. Before 13 November the accused did approach me with a request for transference to sea service and the question as to his capabilities in the firing line was then raised by the accused. Accused told me that he was of very nervous temperament and that he thought he was not fitted for the firing line.

Trevanion then asked Nelson why he had sent Dyett towards the front line:

> I had no other officers available to go up to the firing line on 13 November. Sub-Lieutenant Cowans and Sub-Lieutenant Strickland were not available as they were employed on special duty. Sub-Lieutenant Redmond was not under my command [but] doing duty at the time with the Division. Sub-Lieutenant Walker was our Transport Officer, so he was not available. Sub-Lieutenant Truscott and accused were the only two officers available to be sent forward. I felt some apprehension about sending the accused up into the firing line. I had to send two officers and these were the only two available. I had some misgivings about the accused. I had not the same confidence in him as in Lieutenant Truscott.

When the Prosecutor asked Nelson what he thought Dyett might do, he said that he thought Dyett would obey orders but he had experienced 'misgivings' as to Dyett's possible behaviour. After Nelson's evidence had been read back to him, he left the room.

The court found Dyett guilty of desertion and absence from his battalion, but not guilty on the second charge of 'prejudicial conduct'.

The story which emerged during the court martial was a confusing one. Truscott and Dyett had arrived together at Brigade HQ, where Brigadier General Phillips had given Truscott orders (which applied to both him and Dyett) to join Nelson Battalion at the front. On the way they had met another group of men from different battalions. After Dyett had started arguing with one of them (Herring), Truscott had identified some Nelson men and taken them up to the front. The last Truscott had seen of Dyett and Herring they had still been arguing. Truscott thought Dyett seemed 'normal', with 'nothing strange in his demeanour' or signs of 'cold feet'.

Phillips confirmed what Truscott had said and that, after Dyett had been found wandering around, he had questioned Dyett and placed him under arrest.

Herring stated that the group of men with him when he met Truscott and Dyett had been 'retiring' from the front when, in his view, they should not have been. He implied he had ordered Truscott forward with the Nelson men and that the argument had arisen when Herring had ordered Dyett to follow Truscott and his group. Dyett disputed Herring's authority and said he was returning to Brigade HQ for further orders. Dyett had then, Herring suggested, followed Herring back to the ammunition dump where the latter was based. Herring then sent a message to his captain complaining about Dyett's behaviour. Herring had not thought Dyett seemed 'afraid', 'in a funk' or to be deserting.

Dyett declined to give evidence, call witnesses or say anything in his defence. His defence counsel described him of being of 'neurotic temperament' and confirmed that Dyett had regularly asked to be transferred to reserve forces. He suggested Dyett had not deliberately deserted but had simply wandered around before reporting to Lieutenant-Commander Egerton of Hood Battalion (who had not been asked to give evidence).

When Dyett was found guilty, the court passed the death sentence on him, but recommended mercy due to his young age, lack of battlefield experience and 'circumstances' including the increasing darkness, heavy shelling and the presence of large numbers of men retiring from the front, all of which seemed likely to affect a young man of his temperament.

On 28 December 1916 Nelson left for England on leave. When he returned on 9 January 1917 he learned that Dyett had been executed four days previously. The court's recommendation for mercy had, somewhat unexpectedly, been rejected by Haig.[12]

Edwin Dyett had been blindfolded and tied to a stake. A firing squad of Nelson 'other ranks' aimed for his heart and fired. Dyett, who asked his colleagues to be sure to shoot straight, had, according to the records, died instantaneously.

* * *

Within a few days of his return from leave, Nelson marched his men for 50 miles through rain, sleet and snow to join buses which took them to the new front line at Beaucourt. Nelson was now one of only four Nelson Battalion officers who had fought at Gallipoli and the only non-army officer in charge of a RND battalion.

After spending several days in a shell-pocked, frozen quagmire of trenches being bombarded by German artillery, Nelson and his men were relieved by Hawke Battalion; by then they had lost a dozen men, killed in action or dead from their wounds.

On 3 February Nelson and his men took part in an attack on the German front line east of Beaucourt. During the advance, which took place in the dark, contact was lost between Nelson Battalion and Hawke, which was on its flank. As a result of this and confusion regarding some orders, one Nelson company retired before being relieved by replacement troops.

On the afternoon of 4 February, while Hawke and three Nelson companies were trying to capture a German machine-gun position, Edward Nelson was ordered to hand over to his second in command, Captain Griffiths, and report to Brigade HQ. When he returned just over an hour later he found that a small group of Nelson and Hawke men had seized the German position. Gains had been made but a further nineteen Nelson men had died and almost forty were wounded.

In mid-March, the Nelsons marched for a week to new billets near Béthune, close to the Arras-Vimy Ridge.

On the night of 4–5 April Able Seaman William Attwood of Nelson Battalion was found in the guardroom, dying of a self-inflicted gunshot wound to the head. Attwood, who had a poor disciplinary record, had recently been found guilty of 'prejudicial behaviour' and sentenced to three months of 'Field Punishments', which usually involved being tied up in front of fellow-soldiers (in the tradition of medieval stocks). When Attwood had initially been arrested Nelson (perhaps remembering his own reservations about Dyett's state of mind) had asked for Attwood to be examined by the battalion's Medical Officer to ensure he was fit to stand trial. The MO had found Attwood to be mentally unstable but not of 'unsound mind' or unaware of his actions. The enquiry into

Attwood's death established that he had shot himself while of 'unsound mind' but failed to establish how a loaded gun had come to be in his possession while he was under detention.

During the following week Nelson and his men were held in reserve during Allied attacks on German strongholds around Arras; on one occasion they had been within two hours of being called forward but had been stood down.

On 13 April Nelson was ordered to bring his men forward to the area north of Arras, where, following a night under canvas, they arrived the following morning. Within a few hours of arriving, at noon on 14 April 1917, Nelson was relieved of his command without prior notification or warning.

Edward Nelson left for England that day. At Aubigny, north-west of Arras, he bumped into Arthur Asquith, who had recovered from his most recent injuries and was on his way to rejoin Hood Battalion.[13] He was surprised at the timing of Nelson's departure – and suggested that Nelson could always apply to 'teach the Yanks' who would soon be arriving to support the Allies on the Western Front.

It was almost two years since the President of the United States had protested at the sinking of the *Lusitania*, with the loss of almost 1,200 passengers and crew, including over 100 Americans – and would-be Antarctic explorer J. Foster Stackhouse.

America's entry into the war might, as widely hoped, change everything on the Western Front – but Edward Nelson would need to wait until he arrived in England to see where his next posting would take him.

* * *

In early April 1918 it was reported in *The Times* and newspapers all over Britain that former journalist and war correspondent Lieutenant Bertie John 'B.J.' Hodson had been killed in action in the Somme region. Hodson had signed up for active duty in 1915 after reporting from the Balkans, Antwerp, Ypres and the Dardanelles.[14] When asked what regiment he wanted to join he answered that he would prefer to join one which was 'fighting the Turks'. Despite his wishes, his first tour of duty with the Royal Irish Regiment had been in Ireland, following the Easter uprising. By July 1916 he was with the 1st Royal Irish Rifles on the Western Front. Within ten days of arriving he was shot in the head and shoulder and evacuated to hospital in Boulogne, but by September he was back at the front. Hodson died near St Quentin on 21 March 1918 whilst trying to defend a redoubt with greatly reduced forces.

Reporters wrote warmly of one of their own.[15] It was recalled that Hodson had helped operate a machine gun on the roof of his Antwerp hotel while

Zeppelins passed overhead and had, whilst under fire, joined gunners at a heavy artillery position in Montenegro. One tribute mentioned that Hodson's work had been highly praised by an eminent former war correspondent:[16]

> Lieutenant Hodson was responsible for a number of excellent messages from Belgium ... One of these, which dealt with the fall of Antwerp, won warm praise from Mr. Winston Churchill, who agreed with one of the heads of the Press Bureau that both in matter and manner it might rank with the best written of official dispatches. The tribute, however, did not save it from the very liberal application of the Whitehall blue pencil.

Bertie John 'B.J.' Hodson, who left a wife and two young children, had come a long way since he and Harry Pennell had met in Akaroa in April 1912.

15

Of Scientists, Sailors and Shackleton

━━◦◦◦━━

Raymond Priestley had joined London Regiment's Wireless Section as a Second Lieutenant in September 1914; following spells in Bury St Edmunds, Beccles and Bewdley, he found himself working in Worcester, about 10 miles from his family home in Tewkesbury.[1] Priestley modestly claimed that he had only been offered his current post as second in command after the previously favoured candidate had crashed a 'borrowed' army motorbike, broken his arm and been disciplined for the unauthorised removal of the motorbike.

Priestley's brother-in-law, Silas Wright, had spent much of the war in the wireless section of the Royal Engineers, working in France on the development of wireless equipment which could be used to communicate between trenches.[2] Wright's work had gone well from a technical standpoint but his promotion to lieutenant had been temporarily delayed after his instructions to his men to drive in the centre of the road (rather than risk 'ditching' their vehicles and damaging costly radio equipment) had resulted in a chauffeur-driven staff car being 'ditched' instead.

Wright, knowing that Cherry-Garrard enjoyed receiving news from other 'Antarctics' and sometimes needed cheering up, wrote to him from France:[3]

Am searching diligently now for places where we come nearest to the Bosch trenches … Have seen none of the Expedish since leaving England almost a year ago … Give me, I beg of you of it, (as they say in Turkey?) the address of old Atch – he seems to have been having a feeble time too. Ray Priestley is still cursing me for letting him in to wireless but has a pretty fair job now at Worcester – where the Worcestershire sauce comes from y' know. I must drop a line to old Penelope now that I know his address. Ray is all over himself now he is a prrroud father. Hustle up and get well, old man. Will hope to see you in die *grezt ADVANCE*.

In early July Wright wrote again:[4]

> Sorry to hear you are still groggy. I didn't realize last time I was over that you were
> not up or I'd have made a desperate effort to come over and see you …
>
> Damn the great push – they never push where I am. Hear from Atch
> occasionally. Saw Meares a little while ago &, of all people, Prof. David. He is a
> proper sport – out here with the Aust. Miners as a major & still his same old self.
>
> It's very sad about Penelope. Next to Dr. Bill [Wilson] he's the finest I ever
> met …
>
> It's damned hard lines for you being laid up this way, but there's no use worrying
> about 'being out of it'. I'll bet you are doing much more useful work than I am at
> least … Well, Cherry, here's to a speedy recovery. Keep Cheery and live up to the
> name anyway.

Cherry-Garrard also heard from Frank Debenham, who told him that,
compared to France, there was 'not much happening' in Salonika, where the
city was protected by a huge barbed-wire fence known as the 'Birdcage Line'.[5]

In August 1916 Debenham's regiment was sent to join some 40,000 British
and French troops in the countryside around Lake Doiran, on the Bulgarian
border. Shortly after Debenham helped capture a Bulgarian position, he was
badly injured by a shell, which landed beside him and exploded. His hearing was
also damaged and he was diagnosed as suffering from shell-shock. He was sent
for treatment in England where, while recuperating, he began spending time
with Dorothy Lempriere, a fellow-Australian who was also living in England.
After they became engaged Debenham asked Cherry to serve as best man at his
wedding, which would take place in the New Year.[6]

Cherry had been taking an interest in the increasing use of tanks on the
Western Front. These cumbersome, armour-plated vehicles with caterpillar
tyres bore a family resemblance to the motorised sledges which had been on the
first stage of the South Pole journey in 1911. While Cherry had been driving
his armoured cars, he had been asked to come to London to give his views on a
prototype being developed by RNAS engineers at Wormwood Scrubs.[7] Army
leaders on the Western Front now set great store on armoured tanks which
could drive across trenches and might break the current deadlock.

* * *

In early November 1916 *Terra Nova* veterans Tom Crean and Alf Cheetham
returned to Britain from what Shackleton had, before leaving, described as 'white
warfare'.[8] Crean sailed back to Britain in company with Thomas Orde-Lees,

Frank Wild, Leonard Hussey, James McIlroy, James Wordie, George Marston, Alexander Macklin, Reginald James and Robert Clark. The ship's passenger records showed their most recent residence as 'Sea' and their destination as 'HM Forces'.[9] When Alf Cheetham returned with fellow *Terra Nova* crew member Thomas McLeod, Charles Green, Albert Holness and Walter How, the passenger list showed their prior residence as 'Antarctica'.

Cheetham had, in his absence, gained another daughter, Ella, who had been born six months after he left on the *Endurance*; his eldest daughter, Caroline, had also given him his first grandchild. But Alf's second son, William, was presumed to have gone down with his ship, the collier *Adriatic*, which had been lost with all hands at the end of October, after apparently being struck by a German torpedo in the North Atlantic. William had been 16 years old.

Cheetham and Crean were, everyone knew, lucky to have returned alive and well from Shackleton's latest expedition. After the Weddell Sea had frozen early, the *Endurance* had become trapped in the pack-ice. She had gradually been crushed and had, in November 1915, sunk beneath the ice.

Shackleton and his men had dragged their three lifeboats, the *James Caird, Dudley Docker* and *Stancomb Wills*, to the edge of the ice, then sailed to barren, uninhabited Elephant Island. Shackleton, Crean, Timothy McCarthy, Frank Worsley, Harry 'Chippy' McNish and John Vincent had then rowed the *James Caird* almost 800 miles to South Georgia. After sending a wireless message to England, Shackleton had then set about relieving Alf Cheetham and the other men on Elephant Island. By the time he reached them they had been there for four months.

After ensuring Crean, Cheetham and their shipmates were safely on their way to England, Shackleton and Worsley sailed to New Zealand from where they planned to rescue members of the Ross Sea party, who had been left stranded after the *Aurora* had broken away from her Cape Evans moorings and been driven north by the pack.

Winston Churchill, who had authorised the departure of the *Endurance* in August 1914, was now commanding a regiment on the Western Front. He let it be known that he ranked the rescue of a few men from the land of penguins well below the needs of injured soldiers and the families of those who had died in the war.[10] Cherry-Garrard wrote to *The Times* with assurances that the Ross Sea Party would find the Cape Evans hut well stocked with sledging biscuits, pemmican and other necessities.[11]

When Shackleton and Worsley arrived in Wellington they found the British, Australian and New Zealand governments had collectively spent £20,000 on repairs to the *Aurora*. Joseph Kinsey had been authorised to appoint Mawson's *Aurora* captain, John Davis, as commander for the relief voyage. Shackleton protested but failed to convince Kinsey to appoint either Worsley or his own *Aurora* captain Joseph Stenhouse instead.

On 20 December 1916 Davis and Shackleton sailed south on the *Aurora*, leaving Worsley and Stenhouse to return to Britain to sign up for the war. By New Year's Day 1917 the *Aurora* was through the pack and heading for Cape Evans to rescue the Ross Sea Party.

* * *

On 26 December 1916, Cherry-Garrard learned that his cousin Reginald Smith had jumped to his death from a second-floor window of his London home.[12] Smith, whom *The Times* described as 'a wise and generous publisher', had been suffering for some time from overwork, stress and insomnia. Cherry, other family members and close friends, including Oriana Wilson and Kathleen Scott, attended a private family funeral on 29 December. In early January Cherry, other family members and luminaries from publishing, legal and other circles in which 'Reggie' had worked and moved joined family members for a memorial service.

As there was no one within the family who could replace Reggie within Smith, Elder & Co., an approach was made to John Murray, a long-standing friend and associate whose family owned an even longer-standing publishing house.[13]

At the inquest it had been suggested that Reginald Smith had been feeling depressed about the war. Cherry also sometimes found it difficult to be on the receiving end of what sometimes felt like a constant stream of bad news.

* * *

Teddy Evans appeared to thrive under the pressures of war. By early 1917 he was in command of HMS *Broke*, which had been transferred from the Grand Fleet to the Dover Patrol after Jutland. The *Broke*'s six guns and four torpedo tubes were a welcome addition to the fifty-vessel Patrol, which had recently been supplemented by monitor ship HMS *M24*, a heavily armed vessel commanded by Victor Campbell.[14]

In early 1917 German ships began probing the defence systems in the Channel. On the night of 20 April, Evans (on the *Broke*) and Commander Ambrose Peck (on the *Swift*) were patrolling near the Channel barrage.[15] When they saw flashes they realised that a squadron of German destroyers was bombarding Dover. As *Broke* and *Swift* headed towards the direction of the flashes the German ships slipped away. Evans and Peck resumed their patrolling but when they saw five or six German destroyers just east of Dover they headed straight for them. As German gunners and Peck's men exchanged fire Evans swung the *Broke* round until she was at right angles to the line of German vessels and prepared to ram one of the destroyers.

When his first target was hit by a torpedo (probably from the *Swift*), Evans redirected the *Broke* at *G42*, the next German ship in line. When the *Broke* rammed into the side of *G42* she was travelling at almost 30 knots an hour. The *Broke* continued to move forward, with *G42* attached to her bow. As flames from the *Broke's* damaged fore area spread across to *G42's* deck, some German sailors tried to escape by clambering onto the *Broke's* deck. They were soon driven back by *Broke* crew members wielding pistols, bayoneted rifles and cutlasses which Evans had issued from a stock of weapons he kept under lock and key.

As Evans tried to pull the *Broke* away from the now-sinking *G42* another fire started in the boiler-room. By now a second German destroyer, *G85*, was beginning to sink. Some of her sailors jumped into the water; others clung to the deck and made it clear that they were willing to surrender. When a German sailor fired at the *Broke's* bridge Evans ordered his men to return fire and to torpedo *G85*.

During the hand-to-hand fighting, which lasted less than ten minutes, twenty *Broke* men had died and another thirty had been wounded. Peck, who had only lost one crew member, transported all the captured Germans back to Dover, leaving Evans to anchor his now powerless ship and wait for a relief vessel to take his dead and wounded ashore.

The next day, after the *Broke* had been towed into Dover, Evans visited his wounded men in hospital. The bodies of the German sailors who had died in the raid were transported slowly and respectfully through the streets of Dover, followed by a procession of their captured comrades (accompanied by armed guards) and 300 British seamen, including some from the *Swift* and the *Broke*. A bugler from the Marines played the 'Last Post' over the mass grave in which the Germans were buried. A single wreath, placed on behalf of the Dover Patrol's commanding officer, bore the inscription 'A Tribute to a Brave Enemy'.

That afternoon crowds lined Dover's streets as the funeral procession for seven of the *Broke* seamen passed. The cortège, headed by a gun-carriage and military band, was followed by Evans, Peck and members of their ships' crews, officers and men from other ships of the Dover Fleet and men from Dover garrison.

The story of how the *Broke* and *Swift* had seen off an entire squadron of German destroyers captured the public imagination. The sailors who had fought hand-to-hand on deck 'in the old way' and their commanding officers, now known as 'Evans of the *Broke*' and 'Peck of the *Swift*', became national heroes.

One newspaper published a cartoon showing Evans in polar gear, glaring up at two tiny Germans perched atop a slender iceberg; the captions read 'Got Fritz Up the Pole' and 'Hans and Fritz – Good Evans'.

Evans and Peck were both awarded DSOs and promoted to captain; several *Broke* and *Swift* crew members were decorated, promoted or noted for accelerated advancement. On Saturday, 2 June King George presented Evans and Peck and servicemen with their medals in Hyde Park.[16] Scarlet-coated bandsmen and guardsmen and kilted pipers marched up Constitution Hill into the park and a trumpet fanfare announced the arrival of the king. The monarch was greeted by cheers, salutes and a rousing rendition of the National Anthem; following the presentation ceremony the band played 'A Life on the Ocean Wave' and aeroplanes circled overhead.

According to newspaper reports Evans could not stop smiling. The following week, at a private luncheon hosted by friends at Liverpool's Cotton Exchange, Evans agreed to sketch some penguins on a menu card, so it could be auctioned for charity; such was his celebrity that it raised 1,000 guineas for the Red Cross.[17]

* * *

While the war seemed to suit Teddy Evans' temperament, others were becoming increasingly disillusioned about a conflict which politicians seemed unable or (as some believed) unwilling to bring to a conclusion. During July 1917, Hastings Lees-Smith, an anti-war Liberal MP, brought to the attention of the House of Commons a letter, or 'declaration', written by Second Lieutenant Siegfried Sassoon, DSO. In his declaration Sassoon, who was also a published poet, claimed that the war had changed from one of defence and liberation to one of aggression and conquest.

The Under-Secretary of State for War responded that Sassoon had been examined by a medical board and found to be suffering from the after-effects of a battle-induced nervous breakdown. Given this, he could not be considered responsible for his actions and consequent breach of military discipline. Siegfried Sassoon would, instead of being court-martialled, be sent for psychiatric treatment.

* * *

Sassoon, who moved in the same circles as Brooke's mentor and patron Edward Marsh, would have been aware of the extent of the losses suffered within Brooke's Hood Battalion circle. Patrick Shaw-Stewart had returned to Hood

Battalion in mid-1916 after a period of service in Salonika. In mid-December 1917, following Arthur Asquith's promotion to Brigadier-General of RND's 189th Brigade (which included Hood), Shaw-Stewart replaced him as Hood Battalion commander. On 30 December 1917 he was killed by shells whilst making the rounds of his men in their snow-fringed trenches. His place at the head of Hood Battalion was taken by his friend and Gallipoli comrade-in-arms William Egerton.

Two days after Asquith arrived in his new post a German sniper shot him twice in the same leg.[18] Field hospital doctors amputated his damaged leg then sent him back to London for further treatment. The king visited Asquith in hospital and presented him with a DSO. On 30 April 1918, still on crutches, Asquith married Elizabeth Manners, whom he had known since his schooldays.

Freyberg was also in London recuperating from wounds received at Passchendaele.[19] Still only 28, he was now a brigade commander and held a Victoria Cross for his 'most conspicuous gallantry' at Beaucourt. Since returning to England he had spent much of his time with J.M. Barrie, to whom Kathleen Scott had introduced him.

Freyberg's other regular companion was a young widow, Barbara McLaren, whom he had met (and fallen for) in 1916. Barbara had, at that time, been married to the Hon. Francis McLaren, a pilot who had died in a flying accident during summer 1917. Barbara was connected to Freyberg's friends the Asquiths through her cousin Katherine Frances Horner (of Mells), Raymond Asquith's widow; Barbara and Katherine were also nieces of Gertrude Jekyll, the well-known garden designer.

By December 1917 Edward Nelson had settled into his new role at the Board of Invention and Research in London. The BIR had been established as a branch of the Admiralty in 1915 under the chairmanship of Admiral 'Jackie' Fisher. It had originally operated from some rooms at the Metropole Hotel but now occupied a house in Cockspur Street – which the ebulliently optimistic Fisher had renamed 'Victory House'.[20] BIR was supervised by a board of eminent scientists and naval representatives and staffed by scientists of different disciplines. Nelson now spent his days, as he had done in Antarctica, working with fellow scientists on a range of projects. The Marine Laboratory in Plymouth had also made it clear that he was welcome to return to his work with them when he completed his war service.[21]

* * *

Nelson's erstwhile marine biologist colleague Dennis Lillie had been giving Atkinson, Cherry-Garrard and Debenham cause for concern. Lillie, a conscientious objector, had volunteered for non-combatant scientific work but had gradually become increasingly depressed, delusional and suicidal until, in February 1918, he was admitted to Bethlem Hospital (popularly known as 'Bedlam') for treatment.[22] The hospital usually only accepted patients on a short-term basis, but when the trustees of the Captain Scott Memorial Fund offered to contribute to the costs of treatment, an exception was made. When doctors asked Lillie whether he thought his hardships in Antarctica might have contributed to his state of mind he told them his time with the *Terra Nova* expedition had been amongst the happiest periods of his life.

16

A Norwegian 'Warbird' Keeps his Promise

When Tryggve Gran travelled to London in October 1916 to join the Royal Flying Corps he became the third 'Antarctic' to join Britain's air service.

Cecil Meares had joined the Royal Naval Air Service in April 1915, immediately after resigning from the Northumberland Hussars. He had sat the War Office's languages test and been awarded first-class passes in spoken French, German and Russian and in written French, and second-class passes in spoken German and Russian – something which would make him eligible for additional allowances. He was attached to the RNAS's new 'No. 4 Wing' and was sometimes based at its Dunkirk base – which meant that he regularly passed through Dover and, as he told his wife Annie, sometimes bumped into people he knew:[1]

> Mrs Evans travelled down to Dover with me, she was looking very nice; the country was lovely with all the fruit trees in flower … I dined with Commander & Mrs Evans, they were very kind; Evans … is stationed here in Dunkirk and has several destroyers under his command. Campbell is also coming here in command of the Mohawk.

Jim Dennistoun, with whom Meares climbed Little Mount Peel in 1912, had arrived in England in mid-1915 and joined the Royal Flying Corps in June 1916.[2] His parents were still in England, as was his close friend and erstwhile climbing companion Ada Julius, who had qualified as a VAD nurse. Dennistoun arrived in England just after his younger brother George (whose leg was broken by Pennell's mount at Peel Forest in 1913) had passed through on his way to a new posting on Lake Nyasa.[3]

Dennistoun initially joined the North Irish Horse regiment and, after a period of training at Netheravon Cavalry School, left for France with the 33rd Division of the BEF. At Netheravon he had visited the neighbouring flying school where the Royal Flying Corps trained pilots for front line service. On his return from his tour of duty in France he went for an interview with the RFC (in which his cousin Herbie Russell was already serving). Three months later Dennistoun was ready to join his cousin on sorties, acting as observer.

On 26 June 1916 Russell and Dennistoun climbed into their aircraft, which was equipped with two Lewis guns and loaded with bombs. They flew over the Channel to France, where they were due to rendezvous with four other aircraft at 7,000ft over Arras. From there they would cross the German front line together and release their bombs over the German trenches.

Shortly after take-off, at 5,000ft, their aircraft developed a fault, so they returned to base for a replacement. This time they made it to Arras, but by the time they arrived there was no sign of the other British aircraft. They crossed over the front line and, keeping an eye open for German Fokkers, dropped their bombs.

Suddenly Dennistoun saw a Fokker right on their tail. As the German gunners opened fire, Dennistoun grabbed their aircraft's rear gun and began shooting. While Russell was looking around (in vain) for some cloud cover, Dennistoun was shot in the stomach. Russell tried to throw off the Fokker but the faster machine kept pace behind them and shot Russell's petrol tank, which burst into flames. After Russell was hit in the lung he began to faint, but as his aircraft began to nose dive the rush of cold air brought him round.

Dennistoun was by now unable to operate the heavier rear gun, so Russell suggested he try firing the front gun. As their aircraft plummeted at 75mph, they were both flung clear. By the time they hit the ground, Russell's jacket was ablaze from leaking petrol and Dennistoun had collapsed from his stomach wound.

They had landed in the middle of German lines at Fampoux, east of Arras. Soldiers immediately jumped out of their trenches, wrapped Russell in blankets to extinguish the flames and found a doctor to administer to Dennistoun. The cousins were initially taken to separate hospitals but after Dennistoun had undergone two operations they were transferred to the same hospital. The Germans found an English-speaking nurse to look after Dennistoun and to help him write a letter to his parents in England. During July Dennistoun made some progress but when Russell visited him he could see his cousin was in considerable pain.

On the morning of 9 August Russell popped into Dennistoun's room on his way to have his own dressings changed. Dennistoun was not feeling particularly well and when Russell returned he found his cousin's condition had deteriorated considerably. A doctor came and recommended that a third operation, which had already been planned, should be carried out immediately.

At 12.30 p.m. a doctor came to tell Russell that his cousin had survived the operation but come round feeling 'pretty rotten' and died soon afterwards.

Dennistoun was buried in Germany; Russell returned to duty.

* * *

While New Zealander Dennistoun was flying under British colours, Tryggve Gran was feeling inhibited by Norway's neutrality in terms of his own flying. On 18 October 1916 Gran visited the Norwegian Minister of Defence to request a transfer to the Royal Flying Corps. After Gran had been interviewed at the Norwegian Legation in London, the British War Office and by the commander of the RFC's Home Defence Wing, it was agreed that Gran could be attached to the RFC's 11th Squadron. Given Norway's neutral status, it was decided that he should serve as 'Teddy Grant', a Canadian aviator.

On 7 November Gran reported for duty at Northolt aerodrome, west of London. He obtained clearance to fly solo and, after being appointed as an instructor, went to the Royal Aircraft Factory at Farnborough to collect his aircraft. He was, of course, expected to fly it back:

> It was late in the afternoon ... and it had become twilight. For the first half hour everything went well and I started to look over the side in front of me to detect Northolt. Everything became dark, snow and hail hit me in the face. I cut the motor and went gliding downwards ... at a height of 200 metres, I found myself ... cruising over London ... I turned due west, keeping near the ground, hoping to find a place where I could land ...

But the whole countryside seemed to be flooded:

> Flying at a height of about fifty feet, I followed a railway line westward until I sighted a field apparently free of water. Down I went ... then, suddenly, came a jar and, before I had realised what had happened, the machine and myself shot headlong in the mud – my first experience of night flying thus came to an end.

Despite his shaky start Gran soon passed his official night pilot's test:

> we were taken by motor van to the dark and silent aerodrome. It was a calm night with millions of stars ... Pale, I crawled into the pilot's cockpit which was lit by small electric lamps. I pushed the throttle forward and let the machine rip up above the flares into the darkness. For a time, there was nothing to see, but my eyes became accustomed to the darkness. I kept to my instructions and rose to a

height of 300 metres before I turned back to the aerodrome. Here, I cruised about until they flashed me from the ground [to] 'Land'. I approached the ground in wide circles and, as carefully as possible, glided down between the searchlights to touch my wheels at the first flare. We kept flying for the whole night and when daylight came I was entitled to wear my flying badges.

Gran, who was still technically a member of his own country's air force, was attached to the RFC's 37th Squadron. By day, he practised shooting at targets in the Thames or honed his flying skills; by night, he and his messmates would visit local hotels for music and dancing. On the evening of 26 November, an alarm bell interrupted the music.

Gran and his companions ran to their cars and raced to the aerodrome where the 'Yellow' alert (raised due to Zeppelins having been sighted over London) was raised to Green (due to the rate of sightings increasing to about one a minute). Gran ran to his aircraft, ready for take-off, but before he could do so huge banks of fog began rolling in from the east. He clambered out of his cockpit, returned to his quarters and took a nap. At 5 a.m. orderlies roused him to confirm that there would be no action that night.

When Gran woke he found a note saying that Zeppelins had been dropping bombs on Victoria Street (which he knew well from visits to the *Terra Nova* expedition office) around the time they had received their call to action – it seemed that, even if there had been no fog, they could not have prevented the air raid.

In early December Gran joined the 39th Home Squadron, which was based at a half-finished airfield at Sutton's Farm. Gran tried out his new aircraft, which was painted with the squadron's skull-and-crossbones insignia, but over the next few weeks fog and sleet made flying virtually impossible.

But they were only 15 miles away from London, where 'behind the thick curtains, the lights burned brighter than ever' and music and dancing served 'for a time to fade away all horrible pictures of war from many a soldier's brain'.

By spring 1917, Gran was becoming frustrated that his status as an 'attached' Norwegian officer precluded him from joining his messmates on air raids across the Channel. But when a request was received for a night flying machine to be delivered to the RFC base at St Omer in northern France, Gran volunteered:

There to the right of me lay Ypres, under me lay the Yser Channel shining in the sun, whilst hundreds and thousands of small flashes seemed to be running up and down both sides of the watery way ... Such a flying trip has the effect of a good stimulant and, as cheery as schoolboys just off for a holiday, we made towards St Omer.

When Gran realised that the aircraft he had delivered would soon be flying over enemy lines on moonlit nights, dropping spies by parachute, he decided he must resign as a Norwegian officer and join the RFC in his own right.

But the weather in May was not ideal for night flying activities:

> The rain was pouring down in torrents … flares were lit and two searchlights endeavoured in vain to penetrate the dark drifting clouds. Like drowned rats the mechanics ran around the machine … 'You cannot fly tonight, sir, it's impossible,' said my fitter.

Gran, ignoring the advice, took off into the rain and hail:

> Then suddenly everything turned into a chaos of fog and darkness in which only my instruments could be seen. My machine was terribly chucked about and for a moment I completely lost control … I was flying upside down and with terrible speed … The following three quarters of an hour seemed to me to be like years … [suddenly] it was quite clear … I remembered my orders to patrol the line between London Colney at 12,000[ft] for three hours … For two hours I kept going backwards and forwards and the faint colour of day started spreading over the horizon. Then everything went quiet … the engine had stopped and nothing would make it start again … Then suddenly the clouds disappeared and I saw the earth … and glided into [a] grassy field.

Gran clambered out of his cockpit and ran to the road where some locals told him that the nearest town was Hull. Gran had some difficulties in taking off again but he arrived back at his base to the warmest welcome he remembered ever receiving. It had been a close shave.

A series of Zeppelin attacks on Thames estuary towns in early June suggested a full-scale aerial attack on London might be imminent. On 13 June Gran, in an aircraft which carried three guns and was nicknamed 'The Fortified Terror', took off towards Maidstone to join a daylight sortie against German bombers:

> I saw in the direction of Southend an enemy formation of about six machines. Two British scouts seemed to be attacking continuously, but apparently without any result whatsoever. I tried to get up to the enemy formation, but … after some minutes I lost [them] out of sight … [I then saw] a little formation of aeroplanes which I first believed to be British machines. When I saw dots of smoke appearing around the formation it became clear that I was mistaken and made for them … Undetected I came up in position behind the last one of the enemy fliers and with the sun on my back I managed to approach as near as 50 yards …

During the skirmishes Gran's aircraft was hit several times but he landed safely; whilst waiting for a replacement machine he spent a few nights in a London club. Not long after his arrival he received an urgent telephone call advising him that German aircraft were 'swarming across the channel':

A few moments later I was working like a madman at the starting handle of my car ... Had my car been of German origin, I could have understood that patriotic motives made the machinery strike, but [it] was a full-blood French racer ... I was suddenly pulled together by the sound of half a hundred of the London guns coming into action ... [and] saw over the roofs in a northerly direction a formation of enemy machines.

Gran could see shells exploding all around the twenty or so German aircraft but they stuck to their course. By the time his car motor finally fired and he returned to his base, he was too late for the action, so settled down to enjoy the remainder of a baking hot summer's day.

On 24 July Gran's unit was transferred from 39th Squadron into a newly formed 44th Squadron:

I do not believe that the world has ever seen a finer body of fliers ... acrobatic fliers were inferior to none ... when [an] alarm signal went eighteen first class Sopwith Camels took the air in a most distinguished formation.

Gran, like others, sometimes succumbed to the temptation to show off:

We looped the loop, we spun and flew with head down. The air over London made us quite wild and intoxicated ... [At] the flying ground ... I could not resist the temptation and put my machine into a rolling spin. Downwards it went with lightning speed and very soon the earth was no more than 1,000 feet under me.

Gran tried to neutralise the rudder and pushed the elevator control stick forward to its limit:

But no, round and round went my bus and I thought I was a gonner. Then I remembered ... I put my throttle full on and to my delight the aeroplane came under control again. However the earth was already there and the next moment I heard a bang, saw stars and went out in the land of dreams. When I woke up all the boys were standing round me.

One of Gran's comrades told him he had 'the luck of the devil' – his aircraft was 'smashed to atoms' but he had escaped with only slight concussion.

In early September 1917 Gran arrived on the Western Front and joined the RFC's 70th Squadron, which had been recently re-equipped with brand-new Sopwith Camels which worked 'to perfection'. One evening Gran met Frank Bickerton, who had travelled with Mawson but decided, after taking part in air tractor trials, not to go south with Shackleton on the eve of war.[4]

Bickerton had been in France since the early summer and had recently been flying over the Ypres salient, supporting British troops around Passchendaele and other points in the front line. He suggested that Gran join him and Clive Collett (a New Zealander who was the squadron's top 'ace') on a 'a little expedition' during which they might 'manage to shoot a few penguins together'.[5]

On 8 September Gran, Bickerton, Collett and their comrades relocated (in the midst of a major bombardment) to a new base at Poperinghe. Shortly afterwards Collett's luck finally ran out. His little finger (required to operate aircraft controls) was shot off during a dogfight and he was invalided home. He had shot down fifteen aircraft since July. On 20 September Bickerton was seriously injured; he also lost his little finger, but managed to retrieve it (and the signet ring on it) from the wreckage of his crashed aircraft.

Gran soon discovered that flying over Ypres was a dangerous business:

> our leader suddenly ... changed course and started climbing; in the next minute I heard shooting behind me and ... saw my friend engaging two hostile machines ... Our leader with a lightning manoeuvre, a sharp right hand climbing turn, placed himself and his gun on the tail of one of the German Albatros. I saw the centre of the German machine smoke and fire. Like a dead leaf [it] fell and then suddenly it dived straight down and disappeared like a burning torch ... we continued after this little episode in the direction of Ypres ... [but] seven more Germans caught up in firing range astern ... the German formation divided and turned. Suddenly I saw in front of me at close range a Hun. I gave a round from both my guns and he dived ...

Gran felt almost sorry as he watched his opponent, apparently a 'beginner' like Gran, crash to the ground. Like others in the squadron Gran respected German air aces such as Hermann Goering and Maximilian von Richthofen, whose brightly painted machines were regularly seen wheeling around the sky over the front lines.[6]

But there could also be danger on the ground, as Gran and his messmates discovered one evening during 'a most excellent supper':

> The music stopped ... suddenly someone shouted; 'Hurrah, Huns overhead,' and everybody rushed out of the hut. A few searchlights searched the sky with

their beams. Nearer and nearer came the moaning of the motor and ... and [there] rose a huge smoke column of smoke and flame from the outskirts of the aerodrome.

We ran and threw ourselves down among the trees. Again came a terrible concussion, another one and now not very far away ... something burst with a violent noise almost in our middle. A column of fire almost blinded us and earth and stones were thrown over us between the trunks of the trees. A few minutes afterwards we were all sitting again in the Mess, all of us agreeing that something ought to be done to stop these German fliers careering about on these beautiful moonlight nights.

By late autumn Gran had transferred to 101 Squadron, with which he took part in seventeen (largely successful) night bombing raids. On 30 November, during a low-level night attack on a German column near Cambrai, his aircraft's undercarriage was shot away and he was seriously wounded in the leg. But he and his young observer managed to coax the aircraft back over enemy lines before crash-landing at an emergency landing-ground near Arras.[7]

Gran was treated in a casualty clearing station before being transferred to the Royal Free Hospital, London, where his leg was operated on – and he found out what it was like to be on the receiving end of a night bombing raid:

It was just before Christmas, a wonderful moonlight night; after dinner had been served the alarm went ... A young VAD came over to my bed and asked why I did not get the orderly to carry me downstairs. 'No,' I answered, 'the war has made me believe in fate.' In the same moment the guns of the outer London barrage got into action and before we actually knew what had happened, a blinding flash came through the windows and the house trembled as if an earthquake was going on. The young girl stood pale up against the wall and I in spite of my wounds crawled up in the corner of my bed.

By January 1918 Gran was walking on crutches. He was granted two months' 'rest and recuperation' leave in Norway, where he learned that he had been awarded a Military Cross for his work on the Western Front. By the end of April he was fit enough to return to duty.

Just before doing so he married Lilian Johnson at the registry office in the Strand.[8] Gran's bride was a well-known actress (her stage name was Lily St John), whose latest success had been in *Yes, Uncle!*, a long-running musical comedy at the Prince of Wales Theatre, near Leicester Square.

Flight magazine reported the wedding of 'Captain Grant of the Royal Air Force, formerly Lieutenant Tryggve Gran of the Norwegian Navy' and noted that his best man, fellow pilot Lieut. J. W. Jackson had formerly worked as stage manager at the Alhambra Theatre.

Sharing the page with announcements of Gran's and other weddings were articles devoted to tallies of enemy aircraft and balloons 'downed', details of fatal crashes and lucky escapes and information on those who had died recently. The latter included the sons of newspaper proprietor Lord Rothermere and of firework manufacturer Arthur Brock.

Life in the air could be dangerous but Tryggve Gran's luck had held long enough for him to keep the promise he had made to his friends Oates and Bowers on the Antarctic ice shelf in 1911.

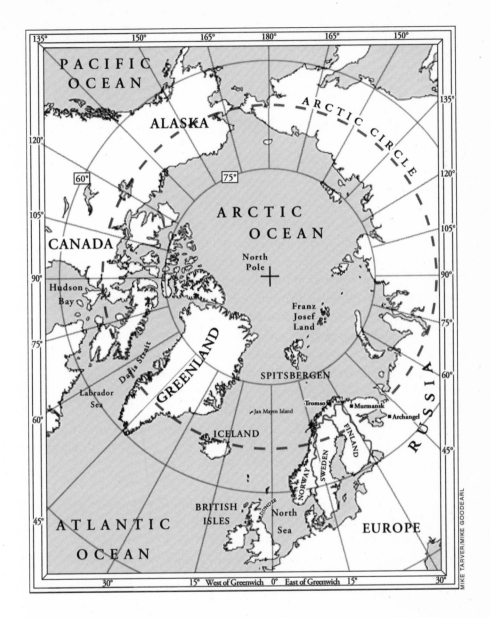

Arctic region, showing Spitsbergen, north Russia, Norway and other surrounding
countries. Map © and courtesy of Michael Tarver and Mike Goodearl.

17

Northward Ho!

———❦———

When Ernest Shackleton returned to London in April 1918, he was eager to find a suitable opportunity to serve his country in the war. One of the possibilities suggested to him was working with Allied troops based near the Arctic Circle at Murmansk and Archangel. They had initially been sent there to provide support and supplies to the Russian army; since the Tsar's abdication in 1917, they had been supporting the Tsar's supporters and other 'White' Russians against their 'Red' Communist opponents.[1]

The situation in Russia had changed again when, on 3 March 1918, Russia's new Bolshevik government signed a peace treaty with Germany at Brest-Litovsk. Now British and Allied forces were protecting their supply bases and supporting the 'Whites' in a bitter civil war.

Shackleton's *Endurance* stalwarts Frank Wild and James McIlroy had been based in Russia since returning from Antarctica. They were, as far as Shackleton knew, alive and well but several of his *Endurance* men had died since signing up for war duties.

Timothy McCarthy (brother of *Terra Nova* helmsman Mortimer McCarthy) had been killed in March 1917 when the oil tanker SS *Narragansett* had been torpedoed and sunk with all hands off Ireland. James 'Scotty' Paton, who had served on the *Morning*, *Nimrod*, *Terra Nova* and *Aurora*, was presumed lost with the *Aurora* when she disappeared after apparently striking a German mine off Australia. Frank Wild's brother Ernest, a member of the Ross Sea Party, had died in March 1918 on a minesweeper in the Mediterranean.

While Shackleton waited for details of his new posting to be finalised he was approached about the possibility of leading a short expedition to Spitsbergen. Shackleton had considered visiting Spitsbergen in 1911, but had been diverted back to his Antarctic activities.[2] During the war, British prospecting activity on Spitsbergen had virtually come to a halt, but Norwegian and Swedish mining companies had continued to extract coal and other minerals. In 1916 Northern Exploration Company and the Scottish Spitsbergen Syndicate approached the British Government about protecting their interests in Spitsbergen. They pointed out that Russia had attempted to annex the island in 1912 and Germany already had a meteorological station there.[3]

When, in early March 1918, an article appeared in *The Times* pointing out that an appendix to the Brest-Litovsk treaty obliged Russia to 'carry out the organization of Spitsbergen … in the sense of German propaganda', everyone seemed to become interested in Spitsbergen.[4]

On 11 March 1918 *The Times* published a letter from NEC's company secretary, J.K. Maples, pointing out that the combined claims of NEC and its Scottish counterpart were, at over 3,000 square miles, threefold those of all other countries combined.[5] It would, Maples concluded, be a 'catastrophe' if Spitsbergen and its minerals fell into German hands.

The expedition Shackleton was asked to lead had been organised by NEC (of which Shackleton's friend, Harry Brittain, was a director) with support from the Admiralty and the Foreign Office. Shackleton secured the release of Frank Wild from his duties in north Russia; James McIlroy, an *Endurance* expedition doctor, also turned out to be available after being invalided out of the army. By way of incentive, NEC offered Shackleton and Wild shares in the company, something which appealed to Shackleton's entrepreneurial spirit.[6]

The Admiralty's representative on the expedition was Lieut.-Comm. Norman Craig (RNVR), Member of Parliament for Thanet. The Admiralty provided an armed merchant ship, SS *Ella*, and the services of a Trinity House pilot; the Foreign Office arranged all necessary permissions and diplomatic contacts in Norway.[7] NEC was represented by its recently appointed managing director, Frederick Salisbury-Jones, company secretary Maples and Noel Davis, son and spokesman of NEC's chairman and major shareholder, Welsh coal magnate Frederick Davis.

Salisbury-Jones, a well-connected 'Africa hand' had, since joining the company, overseen a threefold increase in NEC's share capital to £500,000. He had attracted several new investors, but funds were still required to finance an early resumption of mining operations. Salisbury-Jones wanted to obtain photographic evidence of Spitsbergen's mineral riches and other facilities to show to interested parties. As Shackleton's *Endurance* cameraman, Frank Hurley, was now photographing Australian troops in Europe, Shackleton contacted Herbert Ponting – who had, by happy coincidence, held shares in NEC since 1913.[8]

Ponting, like Shackleton, was above the age limit for active service, but keen to serve his country. During the war his *Terra Nova* expedition films had, gratifyingly, appeared to appeal to people's patriotic spirit, and he had donated copies of the films to the army so they could be shown at the front. These screenings had, according to Rev. F.I. Anderson, Senior Chaplain to the Forces, been a great success:[9]

I cannot tell you what a tremendous delight your films are to thousands of our troops. The splendid story of Captain Scott is just the thing to cheer and encourage out here ... The thrilling story of Oates' self-sacrifice, to try and give his friends a chance of 'getting through', is one that appeals at the present time ... We all feel we have inherited from Oates and his comrades a legacy and heritage of inestimable value in seeing through our present work.

In early August, Ponting and his companions, armed with new passports, left Britain on the *Ella*, sailing in convoy. When they arrived in Tromsø Salisbury-Jones heard rumours that Norwegian and other prospectors had been trespassing on NEC's claims. He and Craig immediately travelled to Christiana to discuss matters with the British Minister to Norway and officials at the Norwegian Foreign Ministry. While the other members of the expedition waited in Tromsø, Shackleton became ill. He refused to let McIlroy examine him properly but decided to return to Britain where he had work to do preparing for his forthcoming mission in north Russia.

Shackleton arrived back in London to discover that Alf Cheetham, who had crossed the Southern Ocean fourteen times during four expeditions, had died in the North Sea. Cheetham had been serving as second mate on SS *Prunelle* when, on 22 August 1918, she was torpedoed by a German U-boat and sank with all of her crew. Alf left his wife Ella with nine children. After their son William had died in 1916, there had been ten, but since then their youngest daughter, Ella, had also died. Another of the couple's sons, the Hull local paper noted, was currently in France, serving at the front.[10] Alf Cheetham had died while trying to keep Britain's supply lines open in time of war.

* * *

On 3 September 1918 Cheetham's *Endurance* shipmate Frank Wild and other members of the NEC expedition entered the unoccupied German weather station on Spitsbergen, dismantled the wireless equipment and ran the Union Jack up the flagstaff.

During his time on Spitsbergen Ponting took hundreds of photographs, including of the captured wireless station, NEC's camps and miners working coal, Salisbury-Jones and other expedition members and Swedish mining operations. While Spitsbergen's summer landscape had little of Antarctica's pristine beauty, Ponting's aim was not to delight the eye but to show potential investors the extent of the island's mineral seams and ice-free inlets from which coal could be shipped to Britain and elsewhere.

By September Ponting, Salisbury-Jones, Maples, Craig, Noel Davis and several other expedition members were preparing to return to London. Wild, McIlroy, Yorkshire miner Bertram Mangham and a team of miners would stay behind to build a new base, Davis Camp (named for Frederick Davis), mine and prospect for coal and other minerals and police NEC's other claims.

The expedition had left Britain quietly but by early October articles began appearing in *The Times* and other newspapers about Spitsbergen's 'enormous' coal and iron deposits.[11] From 8 October *The Financier* ('Britain's oldest financial daily') ran a heavily advertised series of eleven articles on Spitsbergen written by '*The Financier*'s Special Correspondent with the Shackleton Expedition (the only writer who accompanied the Expedition)'.[12] The tone of the articles was optimistic and patriotic:

> A grave danger has been averted by the spirited action of a British Company – namely, the Northern Exploration Company – with the moral and material support of the British Government. The danger was that Germany might gain control of Spitsbergen, oust British interests, which greatly preponderate there, maintain a naval, aerial and coaling station to dominate Northern Europe as Heligoland dominates the North Sea highway to the Baltic and provide her with such mineral deposits which might compensate her for disappointments elsewhere ... If Germany were in control, no selected victim would be safe from her treachery and ruthlessness. Scandinavia would be between the hammer and the anvil ...

The articles described the challenges encountered by Salisbury-Jones and his companions, including claim-jumping and the *Ella*'s collision with an uncharted reef. A wealth of statistics and economic data underpinned NEC's demands that the British government should act to secure Spitsbergen's mineral wealth for Britain. According to one of the articles, expedition members had returned to London 'in the highest spirits, gratified beyond measure by the brilliant success of [their] mission and assured that the mineral riches of Spitsbergen now available for exploitation by British interests far exceeded [their] most sanguine hopes'.

Investors and the financial community were not alone in being interested in Spitsbergen. By mid-October Arthur Spinks, secretary of the Royal Geographic Society, had confirmed with explorer Sir Martin Conway (also the first director of the new Imperial War Museum) that 9 December would be a suitable date for him to present his paper 'The Political History of Spitsbergen' to RGS members.[13] Spinks then contacted Shackleton (as leader of NEC's recent expedition) and William Speirs Bruce (on behalf of the Scottish Spitsbergen Syndicate) inviting them to attend and give an overview of latest developments on Spitsbergen. When Spinks forwarded advance copies of Sir Martin's paper to Shackleton and Bruce he made it clear that they should address geographical rather than 'purely financial or commercial questions'.[14]

On 9 November *The Sphere* published a two-page article on Spitsbergen illustrated by an artist's impression of a bird's eye view of Spitsbergen and four of Ponting's photographs.[15] A map showed that Spitsbergen was approximately 400 miles from Tromsø, 500 from Murmansk, 1,200 from Aberdeen and Archangel and less than 2,000 from London.

The Financier's final article, published on 12 November (the day after the Armistice on the Western Front came into effect), concluded that Spitsbergen's mineral wealth and 'unparalleled combination of advantages' could secure Britain's future economic prosperity. Elsewhere in the paper, articles warned of the 'perfidious methods' which Germany might employ to regain her pre-war industrial dominance of Europe.

On 17 November Ponting wrote to Alfred Hinks about the planned RGS presentation:

> Mr F.W. Salisbury-Jones … tells me that Sir Martin Conway is to give a Lecture on Spitsbergen before the R.G.S. … I have been asked by Mr Salisbury-Jones to read a paper which I am preparing, and to show a series of lantern slides and moving picture films afterwards which will which will illustrate something of the operations of the Expedition …

Ponting asked whether Sir Martin's address could be postponed to allow him time to prepare his 'Kinema Films' for display. Hinks responded that the date was fixed and that Ponting's presentation should last for no more than twenty minutes.

In late November Ponting placed an advertisement in the *Financial Times* for a new double bill of his films at the Philharmonic Hall. Over the past four years he had publicised showings of his Antarctic films at the same venue through small advertisements in *The Times*, which featured drawings of Adelie penguins, but his new advertisement was dominated by the word 'SPITSBERGEN'. Now audiences could enjoy a double bill of 'The Industrial Activities in Spitsbergen' and Ponting's 'World-famous Kinematic Lecture' on Scott's expedition – and see for themselves the contrast between two polar regions.

During the first week of December Alfred Hinks learned that Shackleton's lack of response to his letters was due to his being in north Russia. He and Ponting were by now in regular correspondence about the form Ponting's presentation should take. Hicks had suggested twenty minutes' duration; Ponting wanted thirty minutes. Ponting was keen to show moving images; Hicks wanted a few still pictures to be interspersed within what was a 'contribution to the discussion', not a separate paper. Ponting told Hicks that, although he felt it his duty to 'let people know what Spitsbergen really is', he would 'deal with the Expedition … not touching in any way on the affairs of the Company'.

On Saturday, 7 December *The Financier* published a follow-up article on Spitsbergen. Alongside the main text was a 'Testimony' from Ponting, which included details of his forthcoming RGS presentation and his Philharmonic Hall film showings. Ponting had never, in all his travels, 'seen such geological wonders, and such vast mineral resources'. He confirmed that he had, since returning from Spitsbergen, invested a large part of his life-time savings in NEC shares, which he had purchased on the open market and intended to retain as a long-term investment.

On Tuesday, 10 December *The Times* ran a short report on the previous evening's proceedings at the RGS, accompanied by summaries of Sir Martin Conway's and Ponting's contributions.

Two days later Ponting received a letter from Hinks suggesting that, despite Ponting's earlier assurances, parts of his presentation appeared to have been 'extracts from something which seemed to be an advertising pamphlet' for NEC. Ponting's written response to Hinks' 'totally unwarranted statements' was long, detailed and indignant – as was that of NEC company secretary Maples to Hinks' suggestions that Ponting's presentation amounted to an 'abuse of hospitality' by both Ponting and the company.

Ponting and Maples asked Hinks to withdraw his remarks. When he declined to do so Ponting wrote at length to the RGS president, then to his lawyers, who advised Hinks that his letters to Ponting 'went very near libel'.

During early 1919 Ponting and Maples made their peace with Hinks and the RGS Council, after it was agreed that there had been misunderstandings on both sides and that Ponting had not deliberately tried to 'evade the rules of the Society'.

By then the legal status of Spitsbergen's sovereignty had been added to the agenda for discussion during the Peace Conference at Versailles.

* * *

In late September 1918, as Ponting was completing his assignment on Spitsbergen, Tryggve Gran was heading for Arctic waters. Gran was on a troopship sailing from Dundee to Archangel, where his Royal Flying Corps unit would be supporting Allied ground troops. During the voyage Gran and others suddenly began to feel ill:

the Spanish Flu appeared and took the character of an epidemic. I … lay for days in a high fever. Sometimes I noticed that the boat had stopped for a moment and on asking what was the matter I was told that it was just a soldier who was being buried at sea.

But by the time the ship reached Archangel Gran had recovered and was ready for duty:

For almost three months the town had been in the possession of the allies; the Bolshies had withdrawn up the Dvina and down the railway line towards Vologna. English naval seaplanes had played a great part. They had flown over the town and thrown down pamphlets to good effect and before anybody knew it the Bolsheviks had taken to boats and went up the river … on the other side of the Dvina lay the village of Bacaritza, which is the terminus for the railway from Petrograd. Enormous stores of everything imaginable was to be found here … It was already late in the season and it was clear to all that any decent flying that year would hardly be practicable. Our plan therefore was to make everything ready for the campaign in the Spring [1919].

In late October temperatures suddenly dropped and the Dvina began to freeze over. When Gran's old leg wound began troubling him he went to see the RFC doctor, who advised him to apply for a transfer to a warmer climate.[16]

On 8 November 1918 Gran's tour of duty in north Russia came to an end. When his ship arrived in Norway on 'a wonderful clear night when the north light flamed on a dark blue heaven' a Norwegian naval officer came aboard and announced that an Armistice would be coming into effect on the Western Front on 11 November.

Gran could hardly take the news in: 'An extraordinary feeling poured over me and for a long time I remained on deck staring out in the night towards the flaming sky.'

* * *

At 11 a.m. on 11 November 1918, all over Britain, church bells pealed, flags were waved and people cheered. Now there would be no need to dread the arrival of a telegram or scan lists in newspapers for familiar names. Finally, on the Western Front at least, the war was 'over by Christmas'.

When peace came, Edward Atkinson was no fit state to join in the celebrations. He had returned from France with a DSO to his credit and joined a brand-new ship, HMS *Glatton*.[17] On 16 September, before the *Glatton* put out from Dover on her maiden voyage, there was an explosion on board.[18] As fire spread fore and aft, cutting off parts of the ship, it was feared that the ship might completely blow up at any moment. Most of the ship's officers had been killed or seriously injured in the initial explosion. Atkinson, who had been working in his cabin, was knocked out by the first explosion and came to in a cabin which was now full of thick smoke and flames. As he staggered along the corridor to try to find a ladder to the upper decks, he passed several dead or unconscious colleagues. After locating the only intact ladder he carried two unconscious men up to safety.

While Atkinson was bringing a third man up another explosion blinded him and drove a piece of metal into his leg at such an angle that he was pinned to the ladder. Atkinson extracted the piece of metal and, feeling his way along, managed to place the man he was carrying on the upper deck. Still unable to see, he made his way back down the ladder, felt his way along the corridor, where he found two more unconscious colleagues. After carrying them both to relative safety he collapsed completely on the upper deck.

When Atkinson was found later, he was still semi-conscious but so badly wounded and burned that his fellow doctors had despaired of saving him. But by early October, badly scarred on his face and body and minus an eye, Atkinson was able to scribble a brief pencil note to Cherry-Garrard from Chatham's naval hospital. He thanked his friend for his good wishes and assured him, 'I hope to be out of here pretty soon if all goes well and shall try to see you.'[19]

By November Atkinson had completed a prescribed period of recuperation in Devon and been fitted with an artificial eye. With time on his hands, he had been able to give thought as to how Cherry-Garrard might deal with a difficult aspect of his narrative of the expedition:[20]

> I think you may make trouble with Meares by insisting that we know his orders but have no proof in writing of them. You and I know that he disobeyed orders. I thought unwillingly then that he was flying the white feather and after what I have heard of his conduct in France I know that he was ... if you make a statement to that effect and if it was challenged, you would have to substantiate it in writing ... The Owner [Scott] unfortunately never kept copies of his orders.[21]

There was also the issue of Teddy Evans' planned early departure from the expedition and the scurvy which had resulted in his sledging party's late return from the barrier. But Cherry was still some way from having a draft manuscript which he could show to Lyons and the publications committee.

Atkinson, having missed the final months of the war, was keen to find an alternative to returning to work in a naval laboratory:[22]

> Strictly between ourselves what would you think of flying the South American side of the Antarctic ... I am willing ... Don't let anyone else know.

... the War Office has asked for my services in Russia and if it is not too late I have said I am willing. Please say nothing to anyone about this as nothing is settled at present. I thought I would not go at first but I can clearly see the hand of the Hun behind the whole thing.

In early 1919 Atkinson joined the hospital ship *Lord Morton*, an 1880s' paddle-steamer which had been acquired by the navy in 1918 specifically for the north Russia campaign. When Atkinson arrived, he found that Shackleton and *Endurance* veterans Lionel Hussey, Frank Worsley and Joseph Stenhouse had been there since late October 1918. Shackleton, who was in charge of 'Arctic Equipment and Transport', had been pleased to find two of his expedition doctors, Eric Marshall (*Nimrod*) and Alexander Macklin (*Endurance*), already there. Since arriving, Macklin had been dealing with outbreaks of scurvy, smallpox, typhus, typhoid and influenza.[23]

When Macklin heard Atkinson discussing scurvy with other officers he tried get him to admit that the South Pole party had contracted scurvy before dying. Atkinson had studied the causes and effects of scurvy before going to Antarctica, but had not carried out post-mortems on Scott, Wilson and Bowers. He admitted freely that Teddy Evans had suffered from scurvy but confirmed that Scott had insisted that seal meat and liver and other scorbutics were included in meals and marching rations to guard against the disease.[24]

Terra Nova carpenter Frankie Davies was also now based in north Russia, organising landings and arranging repairs for ships operating on the White Sea and Dvina River. John Mather, now a temporary lieutenant-commander, had transferred to the Royal Engineers to serve in north Russia. He had initially been based at Murmansk, but transferred to a fleet operating on the Dvina River and on Lake Onega, where he had been working with Stenhouse.[25] It seemed that Scott's and Shackleton's men could work together when the need arose.

* * *

By spring 1919 Atkinson was back at Chatham Naval Barracks, from where he wrote to Cherry-Garrard:[26]

I had to go away for some trials and did not get back until last night. Until they send me definitely to Greenwich I am afraid there is no chance of my getting a weekend ... My experience of the Spitsbergen affairs coupled with that of Campbell was not good. Geographical reports were misleading and I quit with luck getting the amounts I had put in through my lawyers.[27]

Atkinson was, it seemed, less enthusiastic than Ponting and others about speculating on the potential future value of Spitsbergen's minerals.

Campbell had arrived in north Russia in July 1918 and been transferred to shore duties the following month. He had spent the previous few months in command of a brand-new flagship, HMS *Warwick*, on which he had taken part in a raid on Germany's U-boat base in Zeebrugge, Belgium. The operation had not been entirely successful, following a change of wind direction which, on two successive days, had blown away the smoke cover set up for HMS *Warwick* and some seventy other ships and left them exposed to enemy fire from shore and sea. There had been heavy losses during the action. HMS *Warwick* was damaged by a mine, but was responsible for ramming and sinking a U-boat; Campbell was mentioned in dispatches and received a bar to his DSO.

When Campbell returned to England in early 1919 he was called to give evidence at a long-delayed enquiry into the Royal Naval Division's 'Antwerp affair'. He also received an OBE for serving 'with distinction both at sea and on shore at Murmansk' and the *Croix de Guerre* for his services in the Channel Fleet.

18

Moving on

—⟨⟨⟨⟩⟩⟩—

On 17 January 1922 *The Times* published an article entitled 'Scott's Dash to the South Pole', in which 'A Correspondent' reminded readers that a decade had now passed since Captain Scott and his companions had planted their Union Jack at 90° South.[1]

Two weeks later newspapers reported the death, on South Georgia, of Ernest Shackleton. He had left London on 17 September 1921 on the *Quest*, accompanied by Antarctic and north Russian stalwarts, Wild, Macklin, Worsley, Hussey and McIlroy. He had suffered a major heart attack in Rio de Janeiro but had insisted that the expedition must continue. After the *Quest* docked in South Georgia on 4 January 1922, Shackleton collapsed again. He died in the early hours of 5 January, a few weeks short of his 48th birthday.

Shackleton's friends had agreed that Hussey would accompany Shackleton's body back to England and Wild would take command of the expedition. While Hussey was in Montevideo waiting for a passage to London he received a cable from Emily Shackleton asking him to take her husband's body back to South Georgia for burial. By April the *Quest* was back in South Georgia, defeated by the ice. When Frank Wild and Shackleton's longest serving shipmates visited their leader's grave, they built a cairn over it. Almost ten years previously Atkinson, Cherry-Garrard and their companions had done the same for Scott, Wilson and Bowers.

* * *

On 3 March 1922 Kathleen Scott married Hilton Young, Viscount Kennet, a former lawyer and journalist and Member of Parliament for Norwich.[2] Victor Campbell had introduced his late leader's widow to Young, with whom he had served during the Zeebrugge raid. During the action, Young had been badly injured, but the subsequent loss of one arm had not prevented him from travelling to north Russia and commanding an armoured train on the line which ran south from Archangel.

The wedding, at which the Bishop of St Albans officiated, was held in the crypt of the House of Commons. The bride was given away by Austen Chamberlain, Leader of the House of Commons, and wore (according to *The Times*) 'a draped fringed gown and cloak of dove-grey chiffon velvet, with a sable collar, and a toque of the same velvet with an upstanding silver plume'. Guests included the bride's 12-year-old son Peter, members of both families, several of Young's political circle and a small number of personal friends.

Kathleen Scott continued to be much in demand as a sculptor of portrait busts and full length statues: her recent subjects included Lloyd George and Arnold Lawrence, younger brother of T.E. Lawrence, whom she had already sculpted, dressed in his Arab robes.[3] She had also been commissioned to make a sculpture of a soldier for a war memorial in the town of Huntingdon, Cambridgeshire.

* * *

On 16 May 1922 Herbert Ponting announced his new invention, the 'Kinatome', which would bring film into the home, as the pianola and gramophone had done for music.[4] He had already intimated that he was working on a new film about the *Terra Nova* expedition which would include previously unseen new footage.[5] He had given over 1,000 lectures and film showings at the Philharmonic Hall, which had, according to *The Times*, made the expedition 'imperishable' and, thanks to his films of penguins and seals, 'added vastly to the gaiety of London during difficult times'.[6] Ponting's account of the expedition, *The Great White South*, had been published in 1921 and was due to be reprinted during 1922.

Cherry-Garrard had delivered a final draft of his account of the expedition in May 1922. It was, following a parting of the ways with the expedition's publications committee, a personal account of the expedition which had at its heart the Cape Crozier expedition and the heroic kindness of Wilson and Bowers. Cherry had been open regarding where he thought things had gone wrong, but he had decided that there would be no villains in his story.

After Pennell had died, Cherry had written a eulogy to him and their equally hardworking friends, Wilson and Bowers.[7] In it Cherry imagined Pennell in his own personal heaven, where everyone worked for thirty hours a day, but from where, Cherry hoped, Pennell might sometimes descend to take him and other friends out for dinner. The passage, like others, was perhaps too personal for publication.

Cherry had told the story of the South Pole journey largely through extracts from Bowers' journal and that of the return of the second returning party through extracts from that of William Lashly. Cherry, knowing Lashly enjoyed reading about his *Terra Nova* companions, sent him a copy of Shackleton's *South*, in which Lashly's friend Tom Crean had been praised by Shackleton.[8]

* * *

By 1922, Frank Debenham's dream of establishing a permanent home for the expedition's scientific papers was beginning to become a reality.[9] The idea had come to Debenham in November 1912 when he and Raymond Priestley had been 'geologising' around Shackleton's *Nimrod* expedition hut at Cape Royds. Debenham had realised that, although their investigations built on work carried out during the *Nimrod* expedition, they were unsure where the *Nimrod* records currently were. When Debenham found some abandoned writing paper in Shackleton's hut he jotted down some ideas for a 'Polar Centre'.

When Debenham and Priestley returned to Cambridge after the war they discussed the idea with Atkinson, Cherry-Garrard, Shackleton, Dr Arthur Shipley, RGS council members and other interested parties. In late 1920 Debenham's detailed plans had been approved by the appropriate university bodies. By 1922 he was installed in an attic office in the Sedgwick Museum (home to a famous earth sciences collection), working to turn his dream into reality. It was early days, but Debenham hoped that one day his polar research institute might have its own building and that he might be its first director.

Dennis Lillie had been discharged from Bethlem Hospital in January 1921 and returned to Cambridge. He had begun lecturing again but by October that year had suffered a relapse and been admitted to Buckinghamshire Mental Hospital. He had been readmitted to Bethlem before Christmas 1921 but there was no sign of improvement in his mental state.

Raymond Priestley had ended the war as a major, in command of the 46th (North Midland) Divisional Signal Company of the Royal Engineers. After writing a history of the signal service, he had returned to Cambridge where he had been awarded a BA for his expedition work on glaciers and been admitted to Fellowship of Clare College. He and Silas Wright were now preparing the final report on their expedition findings for publication.

During the final year of the war a second Priestley brother had been killed. Donald Priestley, a lance corporal with the Artists' Rifles, had died when advancing through waist-deep mud towards a German position in the Ypres salient. Of 500 Artists' Rifles who had gone into battle that morning, only 150 were in fighting condition by nightfall.[10] The 'very beautiful, rolling wooded country [with] very pretty villages' which Cecil Meares described in October 1914 was now a trench-scored, shell-pocked quagmire, punctuated by leafless tree stumps, rubble where buildings had been and a series of makeshift burial grounds.

Wright, who had also risen to the rank of major, had been mentioned twice in despatches for his work on wireless transmission between trenches; he had also been awarded a Military Cross and OBE and been appointed a *Chevalier* of the French Legion of Honour. He was now working at the recently established Admiralty Research Department as assistant to its founding director, Frank Smith.

Priestley's other brother-in-law, Griff Taylor, had remained in Melbourne with his wife and young family, working at the Bureau of Meteorology and writing up his Antarctic research at the city's university. A declared pacifist, he had worked as a meteorologist and lecturer at a flying school, completed a university doctorate and garnered good reviews for his expedition memoir, *With Scott: the Silver Lining*, which had been published in 1916. Since 1920 he had been working in Sydney, where he had established Australia's first dedicated university department of geography.

George Simpson had spent most of the war working in India, but undertaken tours of duty as a meteorological adviser to the British Expeditionary Force in Mesopotamia and as assistant secretary to the Board of Munitions. By 1922 he was back in Britain, working as director of the Meteorological Office, a post Colonel Lyons, of the expedition's publications sub-committee, had held during the war.

Murray Levick had retired from active war service in 1916 on fitness grounds, but subsequently transferred to a military orthopaedic centre in London, developing new uses for electrotherapy, including on trench foot and other war injuries.[11] Since the war he had worked on new methods of rehabilitation and had recently been appointed physiotherapist to a home and craft school for wounded men. The results of Levick's scientific work during the *Terra Nova* expedition had been published before the war. His reports on the social habits of penguins at Cape Adare had been published in both pamphlet and book form, but his shorter paper, 'The Sexual Habits of Adélie Penguins', had only been circulated privately rather than risk offending sensitive nature enthusiasts.[12]

Edward Nelson had, following demobilisation, left his work at the Board of Invention and Research in London and returned to Plymouth and the Marine Laboratory. He had not, however, returned to live with his wife and daughter.[13] In 1921 he had moved to Aberdeen, where he was now working as scientific superintendent of the Fisheries Board for Scotland, supervising a project which used drift bottles to track North Sea currents. This job, which drew on his Antarctic and other earlier work, was proving professionally fulfilling but his marriage appeared to be troubled. His wife, after failing to secure his return to Plymouth by offering to 'let bygones be bygones', was currently seeking a decree of restitution of conjugal rights through the courts.

Edward Atkinson, who had seen little of his beloved 'Missus' during the war, had recently been seconded to the Royal Hellenic Navy as part of a British naval training and organisational mission. Since the war he had been awarded an Albert Medal, for saving lives on HMS *Glatton*, and the Chadwick Medal, awarded every five years to the medical officer in the armed forces who had done most to promote the health of his fellow officers. Atkinson, who continued to undergo treatment and surgery for his burns and other wounds, also managed to find time to write up his *Terra Nova* and wartime scientific findings.

* * *

On 3 May 1922, at St Andrews, on the east coast of Scotland, J.M. Barrie, to whom Scott had written one of his last letters, was installed as Rector of the city's ancient university. Barrie had been born in Kirriemuir, about 30 miles from St Andrews, and educated at schools in Glasgow, Forfar and Dumfries and Edinburgh University. The students of St Andrews had elected Barrie as their rector during Armistice week in November 1919 but his rectorial address had been postponed several times. When Earl Field-Marshall Haig, Barrie's predecessor as rector, was appointed chancellor of the university, it was agreed that the two installation ceremonies would be combined.[14]

New rectors were, by custom, invited to submit names of those whom they felt worthy of receiving an honorary degree.[15] Barrie had suggested Thomas Hardy, 'the chief man of letters living', John Galsworthy and several others from the world of letters and artistic circles. Essayist Charles Whibley's wife was the sister-in-law (and a regular subject) of James McNeill Whistler. Edward Lucas, a regular contributor to *Punch*, worked for publishers Methuen and Co and played in an amateur cricket team established by Barrie and consisting of his writer friends.[16] Sidney Colvin, an art and literary critic, was a long-standing friend of Robert Louis Stevenson (with whom Barrie had corresponded but never met). Scottish cleric William Robertson Nicoll, founder of the London-based *British Weekly*, had given Barrie some of his first writing commissions. Actor-manager Squire Bancroft and much-loved actress Ellen Terry represented the world of theatre, to which Barrie owned much of his fame.[17]

Barrie had also nominated his doctor, Douglas Shields, an Australian who had moved to London from his native Melbourne and also counted amongst his patients Galsworthy, opera singer Dame Nellie Melba, cricketer Don Bradman and members of the British and European aristocracy. Shields had also been knighted for his services as surgeon to Australian forces in France, the Royal Navy and the British Army.

Barrie's final nominee for an honorary degree had been Bernard Freyberg, VC, DSO (and two bars), the highest ranking officer of his age in the British army. Since the war Freyberg had spent much of his time in London living in Barrie's apartment, recovering from his wounds while Barrie was nursed through various bouts of ill health.

Four others were being granted honorary degrees that day. Sir Herbert Lawrence, one of Haig's senior staff officers, had overseen the withdrawal from the Cape Helles sector on Gallipoli. Lord Wester Wemyss, who had family estates in Fife, had been governor of Lemnos, and in charge of the naval base at Mudros harbour during the Gallipoli campaign.[18] Sir James Guthrie was one of Scotland's best known painters and portraitists.[19] The final graduand, Thomas Paxton, was Lord Provost of Glasgow, but had, like Barrie, been brought up near St Andrews.

The day before the graduation Barrie had been warmly and boisterously welcomed by the students and pulled through the streets in a carriage.[20] The morning of the graduation Barrie had attended the unveiling of a new war memorial in the university chapel and been granted the freedom of St Andrews.

In the early afternoon students, staff members and other guests gathered in the Volunteer Hall to hear Barrie's rectorial address.[21] After a humorously self-deprecating introduction, Barrie turned his topic of 'Courage'. He encouraged his younger listeners to engage with the older generation, even though their actions and decisions had led to the recent war. He reminded them that those who died in wars were young and might, in the future, include their as yet unborn children. He suggested that they, the young people of Britain, had more in common with young people of other countries than with old men of their own. He recalled his own early days in London, when, knowing no one and lacking money, he had enjoyed working until nightfall and reminded them that their principal still sometimes burned the midnight oil on their behalf.

After quoting Burns and praising Thomas Hardy (who was receiving his degree *in absentia*) Barrie chastised himself for the number of references he was making to those of his own calling. He then pulled a piece of paper from his pocket. He opened it carefully and began reading the letter which his friend Scott had written to him a decade previously from a tent on the Ross ice shelf: 'We are pegging out in a very comfortless spot. Hoping this letter may be found and sent to you, I write you a world of farewell. I want you to think well of me and my end.'

Barrie paused to explain that Scott's next few sentences were too private to be read out in public, then continued:[22]

Goodbye – I am not at all afraid of the end, but sad to miss many a simple pleasure which I had planned for the future in our long marches … We are in a desperate state – feet frozen, etc., no fuel, and a long way from food, but it would do your heart good to be in our tent, to hear our songs and our cheery conversation ... Later ...

Barrie paused again. After explaining that Scott's closing words were difficult to decipher, he continued: 'We are very near the end ... We did intend to finish ourselves when things proved like this, but we have decided to die naturally without.'

Barrie invited his audience to imagine they were outside Scott's tent, listening to the cheerful songs and conversation. The story of Scott reminded him of that of the young mountaineer who had died after falling down a glacier and whose body had been found years later by his friends, who were by then all old men. Scott and his companions would, like the dead mountaineer, be forever young. The songs and conversations from the tent showed that men of courage could also be light-hearted.

Barrie then told his audience about a young Royal Naval Division officer who had, during the war, been dropped overboard off Gallipoli and swum for two hours in enemy waters. The young man in question had, he told them, regarded the episode as 'a gay affair' rather than a life-threatening exploit. When cheers for Freyberg had died down, Barrie recalled a light-hearted moment he had shared with Scott in Scotland when the latter had tried to rile Barrie by claiming that haggis was nothing but boiled bagpipes. Barrie reminded the students to spend time with friends as well as at lectures and to enjoy the rich heritage of their university. He urged them to be courageous and, in the words of Browning, to 'greet the unseen with a cheer' and to 'fight on' for the 'old red gown' they wore.

Newspapers all over the country reported on the graduation ceremony and quoted from Barrie's speech. Barrie gave permission for Scott's letter (bar the personal passages) to be reproduced so that people could read the explorer's courageous words for themselves.

* * *

Fridtjof Nansen, whom Barrie had also quoted during his rectorial address, was becoming increasingly recognised as an international statesmen. During a wartime visit to the United States on behalf of his country, he had learned of and been impressed by President Woodrow Wilson's 'Fourteen Points for Peace'. In 1919, when serving as a member of the Norwegian delegation at the Versailles Peace Conference, Nansen had become aware of the plight of prisoners and refugees displaced by the war. In his new role as High Commissioner for Refugees to the League of Nations, he worked tirelessly on their behalf, including through the introduction of the 'Nansen Passport' for stateless persons. Nansen was considered as being in line for a Nobel Prize.

The Conference had decided that Svalbard, including Spitsbergen, should become part of Norway, but that Britain, the United States, Sweden, Japan and other treaty signatories, should retain rights to engage in coal mining and other commercial activities. It now seemed unlikely, however, that shares in the Northern Exploration Company would prove to be as profitable an investment as Ponting, George Wyatt and others had once hoped.

Tryggve Gran had returned to Norway in 1921 and rejoined his country's air force. His last years in Britain had not been particularly happy ones: he had joined one of the teams attempting to fly across the Atlantic, but had not been successful; he had damaged his already weakened left leg in a motorcycle accident and his glamorous actress wife had returned to the stage and filed for divorce.[23]

At the end of summer 1922, Roald Amundsen announced that he would attempt to fly over the North Pole during 1923.[24] When he had returned from his Antarctic triumph doubts were being expressed about both Cook's and Peary's claims to have reached the North Pole. During the war Amundsen raised funds for a new expedition by buying and selling ships at a profit. In July 1918 he left Tromsø, but soon became trapped in the ice. Since then he had made little progress, but was determined to attain his goal, either by ship or by air.

* * *

In October 1922 the British Liberal–Conservative coalition government, which had lasted since the war, finally collapsed. When a general election was called for 15 November, Winston Churchill, who had held his Dundee seat for sixteen years, was in hospital recovering from an appendectomy. He finally arrived in Dundee on 11 November, Armistice Day, but could still not stand for long periods of time or address public meetings in his usual fluent manner. He came fourth behind Labour and Prohibitionist candidates and his own Liberal running mate and found himself without a parliamentary seat, a government post or a job.

Churchill had suggested in 1919 that the ruins of Ypres should remain as a monument to the British and Allied soldiers who died defending the city and the channel ports.[25] Others, including the citizens of Ypres, did not agree and in November 1919 Ypres was awarded both the British Military Cross and the French Croix de Guerre.

But memorials and monuments were by now something of a national preoccupation. On 11 November 1920 the body of an unknown soldier had been buried in Westminster Abbey in the presence of the king, members of the government, a guard of honour of VCs (including Freyberg) and 100 women who had lost both husbands and sons in the war. The names of British and Allied war dead were being recorded on memorials and tombstones in graveyards near battlefields on the Western Front and other theatres of war. Memorials, designed by leading architects such as Edwin Lutyens, included one at Tyne Cot, near Ypres. When King George had visited it on 11 May 1922 he had been moved to say:

> We can truly say that the whole circuit of the Earth is girdled with the graves of our dead. In the course of my pilgrimage, I have many times asked myself whether there can be more potent advocates of peace upon Earth through the years to come, than this massed multitude of silent witnesses to the desolation of war.

Graveyards, whether beside memorials or annexed to local cemeteries, were set in gardens based on a designed by Lutyens' friend and collaborator, garden designer Gertrude Jekyll.

Memorials were also being planned in Britain for those who had 'no grave but the sea' or had died fighting on ships. The Admiralty commissioned three identical obelisks to be erected at Plymouth, Portsmouth and Chatham to serve both as memorials and landmarks for shipping.

* * *

On 4 December 1922 Cherry-Garrard's book, *The Worst Journey in the World*, was finally published. Reviews were generally favourable, particularly of Cherry's description of the Cape Crozier journey and the hardships he, Wilson and Bowers had suffered. *The Times* (which regularly published Cherry's letters on Antarctic expeditions and other matters) had recently announced that an exhibition of Wilson's watercolours and drawings from the *Discovery* and *Terra Nova* expeditions would be taking place at London's Whitechapel Gallery.[26]

Teddy Evans had published two books: *South with Scott* was his short, personal account of the expedition; *Keeping the Seas* described his wartime naval exploits. Evans was currently serving in Hong Kong as captain of HMS *Carlisle*. He had recently been awarded a Board of Trade medal for gallantry after swimming from his ship to rescue passengers from SS *Hong Moh*, which had sunk after running aground in poor weather.

Cecil Meares had recently returned from the Far East. After joining the RNAS he had undertaken a number of logistical, intelligence and administrative roles in London, France and Italy. In 1921 he had joined a civilian delegation of former air force officers who had travelled to Japan to give guidance and instruction to the Japanese air force.[27] The delegation was led by William Forbes-Sempill, a Scottish peer who had served in the RFC and RNAS; Thomas Orde-Lees of the *Endurance* expedition was the delegation's parachute expert. Before leaving Japan, Meares had been presented with a sword and awarded the Third-Class Order of the Sacred Treasure.[28]

* * *

On 13 December 1922 Victor Campbell retired from his second naval career and began considering where he might live. He had always like Newfoundland, which he had visited as a young sailor and which, although on a latitude with Norway, had a less extreme climate.[29]

The enquiry into the circumstances of the RND's Antwerp 'affair' had been somewhat inconclusive, given the scope for miscommunication there had been in the confusion surrounding the evacuation of the troops. On 6 June 1919 the Prince of Wales spoke at a final RND parade on Horse Guards Parade in London. He thanked those present for their service 'whether on the slopes of Achi Baba, or on the Somme, or in the valley of the Ancre or, down to the very end, at the storming of the Hindenberg Line.' The prince noted that few of the men his father had inspected in February 1915 at Blandford Camp were still alive. During the war 600 RND officers and almost 10,000 other ranks had died in battle, from injuries or from disease; over 30,000 others had also been wounded.

Rupert Brooke, the RND's most famous recruit had, while based at Blandford Camp, written two prophetic sonnets entitled *The Dead*:[30]

> Blow out, you bugles, over the rich Dead!
> There's none of these so lonely and poor of old,
> But, dying, has made us rarer gifts than gold.
> These laid the world away; poured out the red
> Sweet wine of youth; gave up the years to be
> Of work and joy, and that unhoped serene,
> That men call age; and those who would have been.
> Their sons, they gave, their immortality.

* * *

In the run up to Christmas 1922, Herbert Ponting's *The Great White South* was advertised as being an ideal Christmas gift. At the Philharmonic Hall, where Ponting had shown his expedition films to tens of thousands of people, *Climbing Mount Everest*, a short film about a recent attempt to scale the world's highest mountain, was attracting considerable interest.

George Mallory, a leading member of the expedition, had been a contemporary of Cherry-Garrard at Winchester College. He was already determined to take part in the next attempt to claim the summit (sometimes called 'The Third Pole') for Britain, as was Noel Odell, a geologist with Arctic experience. Odell was keen to recruit for their team a young athlete he had met when climbing in Wales a few years previously.

Andrew 'Sandy' Irvine, born in 1902, was too young to have served in the war but had somewhat surprised the War Office by submitting his designs for a gear which enabled machine guns to be fired from aircraft without damaging the propeller blades. A fine oarsman, he had taken part in a 1919 'Peace Regatta' at Henley and rowed for Merton College, Oxford, and in the 1922 Boat Race. Irvine was now planning to join a 'Merton College Arctic Expedition' to Spitsbergen, which his friend and fellow student George Binney was organising. Binney, who had organised a similar trip in 1921, had already recruited Noel Odell as expedition geologist. He had also asked Tom Longstaff, who had taken part in Binney's previous expedition and in the 1922 attempt on Everest, to act as expedition doctor; Longstaff's late father, a wealthy businessman and friend of Clements Markham, had been a major funder of Scott's *Discovery* expedition.[31]

Andrew 'Sandy' Irvine and George Binney, with assistance from their experienced elders, seemed well-equipped and ready to 'greet the unseen with a cheer', as J.M. Barrie had suggested young people should be prepared to do in the new, post-war world.

Epilogue

—◦◦◦—

Where do stories and histories begin and end? This book spans the time from the beginning of the *Terra Nova* expedition to the end of the year of the tenth anniversary of the reaching of the South Pole and the deaths of the South Pole party.

But the roots and offshoots of these stories continue …

* * *

If Cecil Meares had not sat up overnight with his injured fellow-officer Major Lawrence Johnston in October 1914, perhaps we would not be able to enjoy Hidcote Garden, Johnston's horticultural masterpiece and legacy in the Cotswolds.

Apsley Cherry-Garrard met Johnston in 1923, when they were visiting Bodnant (where Bernard Freyberg and his new wife had recently spent their honeymoon), as members of a gardening club.[1] Cherry-Garrard, the 'Antarctic' who was perhaps most damaged by his experiences and the loss of his friends Wilson and Bowers, had recently published his testament of friendship to them, a work which raised the bar for anyone writing about Antarctic travel.

Harry Pennell, whom Cherry-Garrard so admired, had no children of his own, but his travels inspired descendants of his godson, Lewin Pennell, to visit and work in Antarctica.

The Scott Polar Research Institute is one of the finest legacies Scott and his 'Antarctics' could have hoped for. More recently, Cheltenham's Art Gallery and Museum has been renamed simply as 'The Wilson', in honour of Edward Wilson (whose collection it houses) and his father, who co-founded the town's museum.

Writing this book has convinced me (although I needed little persuasion) that life and death are matters of chance and coincidence. If Bernard Freyberg had, as he wished he had, joined Scott's expedition, might the outcome of the expedition have been different? Might Scott and others have lived, or might Freyberg have died and so not fought with such distinction in the First World War? If Harry Pennell had not met Cecil Prowse in Lyttelton in 1912, perhaps Pennell would not have been on the *Queen Mary* on 31 May 1916. If William James had taken less of a dislike to Prowse, he might have been on the ship during the battle of Jutland. Or perhaps Pennell, like *Terra Nova* stoker Robert Brissenden, was simply in the wrong place at the wrong time.

Alf Cheetham, who had survived so many crossings of the Southern Ocean, seems to have been unfortunate compared to others on the expedition who survived 'near misses': Teddy Evans (scurvy and sea-battles), William Lashly (crevasse falls and a fatally mined *Queen Mary*) and Tryggve Gran (several air accidents).

Several expedition members died, through chance or choice, to save or stay with others: Oates, Bowers, Wilson and Henry Rennick. They join countless others who fell during the war whilst helping fallen or injured comrades.

Anyone who visits Ypres and the Somme cannot, I believe, fail to be moved by the sight of the huge memorials with their lists of names and the graveyards with their rows of immaculate tombstones, interspersed by plants. When I visited Frederick 'Sep' Kelly's grave near Beaucourt someone had placed a note on it saying 'Your music will live forever.' I hope Kelly would have been pleased.

Thanks to Edwin Lutyens, Gertrude Jekyll and the Commonwealth War Graves Commission there are, as Rupert Brooke envisaged, corners of foreign fields that are forever England – or Scotland, Ireland, Wales, Belgium, France, Germany, New Zealand, the United States, Canada, Australia, India, Barbados: the list goes on. But, *pace* Winston Churchill, the people of Ypres were right about their home: the wonderful In Flanders Field Museum (housed in the rebuilt Cloth Hall) is more of a legacy for a new generation than the rubble of people's former homes would ever have been.

A more ephemeral but visually stunning legacy of the war was 'Blood Swept Lands and Seas of Red', an installation of 888,246 ceramic poppies by Paul Cummins and Tom Piper, which filled the moat of the Tower of London for several months during 2014. Some of the millions of people who visited the installation will have noticed, and maybe visited, the Merchant Navy Memorial, across the road from the Tower. Designed by Lutyens, it commemorates the 20,000 men whose names are listed on the memorial; those names include those of 'Alf' Cheetham and his young son William.

Scott and his men lived through times of great change – they trained on sailing ships but lived to plan crossings of polar regions by aircraft. Pennell loved the dynamic buzz of London life, but also enjoyed the peace of Awliscombe and Oddington. His name appears on the war memorials in both villages as well as on the huge naval memorial on the seafront near Portsmouth. He, like three of his 'afterguard' on the deck of the *Terra Nova* on the morning of 1 April 1912, did not survive the war.

This book has proved to be one of connections – the following 'chain' provides, I feel, an appropriate coda. Guests arriving by train for Pennell's wedding on 15 April 1915 would have alighted at Adlestrop, the nearest station to Oddington. Less than a year before Pennell's wedding, on Wednesday, 24 June 1914, a train made an unscheduled stop at the station. One of the passengers was Edward Thomas, a journalist who had recently begun to write poetry. The unexpected stop stayed in his mind:

> Yes. I remember Adlestrop
> The name, because one afternoon
> Of heat, the express-train drew up there
> Unwontedly. It was late June.
>
> The steam hissed. Someone cleared his throat.
> No one left and no one came
> On the bare platform. What I saw
> Was Adlestrop – only the name
>
> And willows, willow-herb, and grass,
> And meadowsweet, and haycocks dry,
> No whit less still and lonely fair
> Than the high cloudlets in the sky.
>
> And for that minute a blackbird sang
> Close by, and round him, mistier,
> Farther and farther, all the birds
> Of Oxfordshire and Gloucestershire

Thomas was on his way to Dymock, Gloucestershire, where he was due to meet Rupert Brooke and other writers and poets. On 9 April 1917 Edward Thomas died near Arras. Five days later, a few miles away, Brooke's former messmate, Edward Nelson, left the battlefield and returned to England.

We will never know whether Nelson read the poem or about Thomas' death and made the connection. But anyone who has visited the site of Adlestrop station will have noticed that the surrounding hedgerows seem to be full of bird song – perhaps 'all the birds of Oxfordshire and Gloucestershire' also sang on the day of Harry Pennell and Katie Hodson's wedding.

* * *

The threads of history seem endless and interwoven.

Just over a century ago Murray Levick dropped a notebook containing lists of exposures he had used when taking photographs in Antarctica; in 2013 the notebook emerged from the ice, the lists of numbers still legible.[2] In April 2015 the negatives and prints of photographs which 'Birdie' Bowers had taken on his way to the South Pole unexpectedly came to auction; they had not been seen for decades.[3] The following weekend, as the centenary of the Gallipoli landings were being commemorated, earthquakes and avalanches in the Himalayas killed thousands, reminding us that nature can be as deadly as weapons of war.[4]

I end this stream of loosely connected thoughts with an apology: I have no ready answers to the 'big questions' about the First World War. But from what I have gleaned about Scott's 'Antarctics', each man did his best according to his abilities and circumstances, whether amongst the ice floes or on the battlefields. In a very different age from our own, they did their duty, fought for their country. They displayed 'Courage' – and, as J.M. Barrie would have expected of Scott's men, greeted the unknown with cheer. They lived up to the epitaph Cherry-Garrard suggested for their own memorial to the South Pole party: 'To strive, to seek, to find and not to yield'.

Surely that is all we can expect of them.

Appendices

—⊂∞∞⊃—

Appendix A: Expedition Personnel

Note: All naval officers are RN unless stated; all Petty Officers ('PO') are RN.

Shore party officers and scientists

Dr Edward Atkinson (RN), 1881–1929, surgeon/parasitologist (nicknames: Atch, Jane)

Lieutenant Henry Bowers (Royal Indian Marine), 1883–1912 (Birdie)

Lieutenant Victor Campbell (retired, Emergency List), 1875–1956 (The Wicked [First] Mate)

Apsley Cherry-Garrard, 1886–1959, assistant biologist (Cherry)

Bernard Day, 1884–1952, motor engineer

Frank Debenham, 1883–1965, geologist (Deb)

Lieutenant Edward Evans, 1881–1957 (Teddy)

Sub-Lieutenant Tryggve Gran (Royal Norwegian Navy), 1889–1980, ski expert (Trigger)

Dr George Murray Levick (RN), 1877–1956, surgeon, scientist

Cecil Meares, 1877–1937, in charge of dogs

Edward Nelson, 1883–1923, marine biologist (Marie)

Captain Lawrence Oates (army), 1880–1912 (Titus, Soldier)

Herbert Ponting, 1870–1935, photographer (Ponko)

Raymond Priestley, 1886–1974, geologist

Captain Robert Scott, 1868–1912 (The Owner)

George Simpson, 1878–1965, meteorologist (Sunny Jim)

T. Griffith Taylor, 1880–1963, senior geologist (Griff)

Edward Wilson, 1872–1912, chief scientist, doctor, zoologist, artist (Uncle Bill, Ted to family)

Charles Wright, 1887–1975, physicist (Silas)

Terra Nova *officers, scientists and senior crew*

Lieutenant Harry Pennell, 1882–1916, navigator/acting captain (Penelope)

Lieutenant Henry Rennick, 1881–1914, surveyor/second-in-command to Pennell (Parny)

Lieutenant Wilfred Bruce (RN reserve), 1874–1953, mercantile marine officer

Francis Drake (RN retired), 1878–1936, paymaster/expedition secretary (Frankie)

Dennis Lillie, 1884–1963, marine biologist

Jim Dennistoun, 1883–1916, in charge of dogs (1911–12 voyage only)

Alfred Cheetham RNR, 1857–1918, boatswain (Alf)

William Williams, 1875–?, chief engine room artificer

Shore party crew

PO George Abbott, 1880–1923

William Archer, 1871–1944, cook/steward (second season)

PO Frank Browning, 1882–1930

Thomas Clissold, 1886–1964, cook/steward (first season)

PO Tom Crean, 1876–1938

Able Seaman Harry Dickason, 1885–1944

PO Edgar Evans, 1876–1912 (Taff)

PO Robert Forde, 1877–1959

Demitri Gerof, 1888–1932, dog driver

Frederick Hooper, 1889–1955, steward

PO Patrick Keohane, 1879–1950

Chief Stoker William Lashly, 1867–1940

Anton Omelchenko, 1883–1932, groom

PO Thomas Williamson, 1877–1940 (second season only)

Leading members of ship's crew and others specifically mentioned

PO Arthur Bailey

Francis Davies, leading shipwright (Frankie, Chippy)

PO (retired) William Heald

PO (RNVR) John Mather

PO Frederick Parsons

Leading Seaman Albert Balson

Leading Stoker Robert Brissenden

Leading Stoker William Burton

Able Seaman William Knowles

Leading Stoker Edward McKenzie

Engine Room Artificer William Horton

Fireman Charles Lammas
Able Seaman and Helmsman Mortimer McCarthy

Other Terra Nova crew

Joseph Leese, Able Seaman; Angus McDonald, Fireman; William McDonald, Able
Seaman; Thomas McGillon, Fireman; Thomas McLeod, Able Seaman; William Neale,
cook/steward; Robert Oliphant, Able Seaman; James ('Scotty') Paton, Able Seaman;
James Skelton, Able Seaman (RNR); Bernard Stone, Leading Stoker;
Charles Williams, Able Seaman (first season only)

Others associated with the expedition

Emily Bowers, mother of Henry Bowers
Hilda Evans, wife of Teddy Evans
Bertie John 'B.J.' Hodson, Central News Agency reporter
Joseph Kinsey, New Zealand expedition agent
Clements Markham, former president, Royal Geographical Society, supporter of Scott
Violet Oates, mother of Lawrence Oates
Kathleen Scott, wife of Captain Scott
Ernest Shackleton, explorer, member of Scott's *Discovery* expedition
Reginald Smith, cousin of Cherry-Garrard, Scott's publisher and friend of Scott and
    Wilson
Oriana Wilson, wife of Edward Wilson
George Wyatt, London expedition agent

Appendix B: Summary Timeline, 1910–19

This is not intended to be comprehensive, but to serve as a background guide
for readers

1910–1913

June 1910: *Terra Nova* expedition leaves London
January 1911: *Terra Nova* arrives in Antarctica
February 1911: *Terra Nova* leaves Cape Evans, Antarctica, for New Zealand
April–December 1911: Landing party lay depots; Antarctic winter; departure for
    South Pole
December 1911: Amundsen reaches South Pole
1912–13: Antarctic expeditions led by Douglas Mawson (Australia), Wilhelm Filchner
    (Germany) and Nobu Shirase (Japan)

January 1912: South Pole party reaches Pole
February–March 1912: *Terra Nova* returns to Cape Evans; leaves for New Zealand
January 1913: *Terra Nova* returns to Cape Evans
February 1913: *Terra Nova* arrives in New Zealand
June 1913: *Terra Nova* returns to Britain

1914

June: Assassination of Archduke Franz Ferdinand of Austria-Hungary
August: Britain declares war on Germany
August: Shackleton's *Endurance* expedition leaves for Antarctica
August–December: British and Allied troops establish Western Front in Europe

1915

Allied attempts to reach Constantinople/Istanbul through Dardanelles
Continuing fighting on Western and Eastern fronts
Shackleton's expedition in Antarctica

1916

Continuing fighting on both European fronts
31 May–1 June: Battle of Jutland, the major naval engagement of the war
November: Shackleton's men begin returning from Antarctica

1917

Continuing fighting on Western Front
March–December: Russian revolution, abdication of Tsar, outbreak of civil war
    between 'Reds' (Bolsheviks) and 'Whites'
April: The United States enters the war

1918

March: Russia signs peace treaty with Germany, with appendix relating to Spitsbergen
January–November: Final offensives on Western Front
November: Armistice signed on Western Front; surrender of German fleet

1919

January–June: Continued fighting in north Russia; Peace conference at Versailles, near
    Paris; final engagements in north Russia

Appendix C: Other Information

Terminology

Icebergs: large chunks (which can be miles long) of ice which have broken off ice shelves or glacier tongues; when an iceberg breaks it is said to 'calve' and gradually disintegrate into 'bergy bits'

Ice shelf: a wide glacier tongue; in this book it (or the word 'barrier') refers to the 400-mile-wide Ross Ice Shelf linking Ross Island (including Cape Evans) to the Beardmore Glacier and Antarctic plateau

Floe: smaller iceberg or 'pancake' of sea ice

Pack-ice ('the pack'):   dense ice covering the ocean, formed from a mixture of sea ice and small floes which have become detached from the land (including glaciers)

Small boat descriptions: A wide range of names are used for small boats used for off-shore or ship-to-shore transportation. The word 'tender' is a more generic term covering vessels of all sizes; others include skiff (lightly built, usually narrow), dinghy (usually with a sail, broader than a skiff) and pram (usually small).

Measurements

Measurements are those current at the time; detailed conversion tables can be found in diaries or online. Distances/speeds are in statute miles unless otherwise indicated. A knot (nautical or 'geographical' mile) equals about 1.15 statute miles/1.85 kilometres. Weights are shown in ounces (oz.), pounds (lbs), stones (1 stone = 14 lbs), etc. Temperatures: shown in degrees Fahrenheit (32°F = 0°C; 0°F = minus 18°C). Winds are shown in miles per hour (mph) or Beaufort scale 'Forces' e.g. Force 8 = strong gale, about 42 mph. Money is shown in pounds (£), shillings (s or /-) and pence (d); present-day equivalents can be obtained through published or web-based tables/calculators.

Names

Place names and spellings of the time are used: the most frequently used ones which have changed completely are Constantinople/Istanbul, Christiana/Oslo and Nyasaland/Malawi (and derivatives); those which vary slightly include Salonika/Thessaloniki and Spitzbergen/Spitsbergen.

Abbreviations

The following abbreviations are used in the text:

RFC:	Royal Flying Corps	**RNAS:**	Royal Naval Air Service
RN:	Royal Navy	**RND:**	Royal Naval Division

The names of well-known military decorations, such as VC for Victoria Cross, have sometimes been abbreviated; others are described in full.

Notes

Documents cited are from archival and private sources in Britain and other parts of the world including those cited in the Acknowledgements section at the beginning of this book. Information on one major source appears below; information on sources relating to specific chapters appears above the notes for that chapter. Every effort has been made to trace and obtain permission from owners and/or copyright holders of documents or images; I apologise for any inadvertent omissions and will, if notified through my publishers, endeavour to incorporate additional acknowledgements in future editions.

Key sources for chapters 1–6 are the journals of Lieutenant (later Commander) Harry L.L. Pennell, who served on the expedition both as navigator and acting captain of the *Terra Nova*. Three volumes of journals covering the period of this book are currently held by Canterbury Museum, Christchurch, New Zealand. The volume designated MS107, running from January 1911 to 1 November 1912, is Pennell's semi-official 'captain's log'. The two volumes designated MS433 run from January 1904 to February 1914 and include more personal observations on the expedition. Pennell also co-authored (with Edward 'Teddy' Evans) a report entitled 'Voyages of the *Terra Nova*', which was published in *Scott's Last Expedition*, Vol. II. I have no knowledge of any journal kept by Harry Pennell following his return to naval duties after the expedition.

I have referenced quotations from or information from Pennell's journals by date of journal entry; dates of the events mentioned are included, where necessary, in the text; I have not referenced widely known events or facts about the expedition (e.g. ports-of-call, locations in Antarctica). I have retained Pennell's use of names, spellings, etc., but have added occasional insertions (e.g. after a nickname) and clarifying punctuation marks (without an accompanying '[sic]' in the interests of fluency). Copies of Pennell's journals were provided by Canterbury Museum; permission to quote and incorporate information from them was kindly provided by them (Sarah Murray) and by David and Virginia Pennell, relatives of Harry Pennell.

In an effort to keep other notes to a manageable level, widely known or uncontested facts about Antarctic expeditions and the First World War are not referenced. Letters to and from Pennell and other expedition members are largely from the collections of the Scott Polar Research Institute ('SPRI') and Royal Geographical Society ('RGS'). Excerpts from documents with SPRI references appear by permission of the University of Cambridge, Scott Polar Research Institute. Where references to books and journals are by short-form title, full details are in the bibliography.

Where a number of newspaper reports have clearly been based on one news agency cable I have cited one or more representative reports; similarly, where many newspapers covered the same event I have generally cited reports from newspapers (e.g. *The Times*, British regional newspapers, Christchurch's *The Press* and other New Zealand newspapers) whose past editions are readily available on electronic databases through libraries or subscription services. Occasionally I have quoted local newspapers (particularly from Cheltenham) or newspapers in my personal possession.

Family and service records have been accessed through www.ancestry.co.uk, the National Archives, Kew and similar sources.

Prologue

1. This incident was related by Gran in his memoirs of the *Terra Nova* expedition, *Tryggve Gran's Antarctic Diary, 1910–13*, and his war experiences, *Under the British Flag*; it is also referred to in Limb and Cordingley, *Captain Oates*, p. 140, and Smith, *I Am Just Going Outside*, pp. 143–4.

1. Southward Ho!

Information on Pennell's early naval career is from sources including David Pennell (Pennell's great-nephew), Pennell's journals, 'Harry Pennell: Scott's Navigator' and 'From the South Pole to Jutland' (articles by Chris Bingham).

1. MS433, 2 August 1909.
2. MS433, 3 and 23 June 1910.
3. Wright, 1993, p. 27.
4. MS433, 23 June 1910 (a long entry written during a stop in Madeira).
5. MS433, 2 October 1910.
6. MS433, 29 November 1910.
7. MS433, 2 October 1910.
8. MS433, 26 October 1910.
9. MS433, 27 December 1910 and 14 April 1911.
10. The incident relating to Rennick was mentioned by Frank Debenham in *The Times*, 26 November 1960.

11. In the Southern Ocean, the 'Roaring Forties' are followed (when sailing south) by the 'Furious Fifties', 'Screaming (or Shrieking) Sixties' and 'Silent Seventies'.
12. MS433, 26 October 1910.
13. MS433, 6 July 1910.
14. Bruce, 1932, p. 6.
15. MS433, 2 October 1910; Strathie, p. 82.
16. There are references to Rennick and the pianola in Scott, *Journals*, entry of 20 January 1911, p. 99, Ponting, *The Great White South,* pp. 23, 129–30, Evans, *South with Scott*, pp. 77–8, and Taylor, pp. 233ff., and on www.pianola.org.
17. MS107, 30 January 1911.
18. The Bay of Whales was discovered and named by Shackleton during the *Nimrod* expedition.
19. MS107, 3–4 February 1911.
20. MS107, 8 February 1911.
21. MS433, 13 February 1911.
22. MS107 (21–22 February 1911); 'The Voyages of the Terra Nova' report (22 February 1911) in Scott, *Scott's Last Expedition*, Vol. II, p. 361; Bruce, *Reminiscences of the* Terra Nova *in the Antarctic.*
23. MS107, 25–26 February 1911.
24. MS107, 28 February–1 March 1911. Coal trimming involves moving the coal around so it does not cause the ship to list but is ready for use in the engine rooms.
25. MS107, 3 March 1911.
26. MS107, 28 March 1911, Pennell's final journal entry covering that voyage.
27. 'While she swims I'll cook' refers to an expression used by Podmore, the cook on Joseph Conrad's fictional ship *Narcissus*.
28. This and subsequent information on the expeditions of Filchner and Mawson are from Turney, *1912: The Year the World Discovered Antarctica* and contemporary newspaper reports.
29. *Evening Post* (Christchurch), 29 March 1911 and other newspapers.
30. MS107, 9 July to 10 October 1911 covers this period.
31. MS433, 11 July 1911.
32. The islands were discovered and named in January 1643 by Dutch explorer Abel Tasman, 3 weeks after he became the first known European to see New Zealand.
33. The wreck of the *Elingamite* and its aftermath were extensively reported in New Zealand newspapers.
34. The *Aurora*, like the *Discovery* and *Terra Nova*, was built in Dundee.

2. Battling Through the Pack

1. MS107, 15 December 1911, and MS433, 5 December 1911.
2. Pennell to Dennistoun, 7 and 11 October 1911, published in Dennistoun, *The Peaks & Passes of J.R.D.*, pp. 212–14.
3. *Scott's Last Expedition*, Vol. II, p. 373.
4. The mules, supplied courtesy of the army in India, replaced ponies which had not been expected to survive the first season on the ice.
5. MS107, 30 December 1911.
6. MS107, 1–8 January 1912.
7. The Northern Party's experiences are described in more detail in Campbell and Hooper.
8. MS107, 9–18 January 1912.
9. MS107, 21–3 January 1912.
10. MS107, 4 February 1912.

11. Strathie, chapter 14; May and Airrless, 'Could Captain Scott have been saved?'.
12. The implications of Meares' late return to Cape Evans and early 1912 departure for New Zealand are referred to in May and Airrless, 'Could Captain Scott have been saved?'.
13. Meares' rescue was described in the *Oregon News*, 23 September 1914. No other references to it have been found, suggesting that Meares told few people about it. The experience may also have contributed to Meares' reluctance to leave Cape Evans for One Ton Depot after the *Terra Nova* had been sighted in early 1912.
14. Ponting, *The Great White South*, p. 4.
15. Ibid., chapter 21.
16. MS107, 11 February 1912.
17. Atkinson to Pennell, 26 October 1911, RGS/HLP/2/2.
18. Bowers to Pennell, 16 and 18 October 1911, RGS/HLP/2/6 and /7.
19. Scott to Pennell, October 1911, RGS/HLP/2/15.
20. Evans to Pennell, 23 October 1911, RGS/HLP/2/10.
21. Emperor penguins, unlike other penguin species, lay their eggs in winter on Antarctic sea ice.
22. MS107, 16 February 1912.
23. The IMD's Director had fallen ill (M. E. Crewe, 2009, *The Met Office Grows Up: In War and Peace*, available at www.rmets.org/sites/default/files/hist08.pdf).
24. Pennell to Wilson, 27 February 1912, RGS/HLP/2/14.
25. MS433, 3 March 1912.

3. Breaking News – and a Mysterious Death

1. MS433, 10 March 1912; this is the last entry in this journal until 18 May in Lyttelton.
2. MS107, 20 March 1912.
3. MS107, 24 March 1912.
4. MS107, 29 March 1912.
5. Pennell to Emily Bowers, 30 March 1912 (SPRI/MS1505/7/2/13) and to Lois Evans, 1 April 1912 (quoted in *Hawera & Normanby Star*, 29 March 1913).
6. MS107, 1 and 3 April 1912 (the last entries until 1 November 1912).
7. Ponting, *The Great White South*, p. 262.
8. Information on Central News Agency ('CNA'), B.J. Hodson and CNA colleagues from Simonis, *The Street of Ink*, and newspapers.
9. Taylor, p. 434.
10. Unused rail passes, including those for members of South Pole party and other members of the landing party still in the south, are held by the Auckland War Memorial Museum.
11. *The Times*, 1 April 1912.
12. *The Press*, 6 April 1912.
13. Information on the homeward voyages of expedition members is from MS433, 3 April 1912, and published ships' passenger lists (www.ancestry.co.uk) and newspaper reports.
14. Dennistoun, *The Peaks and Passes of J.R.D.*, p. 11.
15. Evans, *South with Scott*, chapter 11, p. 162.
16. *The Press*, 23 April 1912.
17. *Hawera & Normanby Star*, 26 April 1912.
18. MS433, 18 May 1912.
19. Dennistoun, *The Peaks and Passes of J.R.D.*, p. 11.
20. Bruce to Lillian Knowles, 11 June 1912 (DSS1–7, Glamorgan Archive, Cardiff); *The Press*, 5 June 1912.

21. Events at French Pass and Elmslie Bay are covered in MS433 (entries 16 June to 21 September 1912) and in MS107 (in one entry, 1 November 1912).

22. MS433, 12 July 1912. Speyer, a wealthy businessman, philanthropist and Privy Councillor, had supported both of Scott's expeditions; his career is covered in Lenton (2013) *Banker, Traitor, Scapegoat, Spy? The Troublesome Case of Sir Edgar Speyer*, London: Haus Publishing.

23. French for holiday, *congé* is Pennell's euphemism for being dismissed.

24. MS433, 4 August 1912.

25. Brissenden's death and the inquest are described in: MS433, 21 August 1912; the coroner's report, COR1912/856 (kindly supplied by Archives New Zealand); an account by William Burton (copy kindly supplied by his grandson Robin Burton); local newspaper reports.

26. Young, *A Great Task of Happiness*, p. 141.

27. *Timaru Herald*, 31 October 1912.

4. Final Journeys

Pennell's journal MS107 concludes with his entry of 1 November 1912. Events in the following chapters are described in his journal MS433 (from the entry of 26 October 1912 onwards) and in memoirs and biographies including those by Cherry-Garrard, Bruce and Evans (*South with Scott*).

1. MS433, 26 October 1912.

2. MS433, 21 November 1912.

3. Teddy and Hilda Evans had been visiting friend and expedition supporter Daniel Radcliffe, a leading member of Cardiff's civic and business community. The king, visiting on the Royal Yacht, had invited Evans aboard to give him a first-hand account of the expedition's progress, following which he promoted Evans to Commander (Johnson, 'Scott of the Antarctic and Cardiff').

4. MS107, 1 November 1912.

5. Elizabeth Acland was born in June 1913; she was brought up in New Zealand, then moved to England, where she married an Englishman, John Pavey; she later returned to live in New Zealand, where she died in Timaru in the mid-1970s.

6. *The Times*, 14, 16 and 22 November 1912; Cheltenham local newspapers.

7. MS433, 15 December 1912. It is not clear whether it struck Pennell or others that this was the anniversary of Amundsen reaching the South Pole.

8. MS433, 23 December 1912.

9. Pennell's mother was a widow, his father having died in September 1907.

10. MS433, 28 December 1912.

11. MS433, 2 January 1913.

12. MS433, 3 January 1913.

13. MS433, 5 February 1913.

14. The words were suggested by Cherry-Garrard, who lent Wilson his copy of Tennyson's *In Memoriam* to take on the South Pole journey (Seaver, *Edward Wilson of the Antarctic*, p. 272, and elsewhere); Tennyson wrote part of *In Memoriam* in Wilson's home town of Cheltenham.

15. MS433, 23 January 1913.

16. Pennell originally wrote 'any effect' but changed it to 'this effect'.

17. By the time the blizzard set in Scott had been unable to walk due to a badly frostbitten foot, but he had continued to write his journal almost to the end (likely to have been the

last days of March 1912). The three men died from lack of food and fuel (needed to melt snow and ice into water) and the cold.

18. Cherry-Garrard, Gran, Nelson, Lashly, Crean, Hooper, Williamson, Keohane and Demitri Gerof were all in the search party.

19. Debenham, *In the Antarctic*, chapter entitled 'Icebergs'.

5. From Oamaru to Awliscombe

1. MS433, 13 March 1913, which covers from 7 February (landing at Oamaru) to leaving for Britain in April; *Terra Nova Arrives at Oamaru* (www.nzhistory.net.nz/media/photo/ night-watchmans-hut-oamaru, Ministry for Culture and Heritage) is one of many other accounts of the landing.

2. Opinions vary as to the number of cables sent from Oamaru and/or Christchurch to London. Pennell refers to one to Kinsey from Oamaru and one to Central News Agency (CNA) from Kinsey's Christchurch office; the report co-authored by Pennell and Evans (*Scott's Last Expedition*, Vol II, pp. 359–407) refers to a 'Commander's cable' from Oamaru to CNA and one encoded cable from Christchurch; Kinsey refers to subsequent cables sent from his office; Jones (*The Last Great Quest*, chapter 4) suggests three cables; historian David Harrowfield of Oamaru, New Zealand, also refers to a series of cables.

3. Scott wrote to Kinsey on 28 October 1911 (Kinsey papers, Alexander Turnbull Library, Wellington) suggesting he did not want Evans to be in charge of the expedition in the event of Scott being delayed (see also Wheeler, *Cherry: A Life of Apsley Cherry-Garrard*, p. 132). The situation regarding leadership was overtaken by events, including Evans' scurvy and promotion and Scott's death.

4. New Zealand newspaper reports, 7 March 1913.

5. MS433, 4–21 March 1913.

6. The expression 'splice the main brace' is used colloquially to mean allowing an extra drink but refers to a difficult repair sometimes needed on sailing ships, following which those involved would be rewarded with an extra 'tot'.

7. MS433, 28 March 1913.

8. MS433, 8 April 1913.

9. Pennell to Atkinson, April 1913, RGS/HLP/2/5.

10. MS433, 15–26 April 1913.

11. MS433, 1 May 1913.

12. Sir Roger Casement, who served as a diplomat in Africa and South America, was investigating malpractices by a British-registered company operating rubber plantations in Peru. He left the diplomatic service later in 1913 to concentrate on obtaining independence for Ireland.

13. Sir William Haggard was the elder brother of Rider Haggard, author of *King Solomon's Mine* and other popular books of the time.

14. MS433, 5 May 1913.

15. MS433, 18 May to 1 June 1913.

16. MS433, 4 June 1913.

17. MS433, 6 July 1913.

18. 24 June is the feast day of St John the Baptist.

19. Henry Lyons (1864–1944) was also a member of the RGS and a Fellow of the Royal Society; he went on to serve as temporary director of the Meteorological Officer and Director of the Science Museum, in which role he sought to make the museum more accessible to children and non-scientists.

20. *The Times*, 1 July 1913.

21. MS433, 6 August 1913.

22. *The Times*, 27 June 1913, refers to a ball of the previous evening (i.e. 26 June); Pennell's journal entry (6 July) suggests 23 June but no reference to a similar ball that week has been traced. The fact that Pennell's name was not listed in *The Times* suggests only that he was not on a guest list issued by the palace before he returned to Britain.

23. The four-act play, first performed in March 1913, was adapted from Bennett's own novel *Buried Alive*. The plot is centred on a world-famous but shy painter who takes on the identity of his dead valet but is unmasked when he paints a portrait of his wife (with whom his valet had previously corresponded through a matrimonial agency). The 'prop' portrait was painted by Sir William Nicholson, a well-known portraitist and father of painter Ben Nicholson.

24. Details from Canadian 1911 census and some pre-1910 entries in Pennell's journal.

25. Pennell's journal MS433, 6 August 1913, *The Times*, Naval and Award Rolls (www.ancestry.co.uk) and Taylor.

26. Clasps were given to those who already had been awarded polar medals.

27. Jones (chapter 8).

28. It is unclear whether Clissold's absence was due to the after-effects of his accident in Antarctica or another ailment.

29. James Montagu Wyatt was the son of a senior civil servant in the War Office and descended from a long line of well-known Anglo-Irish architects, including James Wyatt (1746–1813), the main rival to Robert Adam. 'Miss Wyatt' is Wyatt's elder sister, Katherine Montagu Wyatt, a professional artist. 'Treves' is almost certainly Frederick Boileau Treves (1880–1938), the son of Dr William Treves (1843–1908, an eminent surgeon and physician of Margate) and nephew of Sir Frederick Treves (1853–1923, whose patients included King Edward VII and John Merrick). Frederick Boileau Treves studied medicine at Caius College, Cambridge (as did Edward Wilson); after working in London for several years he returned to Margate to work with his father (*British Medical Journal* obituary and Royal College of Surgeons website).

30. MS433, 22 August 1913.

31. MS433, 4 September 1913. The murals Pennell refers to are still visible in the old church at Oddington.

32. MS433, 17 September 1913.

33. MS433, 22 September 1913.

34. MS433, 24 September and 13 October 1913.

35. MS433, 27 October 1913.

36. MS433, 6 November 1913.

37. A young naval officer's salary was not sufficient to support a wife and family; Pennell, like Scott and Bowers, had a widowed mother and sisters to consider.

38. Jones, *The Last Great Quest*, pp. 139–40 (Evans' predecessors were Stanley, Nansen, Scott, Shackleton and Peary); *The Times*, 22 May 1913 (which lists those present).

39. *The Times*, 10 June 1913.

40. Evans to Emily Bowers, 24 September 1913, SPRI/MS1505/7/2/10.

41. Lecture poster, Jones, p.171.

42. Smith, *I Am Just Going Outside*, chapter 25; Limb and Cordingley, *Captain Oates: Soldier and Explorer*, chapter 11; newspaper reports.

43. RGS journals; *The Times*, 11 November 1913.

44. Information on Mawson's expedition from Turney and Riffenburgh, *Racing with Death*.

45. *Scott's Last Expedition*, p. 622 and Scott, *Journals*, p. 434 and note.

46. Letters quoted from among several which appeared in *The Times* on 4, 7, 8 and 10 November 1913.

47. Jesse Boot had, as a boy, worked in his parents' herbalist shop in Nottingham; the lavish wedding was reported in *The Times* (26 November 1913) and several regional papers; company information from Boots' website.
48. MSS 433, 7 December 1913.
49. *The Times*, 11 December 1913, p.11.
50. MSS 433, 28 December 1913.

6. Ring Out the Old, Ring In the New

The words of the title are a line from Tennyson's *In Memoriam* (see note 14 to chapter 4).

1. MS 433, 18 January and 2 February 1914.
2. MS 433, 24 February 1914.
3. The encounter is described in Huntford, *Shackleton*, pp. 355–7.
4. MS 433, 24 February 1914.
5. By 1914 the Northern Exploration Company ('NEC') and its principals 'staked out' large areas of Spitsbergen, the largest island of the Svalbard archipelago. Spitsbergen was a 'condominium' or '*terris nullis*', which belonged to no country so was subject to claims by explorers, prospectors and investors from, inter alia, Britain, Norway, Sweden, Germany and Russia. William Speirs Bruce (whose *Scotia* Antarctic expedition coincided with Scott's *Discovery* expedition) co-founded the Scottish Spitsbergen Syndicate in 1907; Shackleton was reported in 1911 as contemplating an expedition to Spitsbergen, although this came to nothing. Norway, the nearest country to Spitsbergen, organised conferences in 1910 and 1912 to try to resolve ownership and governance of the island, which Russia at one point tried to annex. Campbell's involvement with NEC is mentioned in Barr et al., *Gold, or I'm a Dutchman* (pp. 126–7) and Kruse (pp. 266–7); his and Barne's 1914 expedition is covered by Erskine, 'Victor Campbell and Michael Barne in Svalbard', and in the introduction to Campbell, *The Wicked Mate*. Information on the NEC's activities also regularly appeared in the newspapers.
6. The UMCA (as it was known) had been founded by members of the Anglican Church at the universities of Oxford, Cambridge, Durham and Dublin in response to a plea by David Livingstone for support for the establishment of mission stations in Zanzibar and Nyasaland (now Malawi).
7. The schistosomiasis (or bilharzia) group of diseases (caused by the parasites Atkinson was investigating) rank second only to malaria in terms of numbers infected worldwide, particularly in Africa and the Far East.
8. *The Times*, 2–27 February 1914.
9. MS 433, 24 February 1914.
10. This is the concluding passage of the last entry in journal MS433. It is not known whether Pennell, who had kept a journal for at least the previous ten years, decided to stop doing so or whether he began another journal.
11. Ponting's letter is quoted in part (without source details) in Arnold, *Herbert Ponting*, pp. 32–3; Francis Drake, recognising Ponting's handwriting, would have returned the letter unopened (Dennistoun, *Peaks & Passes*, pp. 215–6, refers to Drake opening Dennistoun's letter due to not recognising the writing.)
12. *The Looker-On*, 14 February 1914.
13. Ibid., 31 January 1914.
14. *The Times*, 13 May 1914.
15. *The Looker-On*, 30 May, 6 June 1914.

16. *The Looker-On*, 30 May 1914

17. This and other details of the *Duke of Edinburgh's* activities are taken from the ship's log (www.naval-history.net).

18. Pennell to Captain Ramsay, 26 April 1914, ref. 2012/437, Waitaki District Libraries and Archive, Oamaru, New Zealand.

19. Information on the wedding (in St Margaret's Church, Westminster) is from public records, New Zealand newspaper reports and Ponting, *The Great White South*, pp. 129–30.

20. Pennell to Wright, 7 May 1914 (auctioned on 20 September 2011 by Charles Leski Auctions, lot 69).

21. Pennell is alluding to the Franco-British Entente Cordiale (1904).

22. Strange and Bashford, *Griffith Taylor*, pp. 72–6; Sanderson, *Griffith Taylor*, pp. 87–92.

23. *The Times*, 18 November 1913.

24. Speak, *Deb – Geographer, Scientist, Antarctic Explorer*, p. 11.

25. *Washington Post*, 14 March 1914, p. 14.

26. *Our Mutual Girl*, IMDb website; the denial was reported in several newspapers, including in Australia and New Zealand.

27. Newspaper reports, church website and details on Christie's website of Scott's Antwerp medal (www.christies.com).

28. Wheeler, *Cherry*, chapter 8.

29. Rodin sought refuge in Britain in autumn 1914, when Paris appeared under threat from German invasion. He initially (at the suggestion of close friends from Paris) based himself in Cheltenham, arriving in October 1914, three months after the unveiling of the statue of Wilson. Rodin would have passed the statue by his erstwhile pupil every morning on his way from his lodgings to the Town Hall, where war news was posted up. Whilst in Cheltenham Rodin wept when he read about the destruction of Rheims Cathedral and other beautiful medieval buildings in France. Rodin's *Kiss* was shown in Cheltenham's Art Gallery and Museum (The Wilson) in the 1930s (for several years) and again in 2014 (the centenary of his visit).

30. Young, *A Great Task of Happiness*, chapters 11–18.

31. Newspaper reports including *Daily Mail* and *The Times*; Cruden Bay website, www. crudenbay.org.uk.

32. Caird was also well connected in literary and artistic circles through his wife, Sophie Gray, the sister of Effie Gray, who had been married both to John Ruskin (an artist much admired by Edward Wilson) and John Everett Millais.

33. Shackleton, *The Heart of the Antarctic* and *South* (2007, Wordswoth Editions Ltd version), Preface.

34. Haddelsey, chapter 7.

7. From Arctic to Antwerp

1. Erskine, 'Victor Campbell and Michael Barne in Svalbard', pp. 120–21; additional information on Spitsbergen from Kruse, *Frozen Assets*, and Barr et al. *Gold, or I'm a Dutchman* and newspaper reports.

2. Campbell had retired from active naval service soon after his marriage but often travelled partly, it is reported, due to his wife's depression following the drowning, during a family holiday in Norway, of her sister.

3. Kruse, pp. 244–5; *The Press* (Christchurch), 28 August 1913.

4. Sellers, *The Hood Battalion*, p. 8.

5. Quotations from newspapers are from the many reports based on the dispatches of 'B.J.' Hodson of Central News Agency; given the reports are virtually identical they are not

individually cited but can be found by searching for Hodson's byline on the British Newspaper Archive website.

6. Descriptions of the siege of Antwerp are drawn from published and publicly available sources including Sellers, *The Hood Battalion*, and *Royal Naval Division Journals*; the latter includes detailed accounts of the siege by Campbell and others which were given at a later enquiry (National Archives, ADM116/1814).

7. For more information on Kelly's early life see Kelly, *Race Against Time*, and the Australian Dictionary of National Biography (available at http://adb.anu.edu.au). By coincidence Kelly was living in 29 Queen Anne Street at the same time as Pennell and Atkinson were living in 15 Queen Anne Street; in a journal entry of 13 October 1913 Kelly (*Race Against Time*, p. 304) refers to checking to ensure that his piano playing would not be heard by 'the doctors', as the building was not to be used 'as a studio for music, singing lessons or other noise purpose'.

8. Kelly's donation to the expedition is mentioned in Kelly, *Race Against Time*, p. 20; Kelly, *Kelly's War*, pp. 20-47 cover the period during which Kelly served under Campbell in Drake Battalion before joining Hood Battaltion.

8. 'Antarctics' on the Seven Seas

The 'Seven Seas' is used generically here as it has been used at different times and in different areas of the world to refer to a number of seas and oceans. Details of the *Duke of Edinburgh*'s voyages are from the ship's log (www.naval-history.net).

1. Strathie, chapter 4.

2. The engagement on Lake Nyasa (now known as Lake Malawi) is described in articles by Janie Hampton ('Victory in Nyasaland', *History Today*, July 2014) and Tom Rowley ('First World War centenary: the battle on Lake Malawi', *Daily Telegraph*, 6 July 2014).

3. Detailed casualty figures are not given in this book as they would not have been known by those involved in engagements until considerably later, if at all.

4. On his return to Britain in June 1913 Burton joined HMS *Pembroke* at Chatham, was promoted to stoker petty officer, married his long-term girlfriend Florence Cott, set up home in Gillingham, Kent, and joined the *Lowestoft*, a newly commissioned light cruiser. Early in the war the *Lowestoft* sank the German merchant ship *Fernbellin*.

5. Guly, 'George Murray Levick (1876–1956)'.

6. Details of the sinking of the three ships appeared in numerous newspaper reports and in Admiralty documents ADM137/47, /2081 and /2232 and ADM1/8396/356.

7. Learning to swim was not a specific part of naval training.

8. Casualty lists and official reports were usually published in *The Times*, sometimes in piecemeal fashion, usually (but not always) within a few days of the relevant engagement.

9. *Manchester Evening News*, 28 September 1914; Rennick's death was also described in *T P's Journal of Great Deeds of the Great War* (reported in *Otago Daily Times*, 23 March 1915).

10. *New Zealand Herald*, 10 December 1914, and *The Press*, 18 August and 27 November 1914.

11. Ibid.

12. The *Mohawk*'s sister ships included the *Amazon*, the *Cossack* and the *Maori*. Evans wrote extensively about his wartime experiences, including in *Keeping the Seas* and *An Adventurous Life*.

13. *The Times*, 4 November 1914.

14. The ships were given Turkish names but British publications (now as then) tend to use the original names.

15. A description of this event can be found in Nick van der Bijl (2014), *British Military Operations in Aden and Radfan: 100 Years of British Colonial Rule*, Pen and Sword Books, chapter 3.

9. Cavalry Officers, Chateaux and Censors

Letters quoted are in the Cecil Meares Fonds (MS0455), British Columbia Archives, Vancouver, Canada. Information on the Northumberland Hussars is from the regimental war diary (National Archives, WO95/1542/1), 'A Brief History of the Northumberland (Hussars) Yeomanry Cavalry, 1819–1918' (www.bailiffgatemuseum.co.uk) and Howard Pease, *A Brief History of the Northumberland (Hussars) Yeomanry Cavalry, 1819–1918*.

1. Meares to Spengler, undated letter from Lyndhurst camp.
2. Meares to Spengler, 9 October 1914.
3. 'Uhlans' were originally Polish light cavalry, armed with lances, sabres and pistols. The title became used more generically for lancer cavalry regiments in the Prussian (later German), Austrian and Russian armies.
4. General Sydney Lawford, Commanding Officer of 22nd Brigade (nicknamed 'Swanky Syd') was the father of actor Peter Lawford.
5. Huge howitzer shells which, on impact, issue clouds of yellow smoke.
6. Meares to Spengler, undated; based on its order in the Fonds, the address ('A Chateau', with the rest of address scribbled through), and the reference to Major Johnston was probably written on 23 October 1914. Hooge chateau (not a castle in the British sense) was owned by Baron Gaston de Vinck, who continued living there until his home was rendered uninhabitable by Germany shelling.
7. Additional information on Lawrence Johnston from Pearson, *Hidcote*.
8. Meares to Spengler, 29 October 1914.
9. 'Disaster at Hooge', Western Front Association 2012 newsletter (Commonwealth War Graves Commission www.cwgc.org).
10. Ponting to Spengler, 2 November 1914 (also Fonds Cecil Meares).
11. Hodson's reports on Indian troops appeared in *Manchester Courier* (27 October 1914) and *Liverpool Echo* (10 November 1914).
12. Meares to Spengler, 7 November 1914. The word 'Destroy' has been written on the letter but the fact it is in the Fonds suggests it was returned to Meares rather than destroyed.
13. Meares to Spengler, 9 November 1914.
14. The Artists' Rifles included many young men who had recently left public schools or university. Oxford Circus was a trench system near Arras.
15. Meares to Spengler, 13 November 1914.
16. Meares to Spengler, 15, 19 and 26 November 1914.
17. Roberts died of pneumonia at St Omer on 14 November 1914.
18. Meares to Spengler, 7–14 December 1914 (three letters, one of which is undated).
19. When Meares attended Ayr Academy as a boy he had stayed with Mrs Agnes MacDougall, his step-aunt (sister of his father's late second wife); Agnes MacDougall (who by 1914 was married to Rev. James MacDougall, a writer and publisher of Scottish folk tales) had previously been married to a French-born architect Charles de Boinville. 'Mrs Meares' of Edinburgh is Meares' father's third wife.
20. Baker, *The Truce*, and Brown and Seaton, *Christmas Truce: the Western Front, December 1914*, both refer to the Hussars' involvement, which is also evidenced by Harold Robson's photographs in the Imperial War Museum.

21. *London Gazette*, 15 April 1915, and forces records cards (National Archives).

10. Your Country Needs You!

1. Cherry-Garrard, chapters 8 and 9.
2. Speak, p. 11; Priestley, 'Wireless Memories'.
3. The other applicant was Oates.
4. Wheeler, *Cherry*, chapter 8. See also Luci Gosling, 'Messenger Dogs: Lieutenant-Col. Richardson and the British War Dog School' (www.maryevans.com blog); 'Setting up the British War Dog School' (www.bbc.co.uk), E.H. Richardson (1920), *British War Dogs, Their Training and Psychology* (https://archive.org/details/britishwardogsth00richrich).
5. Evelyn Cherry-Garrard to Farrer, 18 August 1914, D/EHR/Z8/111.
6. Cherry-Garrard to Farrer, 23 August 1914, D/EHR/Z8/122.
7. Cherry-Garrard to Farrer, 28 August 1914, D/EHR/Z8/127. Wealthy individuals sometimes offered, or agreed when asked, to put their luxury yachts at the disposal of the government; the *Sheelah*, owned by Lady Beatty, the wife of Admiral David Beatty and daughter of Chicago retailer Marshall Field, was one example.
8. Edie Bowers to Emily Bowers (undated) October, 8 November 1914, SPRI/MS1505/5/1–2; *The British Journal of Nursing*, 31 October 1914 (pp. 345–6).
9. Although I have an aversion to 'spoilers' I would like to reassure readers that Edie Bowers (who makes no further appearance in this book) returned safely to Britain; after a long career as a nurse she retired to Scotland, where she died in her 80s. It is thanks to her that her brother's papers were preserved and are now in the archives of the Scott Polar Research Institute.

11. From Blandford Camp Towards Byzantium

1. Freyberg, chapters 2 to 4.
2. Marsh (*Rupert Brooke*, p. cxxxi) provides Brooke's impressions of fellow officers, including Freyberg.
3. Hedderwick was a distant cousin of Ethel ('Maynie') Hedderwick (see chapter 13).
4. The 'Coterie' also included offspring of the 'Souls', a group of intellectuals and politicians which included the prime minister's second wife (and Arthur Asquith's step-mother), Margot Asquith.
5. Quoted in Sellers, *Hood Battalion*, pp. 37–8.
6. Hassall, *Rupert Brooke*, p. 493.
7. Kelly, *Kelly's War*, journal entry 25 March 1915, pp. 64–5.
8. Sellers (*Hood Battalion*, p. 56) suggests this was a feint intended to divert the Turks from the Dardanelles.
9. Hassall, pp. 495–9; Sellers, *Hood Battalion*, p. 58. It is unclear whether they did discuss poetry or whether Brooke did not want to admit to his friends that Hamilton had encouraged him to accept a staff job (a suggestion which Asquith regularly rejected).
10. From a fragment written in early/mid-April 1915 and quoted in Sellers, *Hood Battalion*, p. 62, and the Rupert Brooke Society website (http://www.rupertbrooke.com/).
11. Kelly, *Kelly's War*, journal entry 14 April 1915, p. 71.
12. *The Times*, 5 April 1915.
13. Information on 'The Soldier' from various sources including Bridget Spiers (Blandford Forum) and Jeff Cooper (Friends of the Dymock Poets).

14. As a guide, 'normal' temperature in an adult is around 98.4°F (37°C).
15. Kelly described events in his journal entries of 23 and 24 April 1915 (Kelly, *Race Against Time*, pp. 381–2).
16. Freyberg, pp. 54–5.
17. Page, chapter 5; Sellers, *Hood Battalion*, chapter 10.
18. Kelly, *Kelly's War*, journal entry of 6 May 1915, pp. 94–5.
19. Page, p. 48.
20. Dr McCracken has been suggested as the author of this often-quoted poem (Sellers, *Hood Battalion*, quotes the poem on pp. 99–100, noting that a copy of it is in McCracken's papers), but references to him as 'Doc' leave the question open; references to casualties place it between 9 May and 3 June (the lack of reference to Freyberg's wound may be for poetic reasons).
21. Members of the 'original' Hawke, Benbow and Collingwood battalions were still under detention in Holland and Germany.
22. Sellers, *Hood Battalion*, chapter 11.
23. His name is also sometimes spelled Crauford-Stuart.

12. Crossing Paths and Keeping in Touch

1. George and Valerie Skinner's website and books provide full details of William Lashly's career (see https://sites.google.com/site/lashlyantarcticexplorer/).
2. Guly, 'George Murray Levick'.
3. Atkinson's report of 13 October 1915, WO95/4290 (from *RND Journal*), Guly, 'Edward Leicester Atkinson'.
4. Atkinson to Cherry-Garrard, 30 September 1915, SPRI/MS559/24/18.
5. Atkinson to Cherry-Garrard, 4 December 1915, SPRI/MS559/24/19.
6. *Sydney Morning Herald*, 18 August 1915.
7. University of Sydney remembrance book, available at www.beyond1914.sydney.edu.au.
8. *London Gazette* No. 29214, 2 July 1915, Gallipoli Campaign.
9. Evans to Daniel Radcliffe, 25 December 1915, Cardiff Central Library, MS3.781.
10. The church was bombed in 1941 (and not rebuilt). St Ermin's was, like many London hotels, partly used as government and related offices during the war.
11. Some newspapers list Rennick as being present; his widow lived in London, so she may have been there.
12. Atkinson to Cherry-Garrard, 1 January 1916, SPRI/MS559/24/20.
13. Atkinson to Cherry-Garrard, 6 January 1916, SPRI/MS559/24/21.
14. Atkinson to Cherry-Garrard, 1 February 1916, SPRI/MS559/24/24.
15. Atkinson to Cherry-Garrard, 17 March 1916, SPRI/MS559/24/27. The 'ship' was the luxury yacht *Liberty*. Originally built for millionaire American publisher Joseph Pulitzer, it had been purchased in 1913 by millionaire Courtney Morgan, Viscount Tredegar, from whom the government had requisitioned it.
16. Atkinson to Cherry-Garrard, 20 March 1916, SPRI/MS559/24/28.
17. Atkinson to Cherry-Garrard, 21 April 1916, SPRI/MS559/24/29.

13. The 'Big Show' – and a Great Loss

There is (for obvious reasons) no ship's log for HMS *Queen Mary* covering most of this period. Information is drawn from sources including Pennell's correspondence, articles by

Christopher Bilham and other publications cited or listed in the biography and publicly available information.

1. *Otago Daily Times*, 28 April 1915. Pennell does not specifically mention these events in letters held in archive collections, but news of the birth of Rennick's son is likely to have been communicated through the 'Antarctics' network.
2. Pennell to Cherry-Garrard, 17 December 1915, SPRI/MS559/101/5.
3. Pennell sent William Burton a bible for his son Lewin (confirmed by Lewin Burton's grandson).
4. Pennell to Cherry-Garrard, 17 December 1915, SPRI/MS559/101/5.
5. Pennell to Emily Bowers, Spinks auction, 14 July 1910 (part of lot 1858).
6. Atkinson to Cherry-Garrard, 8 March 1916, SPRI/MS559/24/26.
7. *Cheltenham & Gloucester Graphic*, 17 April 1915.
8. Information on Hodson brothers from sources including *Gloucester Journal*, 21 August 1915.
9. Although James writes unfavourably about Prowse in his biography of Hall he does not, for unknown reasons, mention Pennell, despite having served with him for several months at a crucial time in the history of the Grand Fleet.
10. James' father-in-law noted in his diary (11 July 1915, soon after his daughter married James): 'It appears that James is getting himself disliked, or rather has a bad name for being constantly onshore. This failing is of long standing. He apparently has the young Lieutenant's view that days off are days when one must go onshore, a very unfortunate view in the case of a Commander.' (DFF/15, National Maritime Museum, quoted in Dreadnought Project biography of James.)
11. Two men had in fact been blown clear and were captured by the Germans.
12. Atkinson to Cherry-Garrard, 5 June 1916, SPRI/MS559/24/31.
13. Atkinson to Cherry-Garrard, 25 May 1916, SPRI/MS559/24/30.
14. Atkinson to Cherry-Garrard, 12 June 1916, SPRI/MS559/24/32.

14. Deaths on the Western Front

Information sources include Swales, Sellers (*Hood Battalion, Death for Desertion, RND Journal*), Page, Freyberg, service and other publicly available records.

1. F.S. Kelly's journal entry (unpublished), 1 March 1916 (information from Thérèse Radic).
2. F.S. Kelly's journal entry (unpublished), 3 March 1916 (information from Thérèse Radic).
3. Confirmed by a member of Nelson's family (2014).
4. Kelly, *Kelly's War*, journal entry of 6 17 May 1916 (pp. 212–13).
5. Sellers, *Hood Battalion*, p. 168; Page, p. 86. Nelson's presence is mentioned by Kelly in his journal entry of 16 September 1916 (Kelly, *Kelly's War*, p. 261–2).
6. Page, p. 87.
7. A.P. Herbert went on to become a famous writer, humourist, satirist and Member of Parliament.
8. From General Sir Ian Hamilton's dispatch of 11 December 1915.
9. Sellers, *Death for Desertion*, p. 52.
10. The attack on Beaucourt is described in considerable detail in Freyberg, chapter 6.
11. For full details of Dyett's court martial see Sellers, *Death for Desertion*, chapter 3.
12. It has been suggested that Haig had decided to make an example of an officer as there had been complaints from other ranks that officers were more likely to receive clemency

if given a death penalty.

13. Page, pp. 109–10.
14. James W. Taylor (2002), *The 1st Royal Irish Rifles in the Great War*, Dublin: Four Courts Press, p. 260.
15. Information from Hodson's obituary in *The Times*, 12 April 1918.
16. *Evening Telegraph & Post*, 12 April 1918, quoting the *Daily News*.

15. Of Scientists, Sailors and Shackleton

Information is from cited documents, Huntford, Smith (Shackleton) and publicly available material.

1. Priestley, 'Wireless Memories Round and About the First World War'.
2. Wright et al., 'Epilogue', in *Silas: The Antarctic Diaries and Memoir of Charles S. Wright*.
3. Wright to Cherry-Garrard, 2 March 1916, quoted in Wright et al., *Silas*, p. 377 (original at SPRI).
4. Wright to Cherry-Garrard, 8 July 1916, quoted in Wright et al., *Silas*, pp. 378–9 (original at SPRI).
5. Debenham to Cherry-Garrard, 10 May 1916, SPRI/MS559/24.
6. The wedding took place on 27 January 1917 at St Phillip's, Kensington.
7. Cherry-Garrard, pp. 179–80.
8. Huntford, *Shackleton*, p. 383.
9. Ship's passenger lists, www.ancestry.co.uk.
10. Referred to in letter of 28 March 1916 from Churchill to his wife Clementine (quoted in part in Tyler-Lewis, pp. 217–8 and endnote, and Huntford, *Shackleton*, pp. 488–9 and note, and in full in Martin Gilbert, *Winston S. Churchill*, Volume Three Companion (Heinemann, 1972) p. 1468.
11. *The Times*, 27 March 1916.
12. Ibid. 29 December 1916, 1 and 10 January, and 27 April 1917.
13. John Murray (which remained a family firm until 2002) published biographies of Wilson and Bowers, something Reginald Smith would have undoubtedly done.
14. Monitor ships carried heavy guns used in bombardments from the water in support of troops.
15. Evans, *Keeping the Seas*; Admiralty and other reports (*The Times*, 23, 25, 26 April 1917).
16. *The Times*, 4 June 1917.
17. *Liverpool Daily Post*, 12 June 1917; 1,000 guineas is £1,050.
18. Events are described from Asquith's and Freyberg's standpoints in Page and Freyberg respectively.
19. Ibid.
20. The BIR is mentioned and described in Nelson's and Brady's service records; see also J.J. Thomson (2011 [1936]), *Recollections and Reflections*, Cambridge: Cambridge University Press, p. 206.
21. Brady, Nelson's supervisor, described him as zealous, hardworking and possessing sound scientific knowledge (Nelson's service records, National Archives, ADM/337/117). Nelson's name appears on the cover of the Plymouth Marine Laboratory's December 1917 journal as a member of staff (despite still being attached to the BIR).
22. 21 February 2011 posting on www.museumofthemind.org.uk (Bethlem Hospital).

16. A Norwegian 'Warbird' Keeps His Promise

Quotations from Gran are, unless otherwise stated, from Gran's journals as reproduced in Gran, *Under the British Flag*, and Barfoot, 'Notes of a Norwegian Warbird'. Other information is from Gran's war records (National Archives, WO 339/103746).

1. Meares to Spengler, undated, but probably April 1916, given references to 'Mrs Evans' (who married Evans in January 1916) and fruit tree blossom in southern England.
2. Dennistoun to Pennell, 21 December 1913, RGS/HLP/2/22; *Dominion*, 2 February 1914; Alpine Club (London) membership records; Dennistoun, *The Peaks & Passes of J.R.D.*, pp. 245–59.
3. George Dennistoun, when serving as captain of the *Gwendolen*, captured the *Hermann von Wissmann* and (after renaming it HMS *King George*) used her to ferry British troops and supplies up and down Lake Nyasa.
4. Haddelsey, chapters 1, 7, 8.
5. Gran, *Under the British Flag*, pp. 58ff. 'Penguins' appear to refer to aircraft or to ground troops who (like penguins in Antarctica) would be relatively easy targets from the air.
6. When Gran met Goering after the war they compared flight logs. Gran wondered if he might have shot Goering down on 8 or 9 September 1917, but it could not be verified.
7. Gran landed the damaged aircraft with assistance from his observer. The RFC 'Casualty Card' (RAF Museum, Hendon) suggests Gran was not blamed for damage to his aircraft.
8. *Flight*, 2 May 1918.

17. Northward Ho!

Information on Shackleton is from Smith, *Shackleton: By Endurance We Conquer*, Huntford, *Shackleton*, and newspaper reports; information on Spitsbergen and NEC is from Kruse, *Frozen Assets*, and Barr et al., *Gold, or I'm a Dutchman*; correspondence relating to Ponting's dispute with the Royal Geographical Society is in the RGS archives (RGS/CB8/Conway).

1. The Bolsheviks' nickname is taken from the colour of the Communist flag; some but not all 'Whites' supported the return of the Tsar.
2. *Dundee Evening Telegraph*, 17 April 1911.
3. This is the German station where Campbell learned about the outbreak of war in 1914.
4. *The Times*, 7 March 1918.
5. Ibid., 11 March 1918.
6. Shackleton and Wild are both recorded as holding NEC shares; Campbell, Barnes and McIlroy may also have been issued with shares.
7. In 1912 Norman Craig booked a first-class cabin on the *Titanic* but changed his plans and did not sail with her (see http://www.encyclopedia-titanica.org/cave-list.html). David Thomson's role in the expedition is mentioned on www.discovergravesham.co.uk.
8. Ponting mentioned a meeting with Shackleton at the RGS event on Spitsbergen in December 1918, RGS/CB8/Conway.
9. Anderson's letter is quoted more fully in Ponting, *The Great White South*, p. 292.
10. *Hull Daily Mail*, 15 February and 2 September 1918. According to public records, Cheetham's son who was serving in France returned home safely.
11. Newspapers including *Dundee Courier*, 1 October 1918.
12. The articles in *The Financier* were advertised in *The Times* of 7 October 1918 and numerous regional newspapers. It has been suggested that Ponting, who had previously worked as a war correspondent, may have written the articles but one article refers to him (in the

third person) arriving on Spitsbergen after other expedition members. Given the range and depth of information in the articles it may be that several writers, including Ponting and/or NEC director Harry Brittain (also a journalist), collaborated in producing them.

13. RGS/C88/Conway.

14. Ibid., 13 November 1918.

15. There appears to be no trace of Ponting's photographs of Spitsbergen. He brought them with him to show at the RGS and took them away again (the RGS usually made their own copy of lecturers' lantern slides). There are boxes with the word 'Spitsbergen' written on them at the Scott Polar Research Institute, but they contain other photographs and SPRI has no record of Ponting's Spitsbergen photographs.

16. Oates' leg wound from the Boer War had troubled him in the low temperatures on the return from the South Pole.

17. Atkinson to Cherry-Garrard, 24 August 1918, SPRI/MS559/24/42.

18. Described in Atkinson's Albert Medal citation (quoted in Guly, 'Edward Leicester Atkinson').

19. Atkinson to Cherry-Garrard, 8 October 1918, SPRI/MS559/24/43.

20. Atkinson to Cherry-Garrard, 17 November 1918, SPRI/MS559/24/44; see chapter 2 for background to Atkinson's reference to Meares' actions in 1911–12 in Antarctica.

21. The basis for Atkinson's reference to Meares and a 'white feather' at Ypres is unclear. While Meares was not decorated or mentioned in dispatches his service records show he resigned his commission; his commanding officer also appears to have been keen to retain his services. Many cavalry officers found conditions difficult in the trenches, as they were unable to fulfil their traditional roles of charging and surveillance. Atkinson and Cherry-Garrard both suffered from the knock-on effects of Meares' decision to leave with the *Terra Nova* in early 1912, but Meares' departure had been signalled by him and anticipated by Scott, Bowers and others. In terms of his personal views on Meares, Atkinson was an exceptionally brave man who appears (like Churchill, and Teddy Evans) to have thrived on the challenge and variety of war.

22. Atkinson to Cherry-Garrard, 5 December 1918, SPRI/MS559/24/45; 11 December 1918 (2 letters), /46 and /47; 31 December 1918, /48.

23. I.D. Levack and S.W. McGowan, 'Alexander Hepburne Macklin: physician, polar explorer, and pioneer', *British Medical Journal*, 18 December 1993, 307(6919), pp. 1597–9.

24. Huntford's description of the encounters between Atkinson and Marshall and Macklin (*Shackleton*, pp. 665–6) do not seem to prove that members of the South Pole party had or died from scurvy. Atkinson's claim that Evans' was an isolated case is backed up by Frank Debenham's comment that 'Teddy really was a very naughty boy and wouldn't eat his seal meat' (referred to in May, 'Could Captain Scott have been saved?').

25. Vennell, 'John Hugh Mather and the north Russian campaign, 1919'.

26. Atkinson to Cherry-Garrard, 15 March 1919, SPRI/MS559/24/49.

27. This suggests that Atkinson may have purchased shares in NEC. Campbell would probably have been issued shares in 1913–14, but may have subsequently purchased more.

18. Moving On

1. *The Times*, 17 January 1922.

2. Young, *A Great Task of Happiness*, chapter 16.

3. The bust of Lloyd George is in the Imperial War Museum; the statue based on Arnold Lawrence is now outside the Scott Polar Research Institute, Cambridge.

4. *The Times*, 16 May 1922.

5. It seems likely that the anonymous article in *The Times* of 17 January was a 'trailer' by Ponting for his article (22 January 1922) about his new film.

6. *The Times*, 19 May and 16 June 1919.

7. Cherry, *The Worst Journey in the World*, p. 188 and endnote.

8. Lashly to Cherry-Garrard, 31 January 1920, SPRI/MS 873/2/12.

9. Speak, *Deb – Geographer, Scientist, Antarctic Explorer*, chapters 3 and 4.

10. *The Regimental Role of Honour and War Record of the Artists' Rifles* (1922), available at https://archive.org/details/regimentalrollof00highiala; Sellers, *Hood Battalion*.

11. Guly, 'George Murray Levick'.

12. Levick, *Antarctic Penguins: A Study of their Social Habits* was published in Britain and North America in 1914. A copy of Levick's paper on the sexual habits of Adelies was rediscovered in the archives of the Natural History Museum in 2012 (following which it was displayed and republished). Levick's photographic records notebook, which he appears to have dropped at Cape Evans during the expedition, emerged out of the ice in 2014. Both these events were the subject of extensive press coverage.

13. *The Times*, 16 January 1923.

14. Although Barrie had not yet visited St Andrews in his new role, one of his plays had recently been performed there. Haig, an avid golfer, was a regular visitor to the city in his capacity as captain of the Royal and Ancient Golf Club.

15. Thanks to Rachel Hart, Muniments archivist and deputy head of Special Collections, Special Collections Division, University of St Andrews, for providing the starting-point for this section; additional information is from the public domain, including the website of the National Portrait Gallery.

16. The team included H.G. Wells, Kipling (Barrie's successor as rector of St Andrews), Arthur Conan Doyle, P.G. Wodehouse, Jerome K. Jerome, G.K. Chesterton and A.A. Milne.

17. As women had only relatively recently been given the vote, J.M. Barrie checked with the principal whether the university awarded honorary degrees to women; the answer was affirmative so Ellen Terry obtained her honorary degree (Letter in University of St Andrews Special Collection).

18. After the war Barrie sometimes hired Stanway House in the Cotswolds, which is owned by the members of the wider Wemyss family. Barrie paid for the pavilion at Stanway cricket ground, which was used by 'his' cricket team.

19. Guthrie had, following the war, been commissioned to paint a group portrait of seventeen wartime political leaders and statesmen, including Asquith, Churchill, Lloyd George, Grey, Balfour, Bonar Law and Kitchener and leading politicians from South Africa, Canada, New Zealand, Australia and India. In 1922 Guthrie was still working on the portrait sketches; he completed the painting in 1930, shortly before his death. The painting and companion portraits of leading navy and army officers (including Wemyss and Haig) by Sir John Stockdale Cope and John Singer Sargent hang in the National Portrait Gallery; Guthrie's portrait sketches are in the Scottish National Portrait Gallery.

20. Details of the day's events were published in several newspapers; there is also a short film which includes some of the proceedings, including an amusing exchange between Barrie and Ellen Terry; see www.britishpathe.com/video/sir-james-barrie.

21. The speech was published in whole or in part in several newspapers and by Hodder & Stoughton (J.M. Barrie, *Courage*, undated but presumed to be 1922).

22. The unpublished sentences refer to an apparent cooling of relations between Scott and Barrie; the words were edited out of 'official' versions of the letter but published (apparently for the first time) in Andrew Birkin, *J.M. Barrie and the Lost Boys*, London: Constable, 1979, pp. 209–10 .

23. *Flight*, 21 October 1920; *Cross & Cockade*, Vol. 24, No. 1, 1993.

24. Amundsen, *My Life as an Explorer*, chapters 4 and 5, and *The Times* (which reported regularly on Amundsen's progress throughout 1922).
25. Commonwealth Military Graves Commission: http://www.cwgc.org.
26. *The Times*, 24 October 1922. The exhibition ran from 5 March to 14 April 1923, and was opened by Sir William Rothenstein, Principal of the Royal College of Art. Rothenstein had, for the past ten years, regularly stayed near Stroud, Gloucestershire, about 15 miles from Wilson's home town of Cheltenham.
27. During the 1920s Sempill was suspected of passing information on the development of British aircraft to the Japanese, but he was not prosecuted (National Archives, KV2/871–4, released for public viewing in 2002); Meares' own papers relating to the mission are in Fonds Cecil Meares, Vancouver (see www.archivescanada.ca). There is no suggestion that Meares, who returned to Britain before Sempill, was aware of what the latter was suspected of doing.
28. *Flight*, 26 October 1922, p. 620.
29. Campbell, *Wicked Mate*, p.13.
30. Brooke's poem was later used as the inscription on the RND memorial in London.
31. The story of Mallory, Irvine and their companions is told in Davis, *Into the Silence*.

Epilogue

1. Pearson, p. 224.
2. New Zealand Antarctic Heritage Trust website, www.nzaht.org/AHT/Levicks-notebook.
3. Lot 242 in auction of 18 April 2015 at Henry Armitage and Son, Devizes.
4. The Gallipoli centenary commemorations took place on 24–25 April 2015; the earthquake which started the avalanches and wrought so much destruction began on 25 April 2015.

Select Bibliography

———❧❧❧———

There are, as anyone interested in the main subject areas of this book will know, numerous books available on the First World War and the Antarctic expeditions. There is also a huge amount of information in the public domain. I have listed books and journals I have consulted, referenced or which have found particularly helpful in terms of background or contextual information.

Amundsen, Roald (1927), *My life as an explorer*, London: William Heinemann

Arnold, H.J.P. (1975), *Herbert Ponting: Another World*, London: Sidgwick and Jackson

Baker, Christopher (2014), *The Truce: The Day the War Stopped*, Stroud: Amberley Publishing

Barfoot, John (1993), 'Notes of a Norwegian Warbird: Tryggve Gran', *Cross & Cockade International Journal*, vol. 24: 1, pp. 12–21

Barr, Susan, Newman, David and Nesterod, Greg (2012), *Gold, or I'm a Dutchman*, Trondheim: Akademica Publishing

Barrie, J. M. (undated, probably 1922), *Courage*, London: Hodder & Stoughton

Bingham, Chris, *Harry Pennell: Scott's Navigator* (*The Review*, Volume 24.4, pp.5-16) and *From the South Pole to Jutland* (*Medal News*, May 2007, pp. 37–39)

Bostridge, Mark (2014), *The Fateful Year: England 1914*, London: Viking

Bowers, Henry R., Lane, Heather, Boneham, Naomi, Smith, Robert D. (eds), Strathie, Anne (Foreword) (2012), *The South Pole Journals*, Cambridge: Scott Polar Research Institute

Brown, Malcolm and Seaton, Shirley (1994), *Christmas Truce: the Western Front, December 1914*, Basingstoke: Papermac

Bruce, Wilfred (2012 [1932]), *Reminiscences of the* Terra Nova *in the Antarctic*, Jaffrey, NH: Erebus & Terror Press

Campbell, Victor and King, H.G.R. (ed.) (1988), *The Wicked Mate: The Antarctic Diary of Victor Campbell*, Norfolk: Bluntisham Books, Erskine Press

Cherry-Garrard, Apsley (2010 [1922]), *The Worst Journey in the World*, London: Vintage Classics

Costello, John and Hughes, Terry (1976), *Jutland 1916*, London: Weidenfeld & Nicolson Ltd

Crane, David (2005), *Scott of the Antarctic*, London: HarperCollins

— (2014), *Empires of the Dead*, London: HarperCollins

David, Saul (2013), *100 Days to Victory*, London: Hodder & Stoughton

Davis, Wade (2011), *Into the Silence: The Great War, Mallory and the Conquest of Everest*, London: Vintage

Debenham, Frank (1952), *In the Antarctic*, London: John Murray

Dennistoun, James and Mannering, Guy (ed.) (1999), *The Peaks & Passes of J.R.D.*, Geraldine, New Zealand: JRD Publications

Erskine, Angus (1994), 'Victor Campbell and Michael Barne in Svalbard: the 1914 voyage of Willem Barents', *Polar Record*, pp. 117–22

Evans, Edward R.G.R. (1920), *Keeping the Seas*, New York: Frederick Warne (on-line pdf version)

— (1953 [1921]), *South with Scott*, London: Collins

— (Admiral Lord Mountevans) (1947), *Adventurous Life*, London: Hutchison & Co.

Freyberg, Lord Paul (1991), *Bernard Freyberg, VC: Soldier of Two Nations*, London: Hodder & Stoughton

Gallipoli Association Journal (various issues and authors)

Gran, Tryggve (1919), *Under the British Flag*, trans. Gran's daughter (from *Under britisk flagg: krigen 1914–18*), Oslo: Gyldendalske Boghandel (copy at Imperial War Museum, ref. 91/41/1)

— (1984), *Tryggve Gran's Antarctic Diary, 1910–13: The Norwegian with Scott*, trans. Ellen Johanne McGhie, Geoffrey Hattersley-Smith (ed.), London: National Maritime Museum

Guly, Henry (2014), 'Edward Leicester Atkinson (1881–1929): Antarctic explorer, scientist and naval surgeon', *Journal of Medical Biography*, 21 March

— (2014), 'George Murray Levick (1876–1956): Antarctic explorer', *Journal of Medical Biography*, 27 June

Haddelsey, Stephen (2005), *Born Adventurer: The Life of Frank Bickerton, Antarctic Pioneer*. Stroud: The History Press

Hassell, Christopher (1964), *Rupert Brooke*, London: Faber & Faber

Hooper, Meredith (2010), *The Longest Winter: Scott's Other Heroes*, London: John Murray (Publishers)

Huntford, Roland (1985), *Shackleton*, London: Hodder & Stoughton

Johnson, Anthony M. (1982, 1983), 'Scott of the Antarctic and Cardiff', *Glamorgan Local History Society Transactions,* vol. 26, pp. 15–52 (Part 1); vol. 27, p. 25–58 (Part 2)

Johnson, Boris (2014), *The Churchill Factor*, London: Hodder & Stoughton

Jones, Max (2003), *The Last Great Quest*, Oxford: Oxford University Press

Jones, Nigel (1999), *Brooke: Life, Death and Myth*, London: Richard Cohen Books

Jones, Nigel (2014), *Peace and War: Britain in 1914*, London: Head of Zeus

Kelly, Frederick Septimus, Radic, Thérèse (ed.) (2004), *Race Against Time: The Diaries of F.S. Kelly*, Canberra: National Library of Australia

Kelly, Frederick Septimus, Cooksey, Jon and McKechnie, Graham (eds) (2015), *Kelly's War: The Great War Diary of Frederick Kelly 1914–1916*, London: Blink Publishing

Kruse, Frigga (2013), *Frozen Assets: British Mining Exploration and Geopolitics on Spitsbergen, 1904–53*, Groningen: University of Groningen

Limb, Sue and Cordingley, Patrick (2009 [1982]), *Captain Oates: Soldier and Explorer*, Barnsley: Pen & Sword Books

MacMillan, Margaret (2014), *The War that Ended Peace*, London: Profile Books

Marsh, Edward (memoir) and Brooke, Rupert (1918), *The Collected Poems of Rupert Brooke: With a memoir*, London: Sidgwick & Jackson

May, Karen (2011), 'Could Captain Scott have been saved? Revisiting Scott's Last Expedition', *Polar Record*, vol. 48: 1, January 2013, pp. 72–90

May, Karen and Airrless, Sarah (2013), 'Could Captain Scott have been saved? Cecil Meares and the 'second journey' that failed', *Polar Record*, vol. 51: 3, May 2015, pp. 260–73

Mills, Leif (2008), *Men of Ice: The Lives of Alistair Forbes Mackay (1878-1914) and Cecil Henry Meares (1877-1937)*, Whitby: Caedmon of Whitby

Nicolson, Juliet (2010), *The Great Game*, London: John Murray

Page, Christopher (1999), *Command in the Royal Naval Division*, Staplehurst: Spelmount

Parsons, Christopher (1993), 'Campbell of the Antarctic: Orders and Medals', *Research Society Journal*, Spring 1993

Pearson, Graham (2007), *Hidcote: The Garden and Lawrence Johnston*, London: National Trust

Pease, Howard (1924), *The History of the Northumberland (Hussars) Yeomanry, 1819–1919*,

London: Constable & Co.

Pennell, Harry, journals, 1904–1914 (three volumes, references MS107 and MS433), Canterbury Museum, Christchurch, New Zealand

Ponting, Herbert (1921), *The Great White South*, London: Gerald Duckworth & Sons

Priestley, Raymond (1971), 'Wireless Memories Round and About the First World War', talk given on 1 May 1971 to the Royal Engineers Signals Association (1914–8), privately printed (copy provided by University of Melbourne Archives)

Quartermain, L.B. (1981), *Antarctica's Forgotten Men*, Wellington, NZ: Millwood Press

Raeside, Adrian (2009), *Return to Antarctica*, Mississauga, Ontario: John Wiley & Sons

Riffenburgh, Beau (2008), *Racing with Death: Douglas Mawson – Antarctic Explorer*, London: Bloomsbury

— (2011), *Terra Nova, Scott's Last Expedition*, Cambridge: Scott Polar Research Institute

Russell, W.S.C. (1911), 'Jan Mayen Expedition of 1911', *Bulletin of the American Geographical Society*, vol. 43: 12, pp. 881–90

Sanderson, Marie (1988), *Griffith Taylor: Antarctic Scientist and Pioneer Geographer*, Ottawa: Carlton University Press

Scott, Robert Falcon, Jones, Max (ed.) (2005 [1910–12]), *Journals: Captain Scott's Last Expedition*, Oxford: Oxford World's Classics

Scott, Robert Falcon and others (1914), *Scott's Last Expedition*, Volumes I and II, London: Smith, Elder & Co.

Seaver, George (1933), *Edward Wilson of the Antarctic: Naturalist and Friend*, London: John Murray

Sellers, Leonard (1995), *The Hood Battalion*, Barnsley: Pen & Sword Books

— (1997–2003), *Royal Naval Division Journals*, 1–24, June 1997–March 2003, available on CD-rom at http://www.crystalpalacefoundation.org.uk/shop/world-war-one-two/royal-naval-division

— (2003), *Death for Desertion: The Story of the Court Martial and Execution of Sub Lt. Edwin Dyett*, Barnsley: Leo Cooper, Pen & Sword Books

Shackleton, Ernest, (2007 [1909; 1919]) *The Heart of Antarctica* and *South*, London: Wordsworth Editions

Simonis, H. (1917), *The Street of Ink: An Intimate History of Journalism*, New York: Funk and Wagnalls (available at http://www.ebooksread.com/authors-eng/h-simonis/the-street-of-ink-an-intimate-history-of-journalism-omi.shtml)

Skinner, George and Valerie, *The Life and Adventures of William Lashly* (published privately, available at https://sites.google.com/site/lashlyantarcticexplorer/new-william-lashly-book)

Smith, Michael (2008), *I Am Just Going Outside: Captain Oates – Antarctic Tragedy*

— (2009), *An Unsung Hero: Tom Crean – Antarctic Survivor*, Cork: Collins Press

— (2014), *Shackleton: By Endurance We Conquer*, London: Oneworld Publications

Speak, Peter (2008), *Deb – Geographer, Scientist, Antarctic Explorer: A Biography of Frank Debenham, OBE*, Guildford: Polar Publishing Ltd, in association with Scott Polar Research Institute

Strachan, Hew (2003–13), *The First World War*, London: Simon & Schuster and Pocket Books

Strange, Caroline and Bashford, Alison (2009), *Griffith Taylor: Visionary Environmentalist Explorer*, Toronto: University of Toronto Press

Strathie, Anne (2012), *Birdie Bowers: Captain Scott's Marvel*, Stroud: The History Press

Sutherland, John and Canwell, Diana (2104), *The Battle of Jutland*, Barnsley, Pen & Sword Books

Swales, Roy (2004), *Nelson at War: 1914–1918*, Barnsley: Pen & Sword Books

Tarver, Michael (2006), *The S.S. Terra Nova (1884–1943): From the Arctic to the Antarctic, Whaler, Sealer and Polar Exploration Ship*, Brixham: Pendragon Maritime Publications

— (2015), *Antarctic Explorer and War Hero, The Man who Found Captain Scott: Edward Leicester Atkinson*, Brixham: Pendragon Maritime Publications

Taylor, Griffith (1916), *With Scott: The Silver Lining*, London: Smith, Elder & Co.

Turney, Chris (2012), *1912: The Year the World Discovered Antarctica*, London: The Bodley Head and Pimlico

Tyler-Lewis, Kelly (2006), *The Lost Men: The Harrowing Story of Shackleton's Ross Sea Party*, London: Bloomsbury

Vennell, Adrian (2006), 'John Hugh Mather and the north Russian campaign, 1919', *Polar Record*, vol. 48: 2, April 2007, pp. 169–171

Wheeler, Sara (2001), *Cherry: A Life of Apsley Cherry-Garrard*, London: Vintage

Williams, Isobel (2008), *With Scott in the Antarctic: Edward Wilson*, Stroud: The History Press

Wilson, David M. (2011), *The Lost Photographs of Captain Scott*, London: Little, Brown

Wilson, David M. and Elder, David B. (2000), *Cheltenham in Antarctica: The Life of Edward Wilson*, Cheltenham: Reardon Publishing

Wright, Silas, Bull, Colin and Wright, Pat F. (eds) (1993), *Silas: The Antarctic Diaries and Memoir of Charles S. Wright*, Ohio: Ohio State University Press

Young, Louisa (2012), *A Great Task of Happiness: The Life of Kathleen Scott*, London: Hydraulic Press of London

Index

—◦◦◦—

Members of the *Terra Nova* expedition who are mentioned in the main text (including by nickname) are indexed, as is the information on them in Appendix A (which also lists other expedition members); introductory material, photographs, maps, notes, other appendices and bibliography are not indexed. Ships are indexed under HMS (Royal Navy), SMS (German navy) or by name. Where a country is indexed, references include the adjectival form where relevant/significant (e.g. Norwegian as well as Norway). Geographical names that appear numerous times (e.g. Antarctica, Germany, France, London) are not indexed.